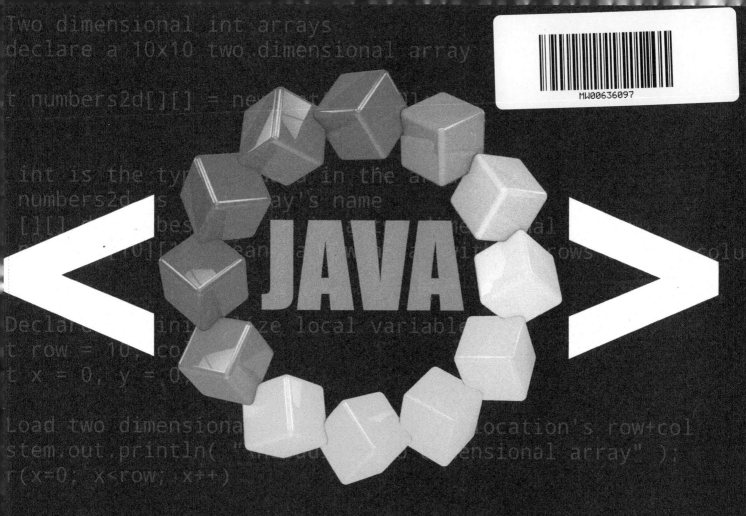

JAVA

Programming Applications

Michael Robinson

Florida International University

Kendall Hunt
publishing company

Kendall Hunt
p u b l i s h i n g   c o m p a n y

www.kendallhunt.com
Send all inquiries to:
4050 Westmark Drive
Dubuque, IA 52004-1840

Contents

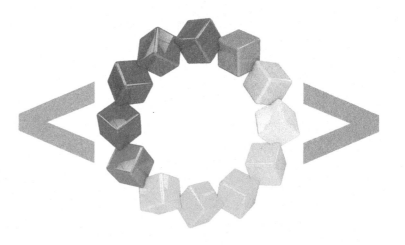

Preface xi

Purpose/Goals. xi
The World's First Computer Programmer xii
Our Logo's Meaning. xiii
Plan Your Work then Work Your Plan xiii
Acknowledgments. xiv
Your Feedback is Needed! xiv
Further Reading xiv
Colophon xiv

Chapter 1: The Basics 1

What is Java?. 1
What is an Operating System? 1
What is a Computer Program Language?. 1
What Do We Need? A computer 2
The Java JDK 2
Editors 2
Graphical User Interface (GUI) 3
IDE Programming Editors 3
NetBeans. 4
Using NetBeans 4
Eclipse. 5
Using Eclipse 5
Text Editors 6
Notepad in Linux 6
Gedit in Linux 7
Nano in Linux. 7

< iii >

Terminal Mode/Command Line 8
Creating Java Programs. 8
What is Compiling in Java? 8
PseudoCode 9
PseudoCode Example 9
Summary. 10
Key Terms 11
Exercises 15
References. 16

Chapter 2: Getting Started   17

Let's Start Programming. 17
Documenting a Program. 17
Javadoc Comments 18
What Are Imports? 18
What is a Class? 19
Creating a Class 19
What is a Method? 20
Creating a Method 20
Indentation 22
Print Commands. 23
    System.out.print 23
    System.out.println 23
    System.out.printf 24
Summary. 25
Key Terms 26
Exercises 31
References. 32

Chapter 3: Basic Tools   33

Numerical Systems 33
    Decimal Numerical System 33
    Binary Numerical System. 33
    Why Binary 34
    8 Bits Byte Samples 34
    Hexadecimal Numerical System. 35
    ASCII Codes Table 35
    ASCII Tables 36
    The Unicode Standard 38
Data Types 38

Primitive Data Types 39

    byte 39

    char 40

    int 40

    short 40

    long 40

    float 40

    double 40

    boolean 40

What Can We Do with Primitives? 41

Problems Choosing the Wrong Date Types 42

Creating a Variable and Assigning a Value to it 43

Numerical Operators 43

Other Operators 44

    Operators > and < 45

    Operators >= and <= 45

    Operators =, ==, != 46

    Operators && 46

    Operators || 46

    Operator % 46

Math Using Primitives 47

Wrapper 55

String Class Data Types 55

First String Program 57

Summary 60

Key Terms 61

Exercises 67

References 68

Chapter 4: Building a House   69

Wrappers 69

Calling Methods 72

    Methods That Do Not Pass Any Data 73

    Methods That Accept Data 75

    Methods That Return Data 77

    Pause Program 80

Variables Scope 82

    Global Variables 82

    Private – Final Variables 83

    Local Variables 84

Reading The Keyboard Using Scanner Class 87

Summary. 91

Key Terms. 92

Exercises 95

References. 96

Chapter 5: if Commands   81

if Command 97

  Plain if 97

  Other Plain if Example. 98

  if_else 100

  if else if 102

  Nested if. 104

  Ternary if 106

Summary. 108

Key Terms. 109

Exercises 111

References. 112

Chapter 6: Loops   113

Loops 113

  for loops 113

  while Loop 116

  Boolean Conditions in while Loops 117

  Endless while Loop 119

  do while Loops 120

  Enhanced for Loops (Summary) 122

Switch Command. 122

  Limitations of the Switch Command. 122

  switch Command Using int as Input 122

  switch Command Using char as Input 126

Summary. 129

Key Terms. 130

Exercises 133

References. 135

Chapter 7: Data Structures – Arrays   137

Data Structures 137

Arrays 137

  One Dimension Array 137

Declaring/Creating One Dimension Arrays: 138
Allocating Space to Declared Arrays: 139
Declare and Allocate at the Same Time: 139
Create, Allocate and Load Data into Arrays: 139
Load Data to a Declared Array 140
Printing all Values Inside this Array 141
Multi Dimensional Arrays 141
Two Dimension Arrays 141
Two Dimensional int Arrays 143
Two Dimensional String Arrays (Using Array's Length) 146
Three Multidimensional Arrays 147
Parallel Arrays 152
Enhanced for Loops 154
String Tokenizer 156
Summary 160
Key Terms 161
Exercises 165
References 166

Chapter 8: Data Structures – ArrayList   167

ArrayList 167
Iterator 172
Using Iterator in an ArrayList 173
Copying Arrays into an ArrayList Modify and Back 182
Object Data Types 188
Summary 191
Key Terms 192
Exercises 195
References 196

Chapter 9: Data Structures – Files   197

What is a File? 197
What is a Record? 198
Catching Errors Exceptions In Data Files 198
Text Files 199
Text Files Using: 199
FileWriter, PrintWriter, FileReader and BufferedReader 199
Text Files Using the File Class 207
Exceptions Handling 210
Text Files Using the Formatter Class 214

Text Files Using the Scanner Class 217

Large Files. Writing and Reading. 221

Printing Numbers Using Decimal Format 225

Binary Files. 227

Summary. 232

Key Terms 233

Exercises 237

References. 238

Chapter 10: External Classes, Methods, This, Constructors   239

External Classes 239

Final Variables 242

toString. 244

What is 'this'? 248

What is a Constructor? 250

Simple Constructors 251

What is a Variable-Length Argument List in Methods? 260

Object Data Types 270

What is the Meaning of main(String arg[])? 272

Summary. 274

Key Terms 275

Exercises 281

References. 282

Chapter 11: GUI Simple Applications   283

What is GUI (Graphical User Interface)?. 283

What are Dialog Boxes? 283

Message Dialog Boxes. 284

Input Dialog Boxes 284

What is a Frame? 291

Creating a Frame. 291

Creating a Small Frame 292

Creating a Full Size Frame 293

Summary. 295

Key Terms 296

Exercises 299

References. 300

Chapter 12: Sorting and Recursion   301

What is Sorting?. 301
Swap - Placing Data in Order. 301
Bubble Sort. 303
Recursion 319
Summary. 322
Key Terms 323
Exercises 325
References. 326

Chapter 13: Inheritance and Polymorphism   327

What is Inheritance?. 327
Polymorphism. 342
Final Methods. 367
Final Classes 369
Protected Classes Methods and Variables 370
Summary. 373
Key Terms. 374
Exercises 377
References. 378

Chapter 14: Interfaces and Abstraction   379

What is an Interface? 379
Data Abstraction. 385
Data Abstraction vs Interfaces 389
Summary. 390
Key Terms. 391
Exercises 393
References. 394

Chapter 15: Data Structures Implementations   395

Linked List 395
Overloading 400
Stacks 402
Queue 408
Summary. 413
Key Terms 414

Exercises 415

References 416

Chapter 16: Complex Programming   417

Caller Program 417

Abstract Classes 417

Classes Inside Classes 418

Interfaces. 423

Extends/Inhereting 427

Summary. 431

Key Terms 432

Exercises 435

References 436

Chapter 17: Miscellaneous   437

Generic Methods 437

Introduction to Java Collection Interface 439

Overriding equals and toString methods 443

How to Reduce Typing. 449

ASCII Codes Program 450

Javadoc 455

Summary. 458

Key Terms 459

Exercises 461

References 462

Glossary   463

Index   505

Preface

Purpose/Goals

The purpose of this book is to teach you computer programming using the Java Language, no previous programming knowledge is required.

Using over 100 of our own very clearly documented Java programs, we teach in detail, and step by step, how to create very useful programs. All programming applications examples presented in this book are based on simple everyday common situations. No math, physics, statistics or other challenging topics are used as examples.

All programs included in this book can be found at robinson.cs.fiu.edu or robinson.dmsdata.com. We recommend that you download any or all programs, compile them, run them and modify them as you see fit. This exercise will help you understand in more detail how every command works.

The knowledge acquired from this book will help you greatly in learning other programing languages. Once you learn one programming language like Java, writing your ideas in another language is easy because the syntax we use in most languages is very similar, the following code is identical in many languages:

```
if( temperature > 150 )
{
    exit
}
```

All Digital Computers, also known as Digital Machines, use a common numerical system called The Binary Numerical System to communicate with humans and other computers. Today's computer programs are written in plain English and then they are automatically converted into Binary by other programs called Compilers and Interpreters.

< xi >

As of this writing the Java language is found everywhere. According to Oracle Corporation, owners of Java https://www.java.com/en/about/

- ▶ 97% of Enterprise Desktops Run Java
- ▶ 89% of Desktops (or Computers) in the U.S. Run Java
- ▶ 9 Million Java Developers Worldwide
- ▶ #1 Choice for Developers
- ▶ #1 Development Platform
- ▶ 3 Billion Mobile Phones Run Java
- ▶ 100% of Blu-ray Disc Players Ship with Java
- ▶ 5 Billion Java Cards in Use
- ▶ 125 Million TV devices Run Java
- ▶ 5 of the Top 5 Original Equipment Manufacturers Ship Java ME

The World's First Computer Programmer

Lady Ada Lovelace, a gifted mathematician and English writer (10th December 1815–27th November 1852) was the world's first computer programmer. Her work on Charles Babbage's analytical engine, an early mechanical general purpose computer, is recognized as the first algorithm to be processed by a machine.

A process to repeat a series of instructions, known today as looping and used in computer programming, was created by Ada Lovelace. She also developed a way to create codes for devices to manage letters, numbers and symbols. Lady Lovelace developed many systems that are fundamental to our current Computer Systems.

She died in London on November 27th, 1852, and was buried next to her father, the famous poet Lord George Gordon Byron, in the Church of St. Mary Magdalene in Nottingham, England.

Drawing © by Pilar Robinson. Image © Everett Historical/Shutterstock.com.

The computer language Ada, created for the United States Department of Defense, was named after Ada Lovelace.

Our Logo's Meaning

Our logo represents exactly what programming is to me. Programming is the development of many blocks of code that work as a single unit. Each block performs a specific logical function. In Java these blocks are called classes. Classes can contain other classes and all classes contain methods. Methods are sections of code with a specific purpose. Methods and Classes can be reused as many times as needed.

Plan Your Work then Work Your Plan

This famous quote used since the 1800s applies very well to programming. To me writing a program is like building a house, and that is precisely how this book was created. First we start with the description of the task at hand, then we write the plans (pseudo code), which is always found at the beginning of each program, followed by the actual programming code called "source code." Finally we test the programs and then we make the necessary corrections. Planning your work well makes for an easy implementation of your projects.

Programmers who usually start programming without the proper planning, spend great amounts of time fixing errors called "debugging the program."

In this book the sequence of topics are presented in a logical manner, all concepts and commands found in all sections are either new or have been learned in previous sections.

All sample programs presented in this book are original, and are to be used as examples of the programs that will be assigned in projects and/or exams.

This book is intended to help my students understand the material that I teach in the classroom.

Be patient, rule number one in Computer Science is: "If a program works the first time, there is something wrong with it."

Happy Programming!!!

—Michael Robinson

Acknowledgments

I want to thank the hundreds of students who used this book, helping me test every program in it, as well as making many suggestions to improve the reading, content and explanations, making this book more interesting and challenging.

My wife, Pilar Robinson, drew the graphical representation of Lady Ada Lovelace, the world's first programmer, used in the Preface section of this book.

The patience and support provided by my wife, Pilar, and my children. The encouragement that I received from many faculty and advising members at Florida International University, Miami Dade College, Miami-Dade and Broward Counties Public Schools, has been invaluable; and the advise and guidance received from Paul Gormley, Senior Managing Editor; Marla W. Swartz, Senior Acquisitions Editor; Bev Kraus, Project Coordinator, and their great team at Kendall Hunt Publishing Company made this book possible.

Your Feedback Is Needed!

This book is an ongoing project. If you find any technical errors or have a comment to make this effort better, please drop me a line at:

michael.robinson@cs.fiu.edu or michael@dmdata.com

Your changes and suggestions may get into future releases.

Further Reading

- Java API Specifications

http://www.oracle.com/technetwork/java/api-141528.html

Colophon

This book was written using LibreOffice Writer with Times New Roman font for the titles and Courier 10 Pitch for the Java programs on a HP 635 laptop, configured with the Ubuntu Operating System. The cover was designed by Kendall Hunt Publishing Company and Michael Robinson.

The Basics

What is Java?

Java has over 3.6 billion installations as of this writing.

The programming language Java is known as "write once run everywhere." This means that we can write our programs on any device, convert it into a standard code and run it in any device that contains a JVM (Java Virtual Machine). Installing JVM in devices and software packages such as Windows has become an industry standard practice.

In theory we can expect to write a program in a Windows PC and run it on a Java enable microwave, cell phone, car, refrigerator, routers, mainframes, etc. without making any modifications. Programs developed in Linux work in Windows and vice versa. However since there are multiple JVM implementations that run on many different systems such as Windows, Linux, Mac-OS, HP-UX, Netware, Solaris, etc., there can be small differences in how a program executes, requiring changes to the program.

What is an Operating System?

Windows, Linux, and Apple are the most popular current Operating Systems. An Operating System is the software that allows the user to control the hardware.

What is a Computer Program Language?

Just as English, Spanish, French, etc. are human languages used by humans to communicate with each other, Computer Programming Languages such as Java, C, Perl, PHP, etc. are used by humans to give instructions to computers. Computers do what we tell them to do through Programming Languages.

< 1 >

There are two general types of Computer Languages, compiled and interpreted languages. A compiled language is a language that when compiled gets translated into a type of code called binary, that the computer can understand. Binary is the natural language of computers.

Compiled Languages are those like C, Cobol, Assembly, etc.

Interpreted languages get translated into binary code when the program runs. Java is an interpreted language.

Since program written using compiled languages are already compiled, they are much faster than program written in interpreted languages.

What Do We Need? A computer

Any computer running Windows, Apple, Linux, Solaris, etc.

© Katousha/Shutterstock.com © Oleksiy Mark/Shutterstock.com © TZIDO SUN/Shutterstock.com

The Java JDK

The Java Development Kit (JDK) is an Oracle Corporation product aimed at Java developers. The JDK has as its primary components, a collection of programming tools for Java. Download (FREE) Java JDK from:

http://www.oracle.com/technetwork/java/javase/downloads/index.html

Make sure you download the proper version for your computer 32 or 64 bits.

Editors

There are two types of editors. One is called IDE and the other Text Editor. Editors are programs that allow you to create your Java programs.

Graphical User Interface (GUI)

©Tinxi/Shutterstock.com

Graphical User Interface (GUI) are used by most people to access their computers. Computers using Windows, Linux, or Apple have beautiful graphical interfaces allowing the users easy management of their computer systems.

©isak55/Shutterstock.com

©manaemedia/Shutterstock.com

IDE Programming Editors

An IDE (Integrated Development Environment) is a programming tool that contains a code editor, a compiler, a debugger, and a GUI (Graphical User Interface) which allows the student to write programs easier. There are some disadvantages in using an IDE, such as all warnings are hidden therefore the student does not know that they exist. The best way to avoid this and other problems is to write the programs using text editors, which we will discuss shortly.

NetBeans

Download (FREE) from:

http://www.oracle.com/technetwork/java/javase/downloads/index.html

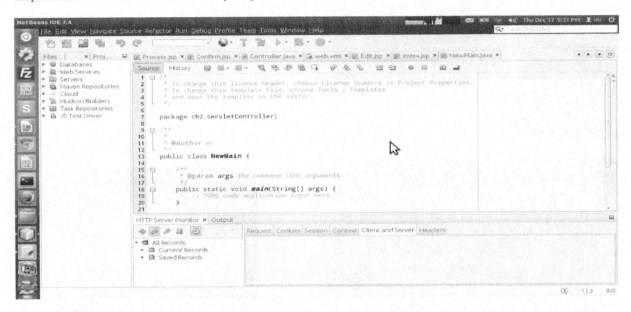

This is a Java program written using NetBeans in Ubuntu Linux Operating System.

Using NetBeans

Find the NetBeans icon and double-click it.

On the top left side of the screen, select File, New Project, Java, Java Application, New. Now enter your project name. Give your project a meaningful name (e.g. myFirstProject). This will create a project which will show on the screen's left column. At this time you can leave the information on Project Location and Project Folder as is; these are the default locations given by NetBeans or you can select different locations. Just remember where you are saving your projects so that you can copy or email your programs. Press Finish and now NetBeans will create what is called a template of the program where you can start writing your program.

To save your program you can select File, Save, or press the picture of a floppy disk on the top left of the screen.

To execute/run your program press the green arrow > on the top the screen. This will compile and run your program, and if you have errors this process will let you know so that you can fix them, save and re-run your program.

For detailed instructions on NetBeans, please refer to its Help section.

Eclipse

Download (FREE) from:

http://www.eclipse.org/downloads/moreinfo/java.php

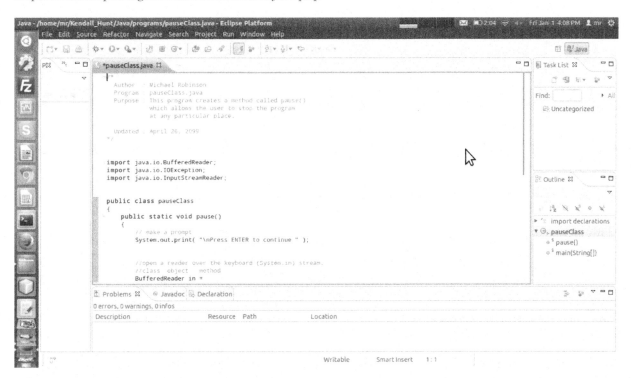

This is a Java program written using Eclipse in Ubuntu Linux Operating System.

Using Eclipse

Select File, New, Project and enter your project name. Give your project a meaningful name (e.g., myFirstProject. This will create a project that will show on the screen's left column.

Double click your project name, right click the folder src inside your project, select file, new, class and enter your class/program name. Give your class a meaningful name (e.g., myFirstProgram). This will create your program which will show inside the src folder.

Run your program. On the command line select Run, or below the command line press the green icon >. If you have errors the program will NOT compile until the errors are fixed.

For detailed instructions on Eclipse, please refer to its Help section.

Text Editors

There are many free text editors available in all operating systems. In Windows we find Notepad and a third-party free editor called Notepad++. In Linux we find Gedit, Nano, Pico, VI and VIM, all free, and in Apple computers we find TextEdit.

Text editors are programs that allow you to create your Java programs in terminal mode. After your first or second semester of programming languages, in my classes, I require that all work be done in terminal mode. The reason is that in most large companies, programmers and scientists prefer, and in some cases, are required to use computers in terminal mode.

Unlike graphical interfaces, terminal mode gives full access to the computer hardware being used.

Notepad in Linux

This picture is a typical Java program written in Notepad under Ubuntu OS.

```java
public class array2rowXcolDIV2
{

    public static void arrays( int rows, int cols )
    {
        int array2dRC[][] = new int[rows][cols];

        int totalRowEven = 0;
        int totalColOdd  = 0;
        int count    = 0;
        int x        = 0;
        int y        = 0;

        for( x=0; x<rows; x++ )
        {
            for( y=0; y<cols; y++ )
            {
                //Load array
                array2dRC[x][y] = (x*y)/2;
                System.out.printf( "%3d", array2dRC[x][y] );
```

Gedit in Linux

Typical Java program using Gedit Text Editor under Ubuntu OS.

Nano in Linux

Typical Java program using Nano Text Editor under Ubuntu OS.

Terminal Mode/Command Line

To use editors such as Notepad, Gedit, VI, VIM, Pico, Nano, and TextEdit.

- Go to the command line of your operating system (Windows, etc.)
- Windows: Start, run, cmd, enter
- Linux Ubuntu: Applications, Accessories, Terminal
- Open the editor of your choice
- Create/Save your program e.g., myFirstProgram.java
- Compile your program as follows: javac myFirstProgram.java
- This command (javac) will create the compiled program called: myFirstProgram.class
- If your program has errors it will NOT compile until all errors are fixed
- Run your compiled program: Java myFirstProgram (note no .class)

> **DO NOT use a word processor to create your programs**

Creating Java Programs

Select an IDE (Integrated Development Environment) such as Eclipse or NetBeans or any editor of your choice. See detailed instructions in the previous corresponding sections.

Once you are inside your code editor, start writing your program's source code file (your typed program). The program name requires three parts: the FirstName, one period/dot, and the word Java. e.g., myFirstProgram.java

What is Compiling in Java?

Compiling a program is to transform your source/program into a language that the hardware can understand. When you compile a Java program its compiler (javac) translates your program (the source code) into instructions that the JVM (Java Virtual Machine) understands. In Java these instructions are known as byte codes and are created in a file that has the same name as your program name and replaces .java with .class at the end of the name.

        e.g.,   program name = myFirstProgram.java
                compiled name = myFirstProgram.class

Java is an interpreted language not a compiled language. The JVM (Java Virtual Machine) in your computer will interpret and execute the byte codes in your myFirstProgram.class program. The advantage of this technology is that most Operating Systems (Windows, Linux, etc.) have their own JVM, capable of executing any Java source code. Therefore you can write your program on a Windows 32 bit computer and re-compile it and run it in a totally different type of computer using different Operating Systems like Solaris, Linux, etc.

If you create your Java program in a Windows computer and want to run it in a Linux computer, you need to transfer your Java source code from the Windows to the Linux computer, and recompile it. This will create a new .class file. Class files compiled in different operating systems are not compatible.

PseudoCode

PseudoCode is the method of writing down the steps to be taken to solve a problem. This is done using regular English words without the use of any programming code.

I highly recommend that you write PseudoCode until you are totally sure that your program will work, before writing your first line of code. This works for any programming language.

Methods similar to PseudoCode are used in many other disciplines with great results. Before a house is built, Architects create detailed plans of how, and with what materials the house will be built. When building highways, civil engineers spend a tremendous amount of time planning how the project is to be done. Computer programming is one of the disciplines where we see students doing trial and error programs. I beg those students not to become architects or civil engineers.

PseudoCode Example

Problem: Implement division by 0 with error trapping.

How:

- Using two variables: FirstNumber and LastNumber
- Ask the user to enter the FirstNumber
- Ask the user to enter the SecondNumber
- If the user enters the value 99 for the FirstNumber or the SecondNumber, you must exit the program immediately,
- If the second number is ZERO inform the user that you CANNOT divide by ZERO, and ask for a correct second number until the user enters a non-zero number
- If the second number is NOT a zero or a 99, do the division, display all numbers on this computation using labels, example: 4 divided by 1 = 4

This PseudoCode gives us the pathway to write a program to solve this problem in any language. Another advantage is that we can change the logic of the program by modifying steps used in the PseudoCode instead of fixing pages of code.

Students who write the PseudoCode of a program before writing a single line of code, finish their work faster and with fewer errors.

Once your program is working the next step is to make it more efficient (faster, smaller).

Summary

Chapter One has been written for people who have no previous knowledge of programming, as well as for experts who have developed many programs in multiple programming languages and like to keep up with some current tools.

We cover some of the hardware used to write Java programs and various currently used software editors that allow us to create the actual Java program source code. We learn to compile and run Java programs using IDE and/or terminal mode editors.

Last but not least, we introduce the use and benefits of writing PseudoCode, before writing our Java program.

This chapter provides a very clear platform to learn the current available tools needed to write program in most languages, making it easy to prepare for a successful Java programming career.

Key Terms

Compiling in Java	Compiling a program is to transform your source/program into a language that the hardware can understand.
	When you compile a Java program its compiler (javac) translates your program (the source code) into instructions that the JVM (Java Virtual Machine) understands. In Java these instructions are known as byte codes and are created in a file that has the same name as your program name and replaces .java with .class at the end of the name.
	program name = myFirstProgram.java
	compiled name = myFirstProgram.class
Computer Programming Language	Just like English, Spanish and French are human languages used by humans to communicate with each other, Computer Programming Languages such as Java, C, Perl, PHP, etc. are used by humans to give instructions to computers. Computers do what we tell them to do through Programming Languages.
	There are two general types of Computer Languages, compiled and interpreted languages.
	A compiled language is a language that when compiled, gets translated into a type of code called binary that the computer can understand. Binary is the natural language of computers. C, Cobol and Assembly are some of the compiled languages.
	Interpreted languages get translated into binary code when the program runs. Java is an interpreted language.
	Since program written using compiled languages are already compiled, they are much faster than program written in interpreted languages.
Creating Java Programs	Select an IDE (Integrated Development Environment) such as Eclipse or NetBeans or any editor of your choice. See detailed instructions in the corresponding section in Chapter 1.
	Once you are inside your code editor, start writing your program's source code file (your typed program). The program name requires three parts: the FirstName, one period/dot, and the word java. e.g., myFirstProgram.java.
Eclipse	A graphical user interface IDE to create Java programs. Download (FREE) from:
	http://www.eclipse.org/downloads/moreinfo/java.php

Editors	There are two types of editors. One is called IDE and the other Text Editor. Editors are programs that allows you to create your Java programs.
Graphical User Interface (GUI)	Graphical User Interface (GUI) are used by most people to access their computers. Computers using Windows, Linux, or Apple have beautiful graphical interfaces allowing the users easy management of their computer systems.
IDE Programming Editors	An IDE (Integrated Development Environment) is a programming tool that contains a code editor, a compiler, a debugger, and a GUI (Graphical User Interface) which allows the student to write programs easier. There are some disadvantages in using an IDE, such as all warnings are hidden therefore the student does not know that they exist. The best way to avoid this and other problems is to write the programs using text editors, which we will discuss in this book.
Java	The programming language Java is known as "write once run everywhere." This means that we can write our programs on any device, convert it into a standard code and run it in any device that contains a JVM (Java Virtual Machine). Installing JVM in devices and software packages such as Windows has become an industry standard practice.
Java JDK	The Java Development Kit (JDK) is an Oracle Corporation product aimed at Java developers. The JDK has as its primary components a collection of programming tools for Java. Download (FREE) Java JDK from: http://www.oracle.com/technetwork/java/javase/downloads/index.html Make sure you download the proper version for your computer 32 or 64 bits.
Netbeans	A graphical user interface IDE to create Java programs. Download (FREE) from: http://www.oracle.com/technetwork/java/javase/downloads/index.html
Operating System	Windows, Linux, and Apple are the most popular current Operating Systems. An Operating System is the software that allows the user to control the hardware.
PseudoCode	PseudoCode is the method of writing down the steps to be taken to solve a problem. This is done using regular English words without the use of any programming code.

Terminal Mode/ Command Line	To use editors such as Notepad, Gedit, VI, VIM, Pico, Nano, and TextEdit using terminal mode in Linux and in Windows.Command Line.
	Windows:
	To go to to the Command Line select:
	Windows: Start, run, cmd, enter
	Linux Ubuntu:
	Applications, Accessories, Terminal.
	Now open the editor of your choice.
	Create/Save your program e.g., myFirstProgram.java
	Compile your program as follows:
	javac myFirstProgram.java
	The javac command creates the compiled program called:
	myFirstProgram.class
	If your program has errors it will NOT compile until all errors are fixed.
	To run your compiled program: Java myFirstProgram (note no .class).
Text Editors	Text editors are programs that allow you to create your Java programs in terminal mode. After your first or second semester of programming languages, in my classes, I require that all work be done in terminal mode. The reason is that in most large companies, programmers and scientists prefer, and in some cases require to use computers in terminal mode.
	There are many free text editors available for all operating systems. In Windows we find Notepad and a third-party free editor called Notepad++. In Linux we find Gedit, Nano, Pico, VI and VIM, all free, and in Apple computers we find TextEdit.

Exercises

1. What is Java?

2. What is an Operating System?

3. What is a Computer Programming Language?

4. What do we need to create a computer program?

5. What is a computer?

6. What is the Java JDK?

7. What are editors?

8. What is Graphical User Interface (GUI)?

9. What are IDE Programming Editors?

10. What is NetBeans?

11. What is Eclipse?

12. What are text editors?

13. What is Notepad in Linux?

14. What is Gedit in Linux?

15. What is Nano in Linux?

16. What is Terminal Mode/Command Line?

17. How do you create Java programs?

18. How do you compile a Java program?

19. How do you run a Java program?

20. What is PseudoCode used for?

21. Write a PseudoCode example.

REFERENCES

- Java API Specifications

    http://www.oracle.com/technetwork/java/api-141528.html

- My Java programs that I use in my Java classes located at robinson.cs.fiu.edu

//END CHAPTER 1: THE BASICS

Getting Started

chapter 2

Let's Start Programming

Every Java program is a CLASS, therefore Java has class, it is a classy language.

Documenting a Program

Java provides us with three ways to document our work, they are called REMARKS. Any documentation with REMARKS is ignored by the Java compiler, and is not part of the program instructions.

The symbols /* begin a documentation area, and ends it with */ and such a section can be of any size, even thousands of pages, e.g.:

```
/*
   Author  : Michael Robinson
   Program : myFirstProgram.java
   Purpose : To present, the Java class, the main method,
             one variable of data type int
             one variable of data type String
             and the three print command of Java
   Updated : November 12th, 2099 by Michael
*/
```

The symbols // can be placed in any line of code, anything written after them is a remark, therefore ignored by the compiler.

< 17 >

```
// Create the variable myFirstName and assign my name to it.
String myFirstName = "Michael"; // This is a String Type variable
```

There is a third documentation procedure called Javadoc which generates html documentation, by adding Javadoc comments in the program code. These are some of the basic Javadoc comments. To see detail Javadoc documentation please see Chapter 17.

Javadoc Comments

The symbols /** .... */ are used by Javadoc. By placing Javadoc comments just before declaration statements, we can add descriptions to classes, methods, variables, and other tools that we have not seen yet such as constructors, and interfaces, e.g.:

```
/** creating JavadocExample class */
/** creating a class called JavadocExample */
public class JavadocExample
{
   /** declaring/creating the variable studentID */
   public int studentID;

   /** declaring the main method */
   public static void main( String arg[] )
   {
      // call all the methods

   }//end public static void main( String arg[] )

}//end public class JavadocExample
```

Every program must be documented fully and in detail, when you update a program that you wrote a month ago, or that was written by someone else, if it is not clearly documented, it is impossible to create proper updates.

What Are Imports?

Java is a very large programming language, when loaded it contains basic utilities that allow us to create a lot of programs. However to create some programs we need to import utilities into Java at the beginning of the program prior to the class header (see next section), e.g., if we want to obtain data from the keyboard we need to "import" a Java utility called Scanner as follows:

```
import java.util.Scanner;
```

If you include the line

```
import java.util.*;
```

Java will load all the commands (classes) in java.util

What is a Class?

In Java all programs are classes, to me a class is equivalent to the perimeter of my house, it has walls, a floor, and a ceiling. Whether it is one bedroom apartment or a 20 room mansion, it has a perimeter. Java programs are of all sizes, and their perimeter is the outside class. A program can be of the size of the Windows operating system (over a million lines of code) or as small as the program that controls the time and temperature of your microwave.

Creating a Class

```
public class nameOfProgram
{

}
```

The first line is called "the header," here the header is:

```
public class nameOfProgram
```

public specifies the type of access, public means that this program can be accessed by any other program.

class means that this program is a class, not a method.

nameOfProgram is the name of this class.

When you save your program to secondary storage (disk, usb, etc.) the program name MUST have the same name as the class name plus one period and the word java, therefore the program name for this class must be: nameOfProgram.java

When choosing a name make it meaningful, e.g., customerName, accountNumber, customerAddress are better than a, b, c.

My preferred naming convention is called camelCase, the first letter of the name is in lowercase, the first letter of the following words are upper case, and the name is as clear as possible to tell me what it means e.g., myFirstProgram, customerFirstName, customerLastName, accountNumber.

The class MUST have two curly braces { }, the opening brace { and the closing brace }. The rest of the program MUST be inside these two braces.

What is a Method?

A method is a section of code inside a program (class) which contains instructions written by you. Methods always go inside a class.

Methods are independent logical units of programming instructions, and can be re-used as often as necessary. If we have an error in a method, it is restricted in that method which makes finding and fixing errors easier.

Methods can not see each other, however they can communicate among themselves by making calls capable of passing and/or receiving data to/from each other.

Creating a Method

Every Java program needs a point to start, so when you start or run a program, Java needs to know where to go. In Java this start method is called main, it is the point of entry. This is how the main method looks:

```
public static void main( String arg[] )
{
     //instructions go here
}
```

public means that the method is visible and can be called from other methods.

static means that the method is associated with the class, and is not a specific instance of that class.

void means that the method is not returning any data to the method that called it. If the method instead of void had float, int, String, etc., it would be returning data of that type to the calling method/program.

main is the name of the method.

(String arg[]) always goes next to main. I will explain the meaning of this when we get to arrays.

All methods MUST have two curly braces { }, the opening brace { and the closing brace }. All instructions MUST be inside these two braces.

The main method MUST go inside the program/class, as follows :

```
public class nameOfProgram
{
    public static void main( String arg[] )
    {
       //instructions go here

    }//end public static void main( String arg[] )

}//end public class nameOfProgram
```

It can only be ONE main method in a class and it can NOT be inside another method. The main method can go anywhere but I recommend that it be located as the last method in the class, and of course inside the class. The reason is that all compiled languages require that the main method be the last method in the program, so if you get used to having the main method at the end, then your programs become standard, regardless of the programming language you are using.

Most programs need to display messages on a monitor/screen or printer to communicate with the user, even microwaves do that. Java uses multiple commands for this purpose. For the moment I will introduce the "println" command so that we can start programming. Later in the "Print Commands" section we will learn in detail how to implement the print, println, and printf commands.

Our first assignment consists in telling the world who we are, using a Java program. We already know what is a class and a main method. Inside the main method we are going to implement our first commands as follows:

```
/*
  Author  : Michael Robinson
  Program : nameOfProgram.java
  Purpose : To present, the Java class, the main method,
            and display my name using
            the Java println command
  Updated : January 14, 2099
*/
```

```
public class nameOfProgram
{
    public static void main( String arg[] )
    {
        System.out.println( "Hello World, my name is Joe" );
        System.out.println( "Have a nice day." );
    }
}
```

Lets break these lines of code:

```
        System.out.println( "Hello World, my name is Joe" );
        System.out.println( "Have a nice day." );
```

System.out.println means display whatever is between the () and inside the " ", then include a "line feed" or "enter" at the end of the text, so this program will produce the following results:

```
Your output (results) will look like this:
```

```
Hello World, my name is Joe
Have a nice day.
```

Every line of code containing a complete command (sometimes we need multiple lines to give a command to the computer) MUST end with a semicolon ; always.

Indentation

Just like a book, programming must follow a structure that allows all persons working in any program to visually understand the sections in it. If every line in a book was left justified, and there were no headings it will be very difficult to read, the same happens in programming.

The class header and its two braces are left justified. All methods inside the class MUST be indented the same amount of spaces, 3, 4, 5 or whatever is best for you. All methods MUST be equally separated by 2 or 3 spaces.

Print Commands

Java uses three distinct commands to print.

`System.out.print,` `System.out.println,` **and** `System.out.printf`

System.out.print

Remember that all statements in Java MUST end with a ;

When a print statement is too long to fit in one line we can split it at the + symbol.

```
System.out.print( "My name is : " + myFirstName +
                  " My ID is : " + myID + "\n" );
```

System.out.print displays whatever is between the () following these rules:

whatever is between " " will be printed

the + adds the contents of the next variable

the + adds what is between the " "

the + adds the contents of the next variable

the + adds the enter key which is \n in Java.

System.out.println

```
System.out.println( "My name is : " + myFirstName +
                    " My ID is : " + myID );
```

System.out.println is exactly the same as System.out.print, except that the command \n does not need to be added inside the (), unless you want an additional line print to be executed, because \n or line print is included in the System.out.println with the letters ln meaning add one line feed or carriage return.

The \n command can be inserted at any location in the print, and as many times as needed, as long as it is inside "", creating an additional line feed or carriage return.

System.out.printf

This is the Java implementation of the ANSI C printf command, it is very powerful, and can do all, and more than the above print and println commands.

When a printf statement is too long to fit in one line we can split it at the ", location.

```java
System.out.printf( "My name is : %s My ID is : %d\n",
                   myFirstName, myID );
```

printf contains several distinct placeholders where the corresponding data variables will display. These placeholders must be inside " " and they look like these:

%d = displays variables of int data type

%s = displays variables of String data type

%c = displays variables of char data type

%f = displays variables of float or double data type

   to these data types (float and double) we can request the

   amount of decimals we want, e.g.

   for a float with 2 decimal we use:

%.2f = displays variables of float data type with 2 decimals.

   We can have as many decimal places as needed.

After the " " inside the printf statement we place a, (comma) and then the corresponding variables in the same sequence as the placeholders. e.g.:

```java
System.out.printf( "My name is : %s My ID is : %d\n",
                   myFirstName, myID );


                   myFirstName uses the first placeholder %s
                   myID uses the second placeholder %d
```

Summary

This chapter shows us how to get organized before writing a program. Once we have written the PseudoCode as explained in Chapter 1, it is very easy for us to build the parts that are required to create our current project/program.

First between /* */ we create a summary to identify program name, author, purpose, and update dates, then we add the necessary imports and create the class section. Inside the class section we create the main method from which we call all the additional methods.

In this chapter we covered three ways of printing in Java. Notice that Java has implemented the System.out.printf command that is used in ANSI C. I personally prefer this command to System.out.print and System.out.println because it allows me to access more functions than the other two.

Finally, indentation is very important. There are different forms of implementing indentation such as:

```java
public static void main( String arg[] )
{
   //call methods
}
```

and, among others

```java
public static void main( String[] args ) {
   //call methods
}
```

I prefer the first sample, which I use it in the entire book. Select whichever is best for you, but make sure to be consistent.

Key Terms

Comments. Javadoc Comments	The symbols /** .... */ are used by Javadoc. By placing Javadoc comments just before declaration statements, we can add descriptions to classes, methods, variables, and other tools that we have not seen yet such as constructors, and interfaces, e.g.: /** creating JavadocExample class */ /** creating a class called JavadocExample */

Documenting a Program	Java provides us with three ways to document our work, they are called REMARKS. Any documentation with REMARKS is ignored by the Java compiler, and is not part of the program instructions.
	The symbols /* begin a documentation area, and ends it with */ Such a section can be of any size, even thousands of pages, e.g.:
	
	``
	/*
	    Author : Michael Robinson
	    Program : myFirstProgram.java
	    Purpose : To present, the Java class, the main
	                    method,
	                    one variable of data type int
	                    one variable of data type String
	                    and the three print command of Java
	
	    Updated : November 12th, 2099
	*/
	``
	
	The symbols // can be placed in any line of code, anything written after them is a remark, therefore ignored by the compiler.

Imports	Java is a very large programming language, when loaded it contains basic utilities that allows us to create a lot of programs, however to create some programs we need to import utilities into Java at the beginning of the program prior to the class header (see next section), e.g. If we want to obtain data from the keyboard we need to "import" a Java utility called Scanner as follows: import java.util.Scanner;

Indentation. Java Indentation	Just like a book, programming must follow a structure that allows all persons working in any program to visually understand the sections in it. If every line in a book was left justified, and there were no headings it will be very difficult to read, the same happens in programming. The class header and its two braces are left justified. All methods inside the class MUST be indented the same amount of spaces, 3, 4, 5 or whatever is best for you. All methods MUST be equally separated by 2 or 3 spaces.
Java Classes	In Java all programs are classes, to me a class is equivalent to the perimeter of my house, it has walls, a floor, and a ceiling. Whether it is one bedroom apartment or a 20 room mansion it has a perimeter. Java programs are of all sizes, and their perimeter is the outside class. A program can be of the size of the Windows operating system (over a million lines of code) or as small as the program that controls the time and temperature of your microwave.
Methods. Java Methods	A method is a section of code inside a program (class) which contains instructions written by you. Methods always go inside a class. Methods are independent logical units of programming instructions, and can be re-used as often as necessary. If we have an error in a method, it is restricted to that method which makes finding and fixing errors easier. Methods cannot see each other, however they can communicate among themselves by making calls capable of passing and/or receiving data to/from each other.
Print Commands	Java uses three distinct commands to print. System.out.print, System.out.println, and System.out.printf
System.out.print	Remember that all statements in Java MUST end with a ; When a print statement is too long to fit in one line we can split it at the + symbol, e.g.: System.out.print("My name is : " + myFirstName + " My ID is : " + myID + "\n"); System.out.print displays whatever is between the () following these rules: whatever is between "" will be printed the + adds the contents of the next variable the + adds what is between the "" the + adds the contents of the next variable the + adds the enter key which is \n in Java.

System.out.printf	This is the Java implementation of the ANSI C printf command, it is very powerful, and can do all, and more than the above print and println commands.
	When a printf statement is too long to fit in one line we can split it at the ", location.
	System.out.printf("My name is : %s My ID is : %d\n", myFirstName, myID);
	System.out.printf contains several distinct placeholders where the corresponding data variables will display. These placeholders must be inside "" and they look like these:

	%d = displays variables of int data type
	%s = displays variables of String data type
	%c = displays variables of char data type
	%f = displays variables of float or double data type to
	      these data types (float and double) we can request the
	      amount of decimals we want, e.g.:
	%.2f displays variables of float data type with 2 decimals.
	%3.2f diplays 3 whole numbers with 2 decimals.

	We can have as many whole and decimal places as needed.
	After the "" inside the printf statement we place a , (comma) and then the corresponding variables in the same sequence as the placeholders, e.g.:
	System.out.printf("My name is : %s My ID is : %d\n", myFirstName, myID);
	myFirstName uses the first placeholder %s myID uses the second placeholder %d

System.out. println	System.out.println("My name is : " + myFirstName + " My ID is : " + myID);
	System.out.println is exactly the same as System.out.print, except that the command \n does not need to be added inside the (), unless you want an additional line print to be executed, because \n or line print is included in the System.out.println with the letters ln meaning add one line feed or carriage return.
	The \n command can be inserted at any location in any of the three print commands, and as many times as needed, as long as it is inside "", creating an additional line feed or carriage return.

Exercises

1. Create a sample documentation section describing the program being written.

2. What are import lines used for in your program.

3. Create a class giving a clear name.

4. Write your main method calling 4 methods.

5. Add the 4 methods being called from the main method

6. The purpose of the imports are _____ (Select all that apply)
   a. To let Java know that we are running in Netbeans
   b. To load into Java, classes that are not loaded by default
   c. Implementation of PseudoCode previously written
   d. Be able to compile the source code

7. What is the purpose of a Java class _____ (Select all that apply)
   a. Make Java into a classy language
   b. To have a blueprint from which programs are created
   c. To be able to convert C++ programs into Java
   d. To create websites

8. Name the require method to create a Java program _____ (Select all that apply)
   a. public class nameOfProgram
   b. public static void main(String arg[])
   c. public static void main(String[] args)
   d. public main()

9. Why should we have indentation when writing programs _____ (Select all that apply)
   a. It is a waste of time, all code should be left justified.
   b. To make programs look like books
   c. It is required by Java
   d. To visually understand the logic of a program and make it easier to find errors.

10. What is a method _____ (Select all that apply)
    a. We only need one method to write all the program, usually the main method
    b. A way of writing imports
    c. A logical section of code with a specific purpose
    d. A section that contains all program documentation only

11. List 3 benefits of a method _____ (Select all that apply)
    a. To write the entire program in the main method
    b. Reuse code, divide and conquer problem, limit errors locations
    c. Easier to add functionality to programs, by adding new methods
    d. Easy to save, can use numbers as names, easy to modify

REFERENCES

- Java API Specifications

> http://www.oracle.com/technetwork/java/api-141528.html

- My Java programs that I use in my Java classes located at robinson.cs.fiu.edu

//END CHAPTER 2: GETTING STARTED

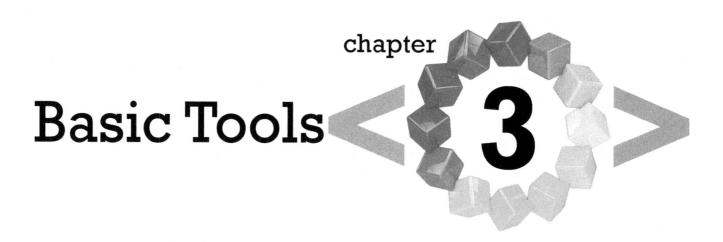

Basic Tools

Numerical Systems

Throughout the existence of humans, we have invented many numeric systems. Here we are going to discuss four types that we will use in this programming class.

Decimal Numerical System

We use this numerical system everyday. It contains 10 digits from 0 to 9 and it is known as base-10 numerical system because it has 10 numbers. Our common daily math computations are done with these 10 digits, e.g.:

```
idNumber = 9876;

x = 5 + 2;

addNumbers( 3, 7, 8, 123, 45 );
```

Binary Numerical System

Computers and all digital systems, such as cell phones, digital cameras, etc. use the binary systems or base-2 numeric system, which has 2 digits, 0 and 1. At first, it is hard to understand, but everything a digital system does, like video, sound, graphics, calculators, etc., is represented in binary. When we use programming languages we write the programs in plain English commands, and the programming language, in this case Java translates our work into binary, which is what digital systems understand, even the decimal system is translated into binary.

< 33 >

Why Binary?

The language of digital equipment is the binary numerical system. Any number can be represented by any sequence of bits (binary digits), which in turn may be represented by any mechanism capable of being in two mutually exclusive states, such as electric or magnetic, on/off.

The first known description of a binary numeral system was presented during the 5th–2nd centuries BC by the Indian scholar Pingala. Since then variations have been presented in China, Africa, France, Germany, and the United States. In 1937, Claude Shannon implemented Boolean algebra and binary arithmetic using electronic relays and switches for the first time in history. In his master's thesis at MIT entitled A Symbolic Analysis of Relay and Switching Circuits, Shannon's thesis essentially founded practical digital circuit design.

A byte is a sequence of bits (binary digits), today we use 4, 8, 16, 32, 64 bit bytes, etc.

8 Bits Byte Samples

Decimal		Binary		
0	=	0 0 0 0	0 0 0 0	
1	=	0 0 0 0	0 0 0 1	
2	=	0 0 0 0	0 0 1 0	
3	=	0 0 0 0	0 0 1 1	
4	=	0 0 0 0	0 1 0 0	
5	=	0 0 0 0	0 1 0 1	
6	=	0 0 0 0	0 1 1 0	
7	=	0 0 0 0	0 1 1 1	
8	=	0 0 0 0	1 0 0 0	
9	=	0 0 0 0	1 0 0 1	
10	=	0 0 0 0	1 0 1 0	
11	=	0 0 0 0	1 0 1 1	
12	=	0 0 0 0	1 1 0 0	
13	=	0 0 0 0	1 1 0 1	
14	=	0 0 0 0	1 1 1 0	
15	=	0 0 0 0	1 1 1 1	
16	=	0 0 0 1	0 0 0 0	
:				
32	=	0 0 1 0	0 0 0 0	
:				
64	=	0 1 0 0	0 0 0 0	
:				
128	=	1 0 0 0	0 0 0 0	
:				
255	=	1 1 1 1	1 1 1 1	

We say that when a bit is ON we represent it with the number 1, when the bit is off then it represented with the number 0. We will use the above line of code (1 1 1 1 1 1 1 1) to explain why its decimal value is 255.

```
255 =    1    1    1    1    1    1    1    1
255 = 128   64   32   16    8    4    2    1
```

As we can see, if we start at the right most location of the byte, every bit to the left is double its value. When we add all the bits, the highest decimal value of an 8 bit byte is 255, which is the highest decimal representation in the ASCII values (please see ASCII Codes Table below). At the present time, to get a stable magnetic state, each bit requires 1,000,000 atoms. To see a detailed explanation of binary numbers and how to convert them to hexadecimal and to decimal numbers, as well to ASCII, please consult the Operating Systems for IT book written by Michael Robinson and published by Kendall-Hunt Publishing.

Hexadecimal Numerical System

This numerical system is base-16 it goes for 0 – F, that is from 0–9 then ABCDEF

```
A = 10
B = 11
C = 12
D = 13
E = 14
F = 15
```

At one time or another we have experienced computer problems where error messages show up on the screen such as:

memory dump at: DA9F011231CCABDEDACF765

What this means is that a RAM memory error occurred at memory location DA9F011231CCABDEDACF765.

The current Oracle SPARC M6-32 Server contains 32 terabytes of RAM memory.
https://www.oracle.com/servers/sparc/m6-32/index.html

ASCII Codes Table

ASCII means American Standard Code for Information Interchange. Every character that a computer makes is assigned a numerical value, the ASCII code is limited to the first 128 characters/numbers, from 0 to 127. There are 33 non-printing control characters like esc, bell, etc. that affects how text and space is processed; 95 are printable characters such as a, b, c, 1, 2, H. Y, T, etc.

The Extended ASCII characters begin at 128 and ends at 255, these group contains non-english alphabetical characters such as:

```
ASCII    Symbol
128  =     ç
164  =     ñ
142  =     À
230  =     µ
145  =     æ
228  =     Σ
```

Work on ASCII formally began on October 6, 1960. The first edition of the standard was published during 1963, a major revision during 1967, and the most recent update during 1986.

A program that prints the ASCII codes can be seen at the Miscellaneous Chapter at section "ASCII Codes Program."

ASCII TABLES

NUMBERS

KEY NAME	ASCII CODE	KEY NAME	ASCII CODE
1	49	6	54
2	50	7	55
3	51	8	56
4	52	9	57
5	53	0	58

ALPHABET

KEY NAME	ASCII CODE	KEY NAME	ASCII CODE
A	65	a	97
B	66	b	98
C	67	c	99
D	68	d	100
E	69	e	101

F	70	f	102
G	71	g	103
H	72	h	104
I	73	i	105
J	74	j	106
K	75	k	107
L	76	l	108
M	77	m	109
N	78	n	110
O	79	o	111
P	80	p	112
Q	81	q	113
R	82	r	114
S	83	s	115
T	84	t	116
U	85	u	117
V	86	v	118
W	87	w	119
X	88	x	120
Y	89	y	121
Z	90	z	122

SOME EXTENDED CHARACTERS

KEY NAME	ASCII CODE	KEY NAME	ASCII CODE
á	160	ü	129
é	130	ñ	164
í	161	Ñ	165
ó	162	¿	168
ú	163	¡	173

To obtain the extended ASCII characters in Windows, press and hold the ALT key and enter the corresponding ASCII code, for instance to obtain Ñ enter ALT 165

To write the letter A in binary, we write its ASCII code

$$A = 65 = 0100\ 0001$$

To find the ASCII value of all/any letter in the English language we need to remember two numbers, 65 and 32. The numeric ASCII value for A is 65, B is 66, C is 67 and so on. The ASCII value for "space" is 32. So if we remember 65 for A and 32 for space, we can figure out the ASCII value for every English letter.

To find the lowercase ASCII value of any uppercase letter, we add 32 to the ASCII value of the uppercase letter:

$$A = 65 \quad a = 97 \qquad B = 66 \quad b = 98 \qquad \text{and so on}$$

To find the uppercase ASCII value of any lowercase letter, we subtract 32 from the ASCII value of the lowercase letter:

$$a = 97 \quad A = 65 \qquad b = 98 \quad B = 66 \qquad \text{and so on}$$

A program that prints the ASCII codes can be seen at the Miscellaneous Chapter at section "ASCII Codes Program."

The Unicode Standard

This is another coding system that can represent over 100,000 characters. The origins of Unicode date back to 1987. The latest version of Unicode consists of more than 109,000 characters covering 93 scripts, a set of code charts for visual reference, display of text containing both right-to-left scripts, such as Hebrew and Arabic, as well as left-to-right scripts.

All the values represented in the ASCII codes are in the same locations in the Unicode Standard.

Data Types

In math we assign numbers to variables such as a, b, c, etc. e.g.,

```
a = 5        where a becomes 5
b = 12.4     where b becomes 12.4
c = a + b    where c becomes 17.4
```

In computer Science a variable is a descriptive name given to a known amount of information, so that we can use such a variable regardless of the value it represents. The value of variables can change during the life of the program.

In Java we do the same, however before assigning a value to a variable, we assign what we call a data type to the variable.

Primitive Data Types

Each Primitive has its own name, occupying a specific amount of Bytes, and containing a minimum and a maximum value. The amount of Bytes and values depend on the computer the program is running on. Large computer systems have different values. The following are the typical values on today's standard personal computers.

Today's Primitive Data Types use the Unicode Standard, all the values represented in the ASCII codes are in the same locations in the Unicode Standard. **These are the primitive data types in Java:**

Name	Bits	Min Val	Max Val
byte	8	-128	127
char	8	-32,768	32,767
int	32	-2,147,483,648	2,147,483,64
short	16	-32,768	32,767
long	64	-9,223,372,036,854,775,808	9,223,372,036,854,775,807
float	32	-+1.701411E-38	-+1.701411E38
double	64	-+1.0E-307	-+1.0E307
boolean	1	true/false	

The following describes each primitive data type:

byte

An eight bit byte allows us to write data values from -128 to 128 or a maximum positive number of 255 by turning all 8 bits on, and then adding them. In this book we will only deal with positive numbers to describe bytes.

```
Bit number      8  7  6  5  4  3  2  1
State on        1  1  1  1  1  1  1  1
Decimal value  128 64 32 16  8  4  2  1 = 255
```

char

The char data type is used to place a single character, such as a letter, number, or symbol. Numbers of char data type are treated as characters not numbers.

int

An int number will hold a whole number. If you placed a number with decimals into an int, the decimals will be dropped.

short

A short number will also hold a whole number but of less value than an int, see table on page 39.

long

A long will also hold a whole number but of greater value than an int, see table on page 39.

float

A float holds whole numbers with decimals, for ranges see table on page 39.

double

A double holds whole numbers with decimals, with much greater values than the float, for ranges see table on page 39.

boolean

The boolean type has only two values, true or false. When we declare a variable of type boolean we can only assign it to be either true or false, e.g.,

```
boolean electricCurrent = true;
boolean electricCurrent = false;
```

To see a more detailed description of the Java Primitive Data Type please see:

http://docs.oracle.com/javase/tutorial/java/nutsandbolts/datatypes.html

What Can We Do with Primitives?

Since primitives are used to represent numbers and single characters, we assign variables/names to each value, e.g.,

```
Type    Name                       Value
double  currentTotalGPA        = 3.68;
char    currentLetterGrade     = A;
int     amountOfCreditsTaken   = 120;
int     maxCreditsPerSemester  = 12;
float   semestersPerYear       = 2.5;
```

If we want to find out how many years it took to obtain the above amountOfCreditsTaken we can do the following:

```
int crYear = ( amountOfCreditsTaken / maxCreditsPerSemester );
int years  = ( crYear / semestersPerYear );

System.out.println( "Amount of years = " + years );
```

In this previous line of code we see + years after the ending ", this means to append the value of years to the data between the "", so the output is:

```
Amount of years = 4
```

The Primitive Data Type int named years, contains the value 4.

As you can see, assigning clear names to variables makes life very easy when programming, even though it takes longer to write:

```
int     amountOfCreditsTaken  = 120;
int     maxCreditsPerSemester = 12;
float   semestersPerYear      = 2.5;

int     crYear = ( amountOfCreditsTaken / maxCreditsPerSemester );
int     years  = ( crYear / semestersPerYear );

System.out.println( "Amount of years = " + years );
```

It is much easier to read and understand the above code than the following code:

```
int    a = 120;
int    b =  12;
float  c =   2.5;
int    y = ( (a / b) / c );


System.out.println( "Amount of years = " + y );
```

Usually five minutes after we write the short code we forget what was the meaning of a or b or c. What about 5 years later when you need to adjust this code to make it run on new technologies?.

Problems Choosing the Wrong Data Types

Notice how we can get into a big problem when we choose the wrong type of primitive to find an answer:

```
Notice that 527 / 18 = 29.27777777

and 29.27777777 /  3 =  9.7592592593
```

But when we do the computations using int instead of float we get 9 not 9.7592592593 which is the correct answer.

Reason: when we divide one integer by another integer and assign the result to another int, Java "truncates" all results, meaning it ignores all decimals. So to avoid this problem, we need to select the correct data types or use a Java tool called "casting."

To cast a variable means to convert or promote its primitive data type to a higher primitive. int to float, int to double, float to double, etc.

When we divide an int by another int we must cast either one of the ints, as shown below, to avoid having the total being truncated and lose all decimal values, therefore instead of:

```
int crYear = ( amountOfCreditsTaken / maxCreditsPerSemester );
```

we declare crYear as a float to be able to accept the computation, and using the casting (float) command we cast either one of the two ints by placing (float) on front of either variables as follows:

```
float crYear = ( (float) amountOfCreditsTaken /
                 maxCreditsPerSemester );
```

```
        or
```

```
float crYear = ( amountOfCreditsTaken /
                 ( float ) maxCreditsPerSemester );
```

The above Java source code makes the value in crYears into a correct float value because we are promoting/casting either int field amountOfCreditsTaken or maxCreditsPerSemester into a float.

Now since crYear is of float type there is not need to cast it. When we do a mathematical operation between numbers of different primitive types the data types, the result is always the larger Primitive Data Type being used in the calculation. In the following example since crYear and semestersPerYear are both of float type, the result in the years variable will not be truncated.

```
float years = ( crYear / semestersPerYear );
```

```
System.out.println( "Amount of years = " + years );
```

Creating a Variable and Assigning a Value to it

In Java we can declare a variable without assigning a value to it, however I recommend that you become used to assigning a value, if necessary zero, because in some languages like ANSI C, if you do not assign a value to a new variable, it assigns the value found at the memory location where the variable gets created, which can cause big problems.

```
double speedOfLight  = 186,282;   //miles per second
float  earthDiameter = 7,926.41;  //miles
int    myAge         = 105;       //my age
float  myHeigth      = 5.9;       //my height
```

Numerical Operators

There are some special symbols called Operators that perform specific operations on one, two or three numbers, giving us a result.

```
In math we say:     x = 3 + 5
but we never say:   x = x + 5
```

In computer science we can say both of the previous examples, the second method needs the following explanation:

```
int basket = 5; //creates variable basket and assign value 5 to it.

basket = basket + 1; //add one to the current value of basket
                     //the new value of basket is 6

basket = basket - 3; //takes 3 from to the current value of
                     //basket the new value of basket is 3
```

In the same manner we can implement multiplication and division.

```
basket = basket * 3; //note * means multiplication
basket = basket / 3; //note / means division
```

The following section shows other ways to use the math operators:

```
=, --, ++, -=, +=, *=, /=
```

```
int counter = 0;      //create and initialize counter to 0

    counter++;        //adds 1 to counter, = 1

    counter *= 6;     //multiply counter by 6, = 6

    counter /= 2;     //divide counter by 2, = 3

    counter--;        //take one from counter, = 2

    counter -= 2;     //take 2 from counter, = 0

    counter += 100;   //add 100 to counter, = 100
```

Other Operators

Variations of -- and ++ before and after the variable.

if we have:

```
int counter = 100;

System.out.println( "counter = " + counter );

prints:  counter = 100
```

and

```
System.out.println( "counter = " + counter++ );

also prints :   counter = 100
```

but the value of counter after the printing, is 101, because counter++ means to add 1 to counter after it prints its value (in this case), but

```
System.out.println( "counter = " ++counter );

will print : counter = 101
```

because ++counter first adds 1 to the counter value, then prints it.

The same happens to the -- commands before and after the variable.

Operators > and <

The operator > means left value is greater than right value e.g.:

```
5 > 2   same as in math, 5 is greater than 2
```

The operator < means left value is smaller than right value e.g.:

```
2 < 5   same as in math, 2 is less than 5
```

Operators >= and <=

The operator >= means left value is greater or equal to right value e.g.:

```
5 >= 5   same as in math, 5 is greater or equal to 5
5 >= 4   same as in math, 5 is greater or equal to 4
```

The operator <= means left value is smaller or equal to right value e.g.:

```
5 <= 5   same as in math, 5 is less or equal to 5
4 <= 5   same as in math, 4 is less or equal to 5
```

Operators =, ==, !=

This is where many people get confused and cause programming errors.

The operator = means the right value is assigned to the left value e.g.,

```
total = 5; // 5 is assigned to the variable total
```

The operator == means equivalence, we check to see if the left value is equivalent to the right value:

```
if( total == 5 ) //if total is equivalent to 5 then
                      //total and 5 have the same value
```

The operator != mean not equal, we check to see if the left value is not equal to the right value

```
if( total != 5 ) //if total is not equal to 5
```

Operators &&

The operator && means logical "and"

```
if( cold && raining ) //if cold and raining
```

Operators ||

The operator || means logical "or"

```
if( cold || raining ) //if cold or raining
```

Operator %

The % operator also known as modulus and mod, means remainder when dividing two numbers, but the result is always an int, which is different than division. Division keeps the decimals in the result, again % gives you and int, dropping/truncating the decimals.

% looks like division but it is NOT

```
5 % 2 = 1 //this is modulus
```

means that 2 exists twice in 5 leaving 1 as the the modulus

```
182 % 3 = 2
```

3 exists 60 times in 182 leaving 2 as the modulus

```
55 % 7 = 6
```

7 exists 7 times in 55 leaving 6 as the modulus

```
2000 % 4 = 0
```

4 exist 500 times in 2000 leaving 0 as the modulus. The % operator is very useful in programming, allowing us to perform very complex operations easily.

Math Using Primitives

Java provide us with already made methods to do many math computations. The math class is called Math.

The following program shows the implementation of some Math methods.

```
/*
  Author   : Michael Robinson
  Program  : mathExamples.java
  Purpose  : To present multiple ways of processing Java build-in
             mathematical functions:
             processAbsoluteValues( i, j, x, y );
             processRoundValues( x, y );
             processCeilingValues( x, y );
             processFlooringValues( x, y );
             processMinimunValues( i, j, x, y );
             processMaximunValues( i, j, x, y );
             processTrigFunctionValues( i, j );
             processExponentialValues();
             processLogValues();
             processPowerValues();
             processSquareRootsValues();
             processRandomValues();

  Updated  : January 14, 2099
*/
```

```java
public class mathExamples
{
    public static void processAbsoluteValues( int i, int j, double x,
                                                double y )
    {
        // Math.abs(i) The absolute value of a number is equal to
        // the number if the number is positive or zero and equal
        // to the negative of the number if the number is negative.
        System.out.println( "|" + i + "| is " + Math.abs(i) );
        System.out.println( "|" + j + "| is " + Math.abs(j) );
        System.out.println( "|" + x + "| is " + Math.abs(x) );
        System.out.println( "|" + y + "| is " + Math.abs(y) );

    }//end processAbsoluteValues(int i, int j, double x, double y )


    public static void processRoundValues( double x, double y )
    {
        // Math.round(x)
        // Truncating and Rounding functions
        // You can round off a floating point number
        // to the nearest integer with round()
        System.out.println( x + " is approximately " +
                    Math.round(x) );
        System.out.println( y + " is approximately " +
                    Math.round(y) );

    }//end processRoundValues( double x, double y );


    public static void processCeilingValues( double x, double y )
    {
        // Math.ceil(x)
        // Ceiling of a number is the smallest integer greater than
        // or equal to the number. Every integer is its own ceiling.
        System.out.println( "Ceiling of " + x + " is " +
                    Math.ceil(x) );
        System.out.println( "Ceiling of " + y + " is " +
                    Math.ceil(y) );

    }//end processCeilingValues( double x, double y );
```

```java
public static void processFlooringValues( double x, double y )
{
    // Math.floor(i)
    // The "floor" of a number is the largest integer less than
    // or equal to the number. Every integer is its own floor.
    System.out.println( "Floor of " + x + " is " +
                        Math.floor(x) );
    System.out.println( "Floor of " + y + " is " +
                        Math.floor(y) );

}//end processFlooringValues( double x, double y )


public static void processMinimunValues( int i, int j, double x,
                                                      double y )
{
    // min() returns the smaller of the two arguments you pass
    System.out.println( "min(" + i + "," + j + ") is " +
                        Math.min(i,j) );
    System.out.println( "min(" + x + "," + y + ") is " +
                        Math.min(x,y) );
    System.out.println( "min(" + i + "," + x + ") is " +
                        Math.min(i,x) );
    System.out.println( "min(" + y + "," + j + ") is " +
                        Math.min(y,j) );

}//end processMinimunValues( int i, int j, double x, double y )


public static void processMaximunValues( int i, int j, double x,
                                                      double y )
{
    // There's a corresponding max() method
    // that returns the larger of two numbers
    System.out.println( "max(" + i + "," + j + ") is " +
                        Math.max(i,j) );
    System.out.println( "max(" + x + "," + y + ") is " +
                        Math.max(x,y) );
    System.out.println( "max(" + i + "," + x + ") is " +
                        Math.max(i,x) );
    System.out.println( "max(" + y + "," + j + ") is " +
                        Math.max(y,j) );
```

```java
    }//end processMaximunValues(int i, int j, double x, double y )


public static void processTrigFunctionValues( int i, int j )
{
    // The Math library defines a couple of useful constants:
    System.out.println( "Pi is " + Math.PI );
    System.out.println( "e is " + Math.E );

    // Trigonometric methods. All arguments are given in radians
    // Convert a 45 degree angle to radians
    double angle = 45.0 * 2.0 * Math.PI/360.0;
    System.out.println( "cos(" + angle + ") is " +
                        Math.cos(angle) );
    System.out.println( "sin(" + angle + ") is " +
                        Math.sin(angle) );

    //Inverse Trigonometric methods.
    //All values returned as radians
    double value = 0.707;
    System.out.println( "acos(" + value + ") is " +
                        Math.acos(value));
    System.out.println( "asin(" + value + ") is " +
                        Math.asin(value) );
    System.out.println( "atan(" + value + ") is " +
                        Math.atan(value) );
    System.out.println( "atan(" + i + ") is " + Math.atan(i) );
    System.out.println( "atan(" + j + ") is " + Math.atan(j) );

}//processTrigFunctionValues(int i, int j, double x, double y )


public static void processExponentialValues()
{
    // Exponential and Logarithmic Methods
    // exp(a) returns e (2.71828...) raised to the power of a.
    System.out.println( "exp(1.0) is "  + Math.exp(1.0) );
    System.out.println( "exp(10.0) is " + Math.exp(10.0) );
    System.out.println( "exp(0.0) is "  + Math.exp(0.0) );

}//end processExponentialValues();
```

```java
public static void processLogValues()
{
    // log(a) returns the natural logarithm (base e) of a.

    System.out.println( "log(1.0) is "     + Math.log(1.0) );
    System.out.println( "log(10.0) is "    + Math.log(10.0) );
    System.out.println( "log(Math.E) is " + Math.log(Math.E) );

}//end processLogValues();


public static void processPowerValues()
{
    // pow(x, y) returns the x raised to the yth power.
    System.out.println( "pow(2.0, 2.0) is " +
                        Math.pow(2.0,2.0) );
    System.out.println( "pow(10.0, 3.5) is " +
                        Math.pow(10.0,3.5) );
    System.out.println( "pow(8, -1) is " + Math.pow(8,-1) );

}//end processPowerValues();


public static void processSquareRootsValues()
{
    // sqrt(i) returns the square root of i.
    int i = 0;
    for( i = -7; i < 10; i++ )
    {
        System.out.println( "The square root of " + i + " is " +
                        Math.sqrt(i));
    }

}//end processSquareRootsValues()


public static void processRandomValues()
{
    // Finally there's one Random method that returns a
    // pseudo-random number between 0.0 and 1.0;
    System.out.println( "Here's one random number: " +
                        Math.random() );
    System.out.println( "Here's another random number: " +
                        Math.random() );
```

```
    }//end public static void processRandomValues()


    public static void main( String args[] )
    {
        int i = 7;
        int j = 9;
        double x = 72.5;
        double y = 0.34;

        processAbsoluteValues( i, j, x, y );
        processRoundValues( x, y );
        processCeilingValues( x, y );
        processFlooringValues( x, y );
        processMinimunValues( i, j, x, y );
        processMaximunValues( i, j, x, y );
        processTrigFunctionValues( i, j );
        processExponentialValues();
        processLogValues();
        processPowerValues();
        processSquareRootsValues();
        processRandomValues();

        System.out.println( "\nEnd of Program" );

    }//end public static void main( String args[] )

}//end public class mathExamples
```

Your output (results) will look like this:

```
|7| is 7
|9| is 9
|72.5| is 72.5
|0.34| is 0.34
72.5 is approximately 73
0.34 is approximately 0
Ceiling of 72.5 is 73.0
Ceiling of 0.34 is 1.0
Floor of 72.5 is 72.0
Floor of 0.34 is 0.0
min(7,9) is 7
min(72.5,0.34) is 0.34
min(7,72.5) is 7.0
```

```
min(0.34,9) is 0.34
max(7,9) is 9
max(72.5,0.34) is 72.5
max(7,72.5) is 72.5
max(0.34,9) is 9.0
Pi is 3.141592653589793
e is 2.718281828459045
cos(0.7853981633974483) is 0.7071067811865476
sin(0.7853981633974483) is 0.7071067811865475
acos(0.707) is 0.7855491633997437
asin(0.707) is 0.785247163395153
atan(0.707) is 0.6154085176292563
atan(7) is 1.4288992721907328
atan(9) is 1.460139105621001
exp(1.0) is 2.718281828459045
exp(10.0) is 22026.465794806718
exp(0.0) is 1.0
log(1.0) is 0.0
log(10.0) is 2.302585092994046
log(Math.E) is 1.0
pow(2.0, 2.0) is 4.0
pow(10.0, 3.5) is 3162.2776601683795
pow(8, -1) is 0.125
The square root of -7 is NaN
The square root of -6 is NaN
The square root of -5 is NaN
The square root of -4 is NaN
The square root of -3 is NaN
The square root of -2 is NaN
The square root of -1 is NaN
The square root of 0 is 0.0
The square root of 1 is 1.0
The square root of 2 is 1.4142135623730951
The square root of 3 is 1.7320508075688772
The square root of 4 is 2.0
The square root of 5 is 2.23606797749979
The square root of 6 is 2.449489742783178
The square root of 7 is 2.6457513110645907
The square root of 8 is 2.8284271247461903
The square root of 9 is 3.0
Here's one random number: 0.5551149570276933
Here's another random number: 0.2810280749677071


End of Program
```

Let's examine this code:

The above program is called: mathExamples.java

At the beginning of the program between /* and */ we have a detailed section that documents what this program does. Every program should have this section.

We then declare this program with the line:

```
public class mathExamples
```

Please note that the entire program lives between { and }

The public static void main(String args[]) is found as the last method in the program. In this method we first declare the necessary variables and assign values to them:

```
int i = 7;
int j = 9;
double x = 72.5;
double y = 0.34;
```

Then, passing variables (data that we created) for most of the methods, we call our own following 12 methods:

```
processAbsoluteValues( i, j, x, y );
processRoundValues( x, y );
processCeilingValues( x, y );
processFlooringValues( x, y );
processMinimunValues( i, j, x, y );
processMaximunValues( i, j, x, y );
processTrigFunctionValues( i, j );
processExponentialValues();
processLogValues();
processPowerValues();
processSquareRootsValues();
processRandomValues();
```

The last thing we do is to inform the user that the program has ended, using the following line of code:

```
System.out.println( "\nEnd of Program" );
```

Notice that at the beginning of each method that we created, we write its own detailed documentation describing what each method does:

```
// Math.ceil(x)
// Ceiling of a number is the smallest integer greater than
// or equal to the number. Every integer is its own ceiling.
```

then we have the code that implements the previous documentation:

```
System.out.println( "|" + i + "| is " + Math.abs(i) );
System.out.println( "|" + j + "| is " + Math.abs(j) );
System.out.println( "|" + x + "| is " + Math.abs(x) );
System.out.println( "|" + y + "| is " + Math.abs(y) );
```

In this section we print the value of 'i' surrounded by ||, the word 'is' and the computation of math class Math.abs(i) which prints the absolute value of the 'i' variable.

All the other methods do similar work.

Remember, learning to program is like learning to drive a car, the more you do it the better you become at it.

Wrappers

As we learned in the primitive data types section, primitives do not have methods, however sometimes we need to perform functions on primitives. To do this Java has given us the wrapper classes. For the eight primitive data types we have eight wrapper classes.

Primitive	Wrapper
byte	Byte
short	Short
int	Integer
long	Long
float	Float
double	Double
char	Character
boolean	Boolean

Notice that the first letter of the Primitives is always lowercase, and the Wrappers first letter is always uppercase.

In Chapter 4 we will cover the detailed implementation of the wrappers classes. To conclude this semester by implementing the string class.

String Class Data Types

To work with numbers we use the primitive data types, to work with characters such as

"aec$ ^%FtaA01982.GA/}]" we use the string class.

The string Java class has over 1,000 methods. This class is used for string variables containing a sequence of characters from 0 to 2gig in length, the characters in it can be the combination of any letters, numbers and/or symbols, e.g.,

```
String myName = " Albert# &(723,.$ Einstein\? ";
```

Some of the differences between primitives and strings are:

```
// Strings accept any character
String address = "123 main street, apt #12 N.Y.";

// Primitives accept only numbers, except for the char data type
// that accepts one character inside to single quotes
char letter = 'a';

// boolen data type that accept true or false
boolean valid = true;
boolean open  = false;
```

However the main difference between primitives and strings is that the string class has methods and Primitives do not.

Because of its methods, strings allows us to do just about anything, if a string contains numbers, using string methods, we can convert the string numbers into primitive numbers and do math with them.

Methods inside the string class are logical sections of code that do many things for us. They are programs already made for us that we can applied to our strings. For instance if I create a string called learning:

```
String learning = "I am learning Java";
```

and I want to convert it to all capital letters, all I need to do is ask the "learning string" to allow me to use its method that does this for me. I do not have to create a program to do it, this is how I would implement it.

```
String learning = "I am learning Java";
System.out.println( learning );

//convert learning to uppercase
learning = learning.toUpperCase();
System.out.println( learning );
```

Now to convert it to lowercase:

```
//convert learning to lowercase
learning = learning.toLowerCase();
System.out.println( learning );
```

The string data type has over 1,000 methods already made that we can use.

To compare two strings we can use the compareTo method in String as follows:

```
"Maria".compareTo( "Maria" ) == 0    // Maria and Maria are equal
"maria".compareTo( "Maria" ) != 0    // maria and Maria not equal
"Maria".compareTo( "maria" ) < 0     // Maria is less than maria
"maria".compareTo( "Maria" ) > 0     // maria is greater than Maria
```

We can prove the previous code by using the ASCII code values that we learned previously in this chapter.

If we select the last line of code above:

```
"maria".compareTo( "Maria" ) > 0     // maria is greater than Maria
```

we notice that the ASCII value of the lowercase 'm' **in maria is = 109**

while the ASCII value of uppercase 'M' in Maria is = 77

since 109 > 77 then this computation is true.

First String Program

Let's write our first Java program. We need to create two variables, one to store my ID number of data type int, called myID, and another to store my name of data type string, called myName.

```
/*
  Author   : Michael Robinson
  Program  : myFirstStringProgram.java
  Purpose  : To present, the Java class, the main method,
             one variable of data type int
             one variable of data type String
             and the three print command of Java
  Updated  : November 12th, 2099 by Michael
*/


public class myFirstStringProgram
{
    public static void main( String arg[] )
    {
        // Creating variable myID, assigning value 777 to it.
        int myID = 777;
```

```java
        // Creating variable myFirstName, assigning my name to it.
        String myFirstName = "Michael";

        // using  System.out.print  to print variables
        System.out.print( "My name is : " + myFirstName +
                            " My ID is : " + myID + "\n" );

        // using  System.out.println  to print variables
        System.out.println( "My name is : " + myFirstName +
                            " My ID is : " + myID );

        // using  System.out.printf  to print variables
        System.out.printf( "My name is : %s My ID is : %d\n",
                        myFirstName, myID );

    }//end public static void main( String arg[] )

}//end public class myFirstStringProgram
```

If you are using an IDE or the command line method to write your program, follow the instructions on the corresponding sections.

Your output (results) will look like this:

```
My name is : Michael My ID is : 777
My name is : Michael My ID is : 777
My name is : Michael My ID is : 777
```

Let's examine this code:

The above program is called: myFirstStringProgram.java

At the beginning of the program between /* and */ we have a detailed section that documents what this program does. Every program should have this section.

We then declare this program with the line:

```
public class myFirstStringProgram
```

Please note that the entire program lives between { and }

Here the public static void main(String args[]) is the only method in this program. In this method we first declare the necessary variables and assign values to them:

```
// Creating variable myID, assigning value 777 to it.
int myID = 777;

// Creating variable myFirstName, assigning my name to it.
String myFirstName = "Michael";
```

Then we use three different type of prints, the first one is:

```
// using  System.out.print  to print variables
System.out.print( "My name is : " + myFirstName +
                  " My ID is : " + myID + "\n" );
```

System.out.print does not print a line feed by itself so we have to add \n at the end of the sentence to have a line feed printed. (a line feed is equivalent to an enter in the keyboard).

Next we use System.out.println which does print a line feed after sentence is printed, therefore we do not need \n here.

```
// using  System.out.println  to print variables
System.out.println( "My name is : " + myFirstName +
                    " My ID is : " + myID );
```

Finally we use System.out.printf which as System.out.print does not print a line feed and \n has to be added at the end.

```
// using  System.out.printf  to print variables
System.out.printf( "My name is : %s My ID is : %d\n",
                   myFirstName, myID );
```

See Chapter 2 for detailed explanation for the printf.

Summary

In this third chapter we learned about the three numerical systems plus the ASCII codes used in digital computers. As humans we daily use the decimal numeric system composed of 10 numbers, from 0 to 9 also known as base 10. We use this system to do mathematical and logical calculations. The language of digital computers is the binary numerical system composed of 2 numbers, 0 and 1 called base 2. The hexadecimal numerical system contains the decimal numerical system (0-9) plus the letters A-F, making it base 16. In computer systems we use the hexadecimal system to assign IPv6 addresses. Memory errors are also described in hexadecimal. Computer keyboards are limited in the amount of keys (letters/numbers/symbols) that can accept. To translate these keys we use the ASCII system to translate each key to a decimal value and then to a binary value that the computer can understand. For detailed information about these numerical systems consult *Operating Systems for IT* written by Michael Robinson and published by Kendall Hunt Publishing.

We also learned about the numerical operators used to implement logic. We discussed the different primitive numerical data types such as int, float, double, etc.

The string class allows us to manage single and strings of characters to form words. We use the string tokenizer to manage all data of string type.

Key Terms

ASCII Codes Table	ASCII means American Standard Code for Information Interchange.
	Every character that a computer makes is assigned a numerical value, the ASCII code that represents the American English Language is limited to the first 128 characters/numbers, from 0 to 127. Codes from 128 to 255 represent other languages like French, Spanish and others. Codes after 255 are called Unicode. At the current time the Unicode has more than 107000 codes representing most of the languages used today.
	The first 255 Unicodes are the original ASCII codes.
	In the ASCII there are 33 non-printing control characters like esc, bell, etc. that affects how text and space is processed; 95 are printable characters such as a, b, c, 1, 2, H, Y, T, etc.
Binary Numerical System	Computers and all digital systems, such as cell phones, digital cameras, etc. use the binary systems or base-2 numeric system, which has 2 digits, 0 and 1.
	At first, it is hard to understand, but everything a digital system does, like video, sound, graphics, calculators, etc., is represented in binary.
	When we use programming languages we write the programs in plain English commands, and the programming language, in this case Java, translates our work into binary, which is what digital systems understand, even the decimal system is translated into binary.
Creating a Variable and Assigning a Value to it	In Java we can declare a variable without assigning a value to it, however, I recommend that you become used to assigning a value, if necessary zero, because in some languages like ANSI C, if you do not assign a value to a new variable, it assigns the value found at the memory location where the variable gets created, which can cause big problems.

	double speedOfLight = 186,282;
	float earthDiameter = 7,926.41;
	int myAge = 105;
	float myHeigth = 9.9;

Data Type Boolean	The boolean type has only two values, true or false.
	When we declare a variable of type boolean we can only assign it to be either true or false.

Data Type byte	An eight bit byte allows us to write data values from -128 to 128 or a maximum positive number of 255 by turning all 8 bits on, and then adding them. In this book we will only deal with positive numbers to describe bytes. Bit number 7 6 5 4 3 2 1 0 State on 1 1 1 1 1 1 1 1 Decimal value 128 64 32 16 8 4 2 1 = 255
Data Type char	The char data type is used to place a single character, such as a letter, number, or symbol. Numbers of char data type are treated as characters not numbers.
Data Type double	A double holds whole numbers with decimals, with much greater values than the float, for ranges see table on page 39.
Data Type float	A float holds whole numbers with decimals, for ranges see table on page 39.
Data Type int	An int number will hold a whole number. If you placed a number with decimals into an int, the decimals will be dropped.
Data Type long	A long will also hold a whole number but of greater value than an int, see table on page 39.
Data Type short	A short number will also hold a whole number but of less value than an int, see table on page 39.
Data Types	In math we assign numbers to variables such as a, b, c, etc. e.g.: a = 5 where a becomes 5 b = 12.4 where b becomes 12.4 c = a + b where c becomes 17.4 In computer science a variable is a descriptive name given to a known amount of information so that we can use such a variable regardless of the value it represents. The value of variables can change during the life of the program. In Java we do the same, however before assigning a value to a variable, we assign what we call a data type to the variable.
Data Types **String Class Data Types**	To work with numbers we use the primitive data types, to work with characters such as "aec$ ^%FtaA01982.GA/}]" we use the string class. The string Java class has over 1,000 methods. This class is used for string variables containing a sequence of characters from 0 to 2gig in length, the characters in it can be the combination of any letters, numbers and/or symbols, e.g.: String myName = " Albert# &(723,.$ Einstein\? ";

Decimal Numerical System	We use this numerical system everyday. It contains 10 digits from 0 to 9 and it is known as base-10 numerical system because it has 10 numbers.
	Our common daily math computations are done with these 10 digits, e.g.:

	idNumber = 9876;
	x = 5 + 2;
	addNumbers(3, 7, 8, 123, 45);

Hexadecimal Numerical System	This numerical system is base-16 it goes for 0 – F, that is from 0–9 then ABCDEF
	A = 10 B = 11 C = 12 D = 13 E = 14 F = 15
	At one time or another we have experienced computer problems where error messages show up on the screen such as:
	memory dump at: DA9F011231CCABDEDACF765
	What this means is that a RAM memory error occurred at memory location DA9F011231CCABDEDACF765.
Math Using Primitives	Java provide us with already made methods to do many math computations. The math class is called Math.
	Please see program mathExamples.java

Numerical Operators	There are some special symbols called Operators that perform specific operations on one, two or three numbers, giving us a result.
	
	In math we say: x = 3 + 5
	but we never say: x = x + 5
	
	In computer science we can say both of the above, the second method needs the following explanation:
	
	//creates variable basket and assign value 5 to it.
	int basket = 5;
	
	//add one to the current value of basket
	
	//the new value of basket is 6
	basket = basket + 1;
	
	//takes 3 from to the current value of basket
	
	//the new value of basket is 3
	basket = basket - 3;
	
	In the same manner we can implement multiplication and division.
	
	basket = basket * 3; //note * means multiplication
	basket = basket / 3; //note / means division
	
	The following section shows other ways to use the math operators: =, --, ++, -=, +=, *=, /=
	
	int counter = 0; //create and initialize counter to 0
	counter++; //adds 1 to counter, = 1
	counter *= 6; //multiply counter by 6, = 6
	counter /= 2; //divide counter by 2, = 3
	counter--; //take one from counter, = 2
	counter -= 2; //take 2 from counter, = 0
	counter += 100; //add 100 to counter, = 100

Numerical Systems	Throughout the existence of humans, we have invented many numeric systems. In this chapter we discuss four types that we will use in this programming class.
Operator &&	The operator && means logical "and" if(cold && raining) //if cold and raining

Operator %	The % operator also known as modulus and mod, means remainder when dividing two numbers, but the result is always an int, which is different than division.
	Division keeps the decimals in the result, again % gives you and int, dropping/truncating the decimals. % looks like division but it is NOT
	5 % 2 = 1 //this is modulus means that 2 exists twice in 5 leaving 1 as the modulus
	182 % 3 = 2 //3 exists 60 times in 182 leaving 2 as the modulus
	55 % 7 = 6 //7 exists 7 times in 55 leaving 6 as the modulus
	2000 % 4 = 0 //4 exist 500 times in 2000 leaving 0 as the modulus.
	The % operator is very useful in programming, allowing us to perform very complex operations easily.
Operator ||	The operator || means logical "or"

	//if cold or raining
	if(cold || raining)

Operators =, == , !=	This is where many people get confused and cause programming errors.
	The operator = means the right value is assigned to the left value e.g.,
	// 5 is assigned to the variable total total = 5;
	Operator = = means equivalence, we check to see if the left value is equivalent to the right value:

	//test if total is equivalent to 5
	if(total == 5)

	The operator != mean not equal, we check to see if the left value is not equal to the right value

	//if total is not equal to 5
	if(total != 5)

Operators >= and <=	The operator >= means left value is greater or equal to right value, e.g.: 5 >= 5 same as in math, 5 is greater or equal to 5 5 >= 4 same as in math, 5 is greater or equal to 4 The operator <= means left value is smaller or equal to right value, e.g.: 5 <= 5 same as in math, 5 is less or equal to 5 4 <= 5 same as in math, 4 is less or equal to 5
Primitive Data Types	Each primitive has its own name, occupying a specific amount of bytes, and containing a minimum and a maximum value. The amount of bytes and values depend on the computer the program is running on. Large computer systems have different values, the following are the typical values on today's standard personal computers. Today's Primitive Data Types use the Unicode Standard, all the values represented in the ASCII codes are in the same locations in the Unicode Standard.
Unicode Standard	This is another coding system that can represent over 100,000 characters. The origins of Unicode date back to 1987. The latest version of Unicode consists of more than 109,000 characters covering 93 scripts, a set of code charts for visual reference, display of text containing both right-to-left scripts, such as Hebrew and Arabic, as well as left-to-right scripts. All the values represented in the ASCII codes are in the same locations in the Unicode Standard.

Wrappers	As we learned in the primitive data types section, primitives do not have methods, however sometimes we need to perform functions on primitives.
	
	To do this Java has given us the wrapper classes. For the eight primitive data types we have eight wrapper classes.
	
	Primitive Wrapper
	  byte Byte
	  short Short
	  int Integer
	  long Long
	  float Float
	  double Double
	  char Character
	  boolean Boolean
	
	Notice that the first letter of the primitives is always lowercase, and the wrappers first letter is always uppercase.

Exercises

1. How is the binary numerical system used.

2. Where do we use the hexadecimal numerical system.

3. Where do we use the ASCII system.

4. List Java's primitive data types.

5. Describe the numerical operators in Java.

6. Numerical Operators allow us to _____ (Select all that apply)
   a. Compare decimal to hexadecimals
   b. Evaluate values of primitive data types
   c. Find the numerical ASCII values of characters
   d. Analyze logical comparison of functions

7. What happens if we choose wrong data types _____ (Select all that apply)
   a. It does not matter, Java adjusts it automatically
   b. Java will give us wrong answers
   c. Java programs will probably not compile
   d. Eclipse and NetBeans will accept the code

8. What is similar between boolean and binary _____ (Select all that apply)
   a. Boolean is true or false, binary is base 10
   b. Binary has two values with similar meaning to boolean
   c. Nothing
   d. Boolean is base 2, binary is also base 2

9. The binary numerical system _____ (Select all that apply)
   a. Is base 16 and is use for digital computers
   b. Is the language of digital systems
   c. Is used to do math in elementary school
   d. Is usually used to give us the memory errors

10. What is the difference between a wrapper and a primitive data type _____
    a. Wrappers contains strings
    b. Primitive data type do not contain methods
    c. Wrappers contain information about complete classes
    d. Wrappers are classes for binary numbers only

REFERENCES

- Java API Specifications
  http://www.oracle.com/technetwork/java/api-141528.html

- My Java programs that I use in my Java classes located at robinson.cs.fiu.edu

//END CHAPTER 3: BASIC TOOLS

Building a House

chapter 4

Wrappers

As we learned in the primitive data types section, primitives do not have methods, however sometimes we need to perform functions on primitives. To do this, Java has given us the wrapper classes. For the eight primitive data types we have eight wrapper classes.

Primitive	Wrapper
byte	Byte
short	Short
int	Integer
long	Long
float	Float
double	Double
char	Character
boolean	Boolean

Notice that the first letter of the Primitives is always lowercase, and the wrappers first letter is always uppercase.

```
/*
  Author   : Michael Robinson
  Program  : wrappersClass.java
  Purpose  : To present how to use the wrappers and some
             of their classes.
             Java creates wrapper classes for all primitives:

             Primitive   Wrapper
             byte        Byte
```

< 69 >

```
            short       Short
            int         Integer
            long        Long
            float       Float
            double      Double
            char        Character
            boolean     Boolean

            Integer     -> int
            Float       -> float
            Double      -> double
            Character   -> char
            Boolean     -> boolean

            Wrappers have many methods, and some allow us to
            UN-WRAP its values, for example an Integer wrapper
            can become a primitive int

      Updated : April 26, 2099
*/


public class wrappersClass
{
    public static void main( String arg[] )
    {
        int number = 10;              //regular primitive int
        Integer wNumber = 5;          //wrapper Integer class
        String stringNumber = "123"; //numbers as string

        //print the float value of an Integer wrapper
        System.out.println(
            "float value of Integer wrapper wNumber 5 = " +
            wNumber.floatValue());

        //we can add int and Integer
        System.out.println(
            "Adding int number 10 + wrapper wNumber 5 = "   +
            ( number + wNumber ) );

        //convert a String into an int and then print both
        number = Integer.parseInt(stringNumber);
        System.out.printf(
            "String %s converted to Integer %d\n",
            stringNumber, number );
```

```
        //convert an int into an object Integer and then print both
        Integer wNumber2 = new Integer(number);
        System.out.printf( "Convert int number %d into Integer " +
                        "wNumber2 %d\n", number,  wNumber2 );


        //convert Integer into an int and then print both
        int temp = wNumber2;
        System.out.printf( "Convert Integer wNumber %d into " +
                        " int temp %d\n", wNumber2, temp );


    }//end public static void main( String arg[] )


}//end public class wrappersClass
```

Your output (results) will look like this:

```
float value of Integer wrapper wNumber 5 = 5.0
Adding int number 10 + wrapper wNumber 5 = 15
String 123 converted to Integer 123
Convert Integer number 123 into Integer wNumber2 123
Convert Integer wNumber 123 into int temp 123
```

Let's examine this code:

```
In this program we create three variables:
int number = 10;              //regular primitive int
Integer wNumber = 5;          //wrapper Integer class
String stringNumber = "123"; //numbers as string
```

We then use the following wrapper functions to present some of the possible implementations:

```
//print the float value of an Integer wrapper
System.out.println( "float value of Integer wrapper wNumber 5 = " +
wNumber.floatValue() );


wNumber is the Integer and floatValue() is the function that
converts it to float


//we can add int and Integer
System.out.println( "Adding int number 10 + wrapper wNumber 5 = "  + (
number + wNumber) );
```

When we add an int with an Integer we get an int

```
//convert a String into an int and then print both
number = Integer.parseInt( stringNumber );
        System.out.printf( "String %s converted to Integer %d\n",
                            stringNumber, number );
```

Integer.parseInt converts the stringNumber into an int

```
//convert an int into an object Integer and then print both
Integer wNumber2 = new Integer(number);
System.out.printf( "Convert Integer number %d into Integer wNumber2
%d\n", number,  wNumber2 );
```

```
new Integer(number)
converts number into a new Integer
```

```
//convert Interger into an int and then print both
int temp = wNumber2;
System.out.printf( "Convert Integer wNumber %d into int temp %d\n",
wNumber2, temp );
```

```
int temp = wNumber2
converts the Integer Wnumber into an int
```

Calling Methods

In programming it is very important to be organized, good use of methods is the best way to achieve organization in Java.

In Java we can have as many methods as we want. The main(String arg[]) method is the entry point of Java. I use it to create variables and as the central control point from where I call all methods, we can also call methods from inside another methods.

To show how to use methods I say that Java has three types of methods with variations: methods that do not accept any data, methods that accept data, and methods that return data.

Let's use four regular methods called printMyInfo1, printMyInfo2, printMyInfo3, and printMyInfo4 to implement the three different types of methods mentioned above.

Methods That Do Not Accept Any Data

Methods that do not accept any data are methods that can be called without needing any data from the calling statement.

The following program called noDataPassProgram.java contains two methods main and printMyInfo1()

```java
/*
  Author   : Michael Robinson
  Program  : noDataPassProgram.java
  Purpose  : To present, the Java class, the main method,
             calling printMyInfo1() method
  Updated  : November 12th, 2099 by Michael
*/


public class noDataPassProgram
{
    public static void printMyInfo1()
    {
        System.out.print( "Hi I am at the printMyInfo1() method\n" );

    }//end public static void printMyInfo1()


    public static void main( String arg[] )
    {
        //calls method NOT passing any data to printMyInfo1
        printMyInfo1();

        System.out.print( "Hi I am back at main from printMyInfo1()"+
                          " method\n" );

    }//end public static void main( String arg[] )

}//end public class noDataPassProgram
```

Your output (results) will look like this:

```
Hi I am at the printMyInfo1() method
Hi I am back at main from printMyInfo1() method
```

A variable or a method that is declared public is publicly accessible by any part of the project. Any class or method can freely access other public methods and variables of another class.

Let's examine this code:

The above program is called: **noDataPassProgram.java**

At the beginning of the program between /* and */ we have a detailed section that documents what this program does. Every program should have this section.

We then declare this program with the line:

```
public class noDataPassProgram
```

Please note that the entire program lives between { and }

Now if we look in the main method the line that calls method printMyInfo1

```
//calls method NOT passing any data to printMyInfo1
printMyInfo1();
```

does NOT have any data between the parenthesis (), this means that it is calling a method NOT passing any data.

Now let's notice that the public static void printMyInfo1() method is NOT receiving any data inside the parenthesis ( ). That is why we call this method: a method that does NOT accept any data.

After the printMyInfo1() method finish executing, it returns to the main menu (the method that called it) and executes the following line of code, before ending.

```
System.out.print( "Hi I am back at main from printMyInfo1()"+
                  " method\n" );
```

Methods That Accept Data

Methods that accept data are methods that are called by other methods that are passing/sending data of any type to the receiving methods, as shown in the following program.

```java
/*
  Author   : Michael Robinson
  Program  : passingDataProgram.java
  Purpose  : To present, the Java class, the main method,
             one variable of data type int
             one variable of data type String
             and the three print command of Java
             Calls four methods

  Updated  : November 12th, 2099 by Michael
*/



public class passingDataProgram
{
    public static void printMyInfo2( String myFirstName, int myID )
    {
        System.out.print(
          "\nHi I am at printMyInfo2(String myFirstName, " +
          "int myID ) method\n");

        System.out.print(
          "\nMy name is : " + myFirstName + " My ID is : " + myID +
          "\n" );

        System.out.println(
          "My name is : " + myFirstName + " My ID is : " + myID );

        System.out.printf(
          "My name is : %s My ID is : %d\n", myFirstName, myID );

    }//end public static void printMyInfo2


    public static void main( String arg[] )
    {
        int     myID       = 777; //I am creating variable myID, and
                                  //assigning value 777 to it.
```

```
//Create the variable myFirstName and assign my name to it.
String myFirstName = "Michael";

//Methods that pass data
//calls method passing myName and myID to printMyInfo2
printMyInfo2( myFirstName, myID );

System.out.print("\nHi I am back at main from public static"+
                " void printMyInfo2( String myFirstName," +
                " int myID ) method\n" );

    }//end public static void main( String arg[] )

}//end public class passingDataProgram
```

Your output (results) will look like this:

```
Hi I am at printMyInfo2(String myFirstName, int myID ) method
My name is : Michael My ID is : 777
My name is : Michael My ID is : 777
My name is : Michael My ID is : 777
Hi I am back at main from public static void printMyInfo2( String
myFirstName, int myID ) method
```

A variable or a method that is declared public is publicly accessible by any member of the project. Any class or method can freely access other public methods and variables of another class.

Let's examine this code:

In the main method we declare two variables, an int and a string, before calling the following method:

```
//Methods that pass data
//calls method passing myName and myID to printMyInfo2
printMyInfo2( myFirstName, myID );
```

As we see this method contains the variables "myFirstName, myID" inside the parenthesis ( ). This is called "Calling a method passing data." Then we see that the following method:

```
public static void printMyInfo2( String myFirstName, int myID )
```

is receiving the variables that were send/passed from the main method. In this method we accept the data and print it using the three print statements that we learned in Chapter 2.

After the printMyInfo1() method finish executing, it returns to the main menu (the method that called it) and executes the following line of code, before ending.

```
System.out.print("\nHi I am back at main from public static"+
                " void printMyInfo2( String myFirstName," +
                " int myID ) method\n" );
```

Methods That Return Data

Java also has methods that return data to its calling statements/methods. Note that in this example, in main we are making this type of call:

```
int result1 =  printMyInfo3( myFirstName, myID );
```

Also note the first line of the called method:

```
public static int printMyInfo3( String myFirstName, int myID )
```

Notice that instead of "void" we have "int" which means that this method will return a variable of data type "int".

The last line in this method is:

```
return ( myID * 2 );
```

which means that it is returning the value of (myID * 2) which in this case is an int. The following are several examples of methods that return data:

```
/*
  Author  : Michael Robinson
  Program : returnDataProgram.java
  Purpose : To show how to to return data to the
            calling statement.

  Updated : January 14, 2099
*/
```

```java
public class returnDataProgram
{
    //Calls method myInfo1 passing myName and myID and
    //expects data to be returned to the int result variable
    public static int myInfo1( String name, int myID )
    {
        System.out.print( "\nHi I am at myInfo1\n" );

        System.out.printf( "My name is : %s My ID is : %d\n",
                            name, myID );

        System.out.printf( "returning to main() %d * 2 to be" +
                            " printed\n", myID );

        return( myID * 2 );

    }//end public static int myInfo1


    //calls method NOT passing data to myInfo2
    //and expects data to be returned to the int result variable
    public static int myInfo2()
    {
        System.out.print( "\nHi I am at the public static int " +
                            "myInfo2() method\n" );

        System.out.print( "returning the value 999 which will " +
                            "be printed at main\n" );

        return( 999 );

    }//end public static int myInfo2()


    public static void main( String arg[] )
    {
        int     myID = 777; //create variable myID with value 777

        String name = "Michael";  //create name value Michael

        //methods can return data to calling statement as follows:
        int result1 =  myInfo1( name, myID );

        System.out.printf( "\nAt main() received %d\n", result1 ) ;
```

```
    //calls method NOT passing data to myInfo2
    int result2 =  myInfo2();

    System.out.printf( "\nAt main() received %d\n\n", result2 );

}//end public static void main( String arg[] )

}//end public class returnDataProgram
```

Your output (results) will look like this:

```
Hi I am at myInfo1
My name is : Michael My ID is : 777
returning to main() 777 * 2 to be printed
At main() received 1554
Hi I am at the public static int myInfo2() method
returning the value 999 which will be printed at main
At main() received 999
```

A variable or a method that is declared public is publicly accessible by any member of the project. Any class or method can freely access other public methods and variables of another class.

Let's examine this code:

The previous program "passingDataProgram" is very similar to this program called "returnDataProgram". The main difference is that this program contains the method "public static int **myInfo1(String name, int myID)**" which returns an int value "public static int":

```
    return( myID * 2 );
```

to the calling statement, in this case in the main method:

```
        //methods can return data to calling statement as follows:
        int result1 =  myInfo1( name, myID );
```

into the int result1 variable, and then it prints the received data:

```
    System.out.printf( "\nAt main() received %d\n", result1 ) ;
```

This program does the same for the myInfo2() method:

```
        //calls method NOT passing data to myInfo2
        int result2 =  myInfo2();


        System.out.printf( "\nAt main() received %d\n\n", result2 );
```

Pause Program

In programming we need to stop our programs at any place so that we can see what the program is doing, this is called debugging. Java has a class called wait() which allows us to stop a process for a specific amount of time, but it can be interrupted by other processes through a class called threads. However, when debugging we want the program to stop until we tell it to continue, we need total control.

For this purpose I created a program called pauseClass.java which has a method called pause. I use this method all the time to do my debugging, and I think it will be useful to you. So here it is:

```
/*
  Author   : Michael Robinson
  Program  : pauseClass.java
  Purpose  : This program creates a method called pause()
             which allows the user to stop the program
             at any particular place.

  Updated  : April 26, 2099
*/



import java.io.BufferedReader;
import java.io.IOException;
import java.io.InputStreamReader;



public class pauseClass
{
    public static void pause()
    {
        // make a prompt
        System.out.print( "\nPress ENTER to continue " );

        //open a reader over the keyboard (System.in) stream.
        //class                 object    method
        BufferedReader in =
```

```
        new BufferedReader( new InputStreamReader( System.in ) );

        //checking for errors
        try //execute the following line of code
        {
            String line = in.readLine(); // read one line.
        }
        catch (IOException ioe)
        {
            //if an error was detected execute the following
            System.out.println( "Something went wrong reading IO:" );
            ioe.printStackTrace();
        }

    }//end  public pause()

    public static void main( String arg[] )
    {
        pause();

        System.out.println( "\n  Thank you!\nend of program" );

    }//end public static void main( String arg[] )

}//end public class pauseClass
```

Your output (results) will look like this:

Press ENTER to continue

  Thank you!

end of program

Let's examine this code:

Notice that in this pauseClass program, there is a method called:

```
public static void pause()
```

Since we are beginning to write bigger programs, we are going to encounter errors more frequently. A very useful technique to track the errors (also called debugging) is to print the values of all current variables and then stop the program on or before the line where the error is found, to see the current status of the program.

Most programming languages have a command to stop the processing, called "wait" or "pause." Unfortunately Java does not provide either one that will give you full stop of the program, therefore this pause method that I wrote can be added into any of your Java programs, and just call it from anywhere. To stop your program at any place use the pause method as shown in the main method:

```
pause();
```

When this method gets called you will receive this message:

```
Press ENTER to continue
```

Do not worry about understanding the entire code in this program at this time. You will be able to totally understand it in Chapter 9.

To allow your program to continue processing just press any key on the keyboard. You can place the pause() command at any location in you program and you can call it as many times as needed.

Variables Scope

Variables in Java have an area inside the program where we can access them. This is called the scope of a variable. Java has global and local variables.

Global Variables

In the Methods section we learned that methods do not see each other, however they can communicate with each other by passing and returning data to each other. Java in general has two types of variables, global and local. The global variables are declared/created outside of all methods and they can be declared only once. The advantage of global variables is that they can be seen by all methods, at the same time the disadvantage is that they can be modified by any method, to solve that problem we can make any variable global or local variable into a constant variable so that it can only be read but not changed (see Private – Final Variables section).

```
public static String firstName = "Joseph";
```

Private – Final Variables

These types of variables are also called constant variables because they do not change value once they are created.

The following program shows how to create and use constants.

```
/*
  Author   : Michael Robinson
  Program  : finalStatic.java
  Purpose  : To present the constant data type
             data type that can not be changed
             once they are declared and a value is assigned

  Updated : May 1, 2099
*/


public class finalStatic
{
    public static final double  monthlyRent = 950;
    public static final Integer yearsLeased = 30;

    public static void main( String arg[] )
    {
        System.out.printf( "Monthly Rent  %.2f\n", monthlyRent );
        System.out.printf( "Years Leased  %d\n",   yearsLeased );

        System.out.printf( "Total Rent Income :  %.2f \n",
                      ( monthlyRent * yearsLeased * 12 ) );
    }

}//end public class finalStatic
```

Your output (results) will look like this:

```
Monthly Rent  950.00
Years Leased  30
Total Rent Income :  342000.00
```

Let's examine this code:

Notice that we have declare two global variables outside of any method:

```
public static final double  monthlyRent = 950;
public static final Integer yearsLeased = 30;
```

Then notice that we can access those variables from inside the main method:

```
public static void main( String arg[] )
{
    System.out.printf( "Monthly Rent  %.2f\n", monthlyRent );
    System.out.printf( "Years Leased  %d\n",  yearsLeased );

    System.out.printf( "Total Rent Income :  %.2f \n",
                     ( monthlyRent * yearsLeased * 12 ) );
}
```

This is the purpose of the global variables.

Local Variables

Variables are created in, or passed to a method. Once accepted by a method the variable is called a local variable. What is usually hard to understand is that we can have local variables that have the same name in multiple methods, and they are different. The easiest example to explain this is: We get 200 persons called Maria and we send them to 200 different cities. Each Maria in each city is different. Think of Maria as the name of the variable, and each city as a method.

This is an interesting example:

```
/*
  Author  : Michael Robinson
  Program : variables.java
  Purpose : To show the global and local variables

  Updated : May 4, 2099
*/
```

```java
public class variables
{
    static double interestRate = 3.5;

    public static void firstLoan( int loanAmount )
    {
        interestRate = interestRate + .25;
        System.out.printf( "I borrowed %d at %.2f interest.\n",
                            loanAmount, interestRate );
    }


    public static void secondLoan( int loanAmount ) ***
    {
        interestRate = interestRate + .25;
        System.out.printf( "I borrowed %d at %.2f interest.\n",
                            loanAmount, interestRate );
    }


    public static void thirdLoan( int loanAmount )
    {
        interestRate = interestRate + .25;
        System.out.printf( "I borrowed %d at %.2f interest.\n",
                            loanAmount, interestRate );
    }


    public static void fourthLoan( int loanAmount )
    {
        interestRate = interestRate + .25;
        System.out.printf( "I borrowed %d at %.2f interest.\n",
                            loanAmount, interestRate );
    }


    public static void main( String arg[] )
    {
        firstLoan( 100 );
        secondLoan( 200 );
        thirdLoan( 300 );
        fourthLoan( 400 );
```

```
        int loanAmount = 500;
        interestRate = interestRate + .25;
        System.out.printf( "I borrowed %d at %.2f interest.\n",
                        loanAmount, interestRate );


   }//end public static void main( String arg[] )


}//end public class variables
```

Your output (results) will look like this:

```
I borrowed 100 at 3.75 interest.
I borrowed 200 at 4.00 interest.
I borrowed 300 at 4.25 interest.
I borrowed 400 at 4.50 interest.
I borrowed 500 at 4.75 interest.
```

Let's examine this code:

As we can see interestRate is a global variable that can accessed and changed in every method.

```
static double interestRate = 3.5;
```

In all methods we have a method called loanAmount, and even though they have the same name, the amounts are different. Therefore they are different and they are local to each method. Also they cannot see each other because they are at different address locations in RAM.

```
    public static void firstLoan( int loanAmount )
    {
        interestRate = interestRate + .25;
        System.out.printf( "I borrowed %d at %.2f interest.\n",
                        loanAmount, interestRate );
    }
```

Passed from the main method:

```
        firstLoan( 100 );
        secondLoan( 200 );
        thirdLoan( 300 );
        fourthLoan( 400 );
```

Reading the Keyboard Using Scanner Class

We need to be able to communicate with the keyboard. The easiest way is to use the scanner class.

In the following program we will obtain input from the keyboard of three different data types: int, double and string.

```
/*
  Author   : Michael Robinson
  Program  : scannerClass.java
  Purpose  : To present the Scanner class to read from KB
             Scanner myScanner = new Scanner(System.in);
             Accepts                              Returns
             byte x   = myScanner.nextByte();     byte
             double x = myScanner.nextDouble();   double
             int x    = myScanner.nextInt();      int
             float x  = myScanner.nextFloat();    float
             String x = myScanner.nextLine();     String
             long x   = myScanner.nextLong();     long
             short x  = myScanner.nextShort();    short

  Updated : May 7, 2099
*/


import java.util.*;
import java.util.Scanner;



public class scannerClass
{
    public static void readTheKeyboard()
    {
        //create an object to read the keyboard
        //class    object                     method
        Scanner myScanner = new Scanner( System.in );

        System.out.print(
        "Hi I am Scanner, please enter your name : " );

        //user input get assigned to name
        String name = myScanner.nextLine();

        System.out.printf( "Hi %s, nice meeting you\n", name );
```

```java
System.out.print( "\nNow we are going to do some math." );

double fnum, answer;
int snum;

System.out.print( "\nEnter first number : " );

//user input get assigned to fnum
fnum = myScanner.nextDouble();

System.out.print( "Enter second number: " );

//user input get assigned to snum
 snum = myScanner.nextInt();

System.out.printf( "\nAdding        %.2f + %d = %.2f\n",
                   fnum, snum, (fnum + snum) );

answer = fnum * snum;

System.out.println(
"Multiplying: " + fnum + " by " + snum + " = " + answer );

String input;            //to hold a string line of input

char singleCharacter; //to hold a char from String input

//ask user a question
System.out.print(
"\n\n\tAre we having fun? y=Yes N=Not ? " );

//java PROBLEMS:
//this line is needed to clear the keyboard buffer
//READS KB BUFFER WHICH HAS CR FROM PREVIOUS
//myScanner.nextInt() and myScanner.nextDouble DOES NOT read
//the CR at end of input, but reads the CR at beginning, left
//from last Scanner clears CR at beginning of keyboard buffer
input = myScanner.nextLine();
input = myScanner.nextLine(); //reads user keyboard input

//takes first char from user input and makes it uppercase
singleCharacter = input.toUpperCase().charAt(0);
```

```java
        while( singleCharacter != 'Y' && singleCharacter != 'N' )
        {
            System.out.println(
            "\tYou must be dreaming, just answer Yes or No." );

            //ask user a question
            System.out.print(
            "\n\n\tAre we having fun? y=Yes N=Not ? " );

            //reads user keyboard input
            input = myScanner.nextLine();

            //makes first char from user input into uppercase
            singleCharacter = input.toUpperCase().charAt(0);

        }

        System.out.println( "\n\tYour FULL answers is         : " +
                            name );

        System.out.println( "\tThe First UpperCase letter is : " +
                            name.toUpperCase().charAt(0) );

        if( singleCharacter == 'Y' )
        {
            System.out.println( "\tI am very happy to hear that." );
        }
        else //if( singleCharacter == 'N' )
        {
            System.out.println( "\tI am sorry to hear that." );
        }

    }//end public static void readTheKeyboard()


    public static void main( String arg[] )
    {
        readTheKeyboard();
        System.out.println( "\n\nEnd of program\n" );

    }//end public static void main( String arg[] )

}//end public class scannerClass
```

Your output (results) will look like this:

```
Hi I am Scanner, please enter your name : michael
Hi michael, nice meeting you

Now we are going to do some math.
Enter first number : 5
Enter second number: 4
Adding        5.00 + 4 = 9.00
Multiplying: 5.0 by 4 = 20.0

        Are we having fun? y=Yes N=Not ? y

        Your FULL answer is        : michael
        The First UpperCase letter is : M

        I am very happy to hear that.

End of program
```

Since this program is very well documented, please read the program carefully to understand what each line does.

Let's examine this code:

This **scannerClass** program is very useful and easy to implement. Its main purpose is to be able to communicate with the user by asking questions and accepting input from the keyboard.

We first have to include in the program two import commands:

```
import java.util.*;
import java.util.Scanner;
```

The scanner handles all the communications of the user with the keyboard as follows:

```
        //create an object to read the keyboard
        //class    object                    method
        Scanner myScanner = new Scanner( System.in );
```

The class is called "Scanner" and the "System.in" is the method that reads the keyboard. In this example "myScanner" is the variable that will contain the data entered by the user. This program is internally very well documented. Please read the instructions.

Summary

I see methods as parts of a larger structure, each method having a specific purpose. My best comparison is my car. In my car I see the radio as a "method" that has a specific function, it makes me happy and keeps me informed. Programs are made with methods, each method having a specific purpose. Three of the best benefits of methods are: Divide and conquer, which allow us to take a large problem and divide it into small unique parts/methods. If a method has an error, it can be blocked allowing the rest of the program to work, until the error is fixed. It can be re-used at any time, just like the radio in my car.

There are multiple types of methods, therefore they are flexible and we can select which type to use for a particular use.

In this chapter we also learned about the scope/life of variables such as: global variables which can be accessed from any method, and local variables which can only be accessed inside the method where it was created, unless they are being passed and returned from one method to another. We also covered private/final variables whose values can not be modified.

I created a method called pause(), which I find very useful when I am debugging my programs.

Finally, we learned to read the data inputed by the user in keyboard using the scanner class, presented in the pauseClass.java program using the pause() method.

Key Terms

Methods That Accept Data	Methods that accept data are methods that are called by other methods that are passing/sending data of any type to the receiving methods, as shown in the following program. Please see program passingDataProgram.java
Methods That Do Not Accept Any dData	Methods that do not accept any data are methods that can be called without needing any data from the calling statement. Program noDataPassProgram.java contains two methods main and printMyInfo1()

Methods That Return Data	Java also has methods that return data to its calling statements/methods.
	
	Note that in this example, in main we are making this type of call:
	
	int result1 = printMyInfo3(myFirstName, myID);
	
	Also note the first line of the called method:
	public static int printMyInfo3(String myFirstName, int myID)
	
	Notice that instead of "void" we have "int" which means that this method will return a variable of data type "int".
	
	The last line in this method is:
	return(myID * 2);
	returning the int value of (myID * 2)

Methods. Calling Methods	In programming it is very important to be organized, good use of methods is the best way to achieve organization in Java. In Java we can have as many methods as we want. The main(String arg[]) method is the entry point of Java. I use it to create variables and as the central control point from where I call all methods. We can also call methods from inside another methods. To show how to use methods I say that Java has three types of methods with variations: methods that do not accept any data, methods that accept data, and methods that return data. Let's use four regular methods called printMyInfo1, printMyInfo2, printMyInfo3, and printMyInfo4 to implement the three different types of methods mentioned above.

Pause Program	In programming we need to stop our programs at any place so that we can see what the program is doing, this is called debugging. Java has a class called wait() which allows us to stop a process for a specific amount of time, but it can be interrupted by other processes through a class called threads. However, when debugging we want the program to stop until we tell it to continue, we need total control. For this purpose I created a program called pauseClass.java which has a method called pause. I use this method all the time to do my debugging, and I think it will be useful to you.
Scanner Class Reading The Keyboard Using Scanner Class	We need to be able to communicate with the keyboard. The easiest way is to use the scanner class. In the program scannerClass.java we obtain input from the keyboard of three different data types: int, double and string.
Variables Scope	Variables in Java have an area inside the program where we can access them. This is called the scope of a variable. Java has global and local variables.
Variables. Global Variables	In the Methods section we learned that methods do not see each other, however they can communicate with each other by passing and returning data to each other. Java in general has two types of variables, global and local. The global variables are declared/created outside of all methods and they can be declared only once. The advantage of global variables is that they can be seen by all methods, at the same time the disadvantage is that they can be modified by any method. To solve that problem we can make any variable global or local variable into a constant variable so that it can only be read but not changed (see Private – Final Variables section). public static String firstName = "Joseph";
Variables. Local Variables	Variables are created in, or passed to a method. Once accepted by a method the variable is called a local variable. What is usually hard to understand is that we can have local variables that have the same name in multiple methods, and they are different. The easiest example to explain this is: We get 200 persons called Maria and we send them to 200 different cities. Each Maria in each city is different. Think of Maria as the name of the variable, and each city as a method. Please see the following interesting example: Program : variables.java

Variables. Private – Final Variables	These types of variables are also called constant variables because they do not change value once they are created. The following program shows how to create and use constants. Program : finalStatic.java

Wrappers	As we learned in the primitive data types section, primitives do not have methods, however sometimes we need to perform functions on primitives.
	
	To do this, Java has given us the wrapper classes.
	
	For the eight primitive data types we have eight wrapper classes.
	
	Primitive Wrapper
	  byte Byte
	  short Short
	  int Integer
	  long Long
	  float Float
	  double Double
	  char Character
	  boolean Boolean
	
	Notice that the first letter of the primitives is always lowercase, and the wrappers first letter is always uppercase.

Exercises

1. Create a class with the mandatory method to create a Java program.

2. Create a program with a method that will accept and display two numbers from main, multiplies one by the other and returns the total to the calling statement.

3. Write a method that reads 5 primitive global numbers and do mathematical calculations using your choice of operators (* % - + /).

4. Write a method that will use private – final variables to do modules.

5. What is the difference between final and global variables.

6. What is a method _____ (Select all that apply)
   a. A way of doing anything
   b. Where you call the imports from
   c. A section of code with a specific purpose
   d. Section of code that can be re-used

7. Can a method call another method _____ (Select all that apply)
   a. No, the program will get confused
   b. Yes methods call other methods, make sure not to get into an endless loop
   c. Only if they know each other
   d. No, only the main method can call other methods

8. Difference between global and local variables _____ (Select all that apply)
   a. There is no difference
   b. Global variables can be accessed from any method, locals only locally
   c. Global variables can be accessed locally, locals from any method
   d. All variables are global

9. What is a method that returns a value _____ (Select all that apply)
   a. This type of method does not exist
   b. A method that returns a value to the calling statement
   c. A method that obtains data from other method
   d. Methods that accept data from another method

10. What are methods that accept data _____ (Select all that apply)
    a. They do not exist
    b. Methods that pass data to another methods
    c. Method that will receive data from calling statements
    d. Methods that return data to the calling statements

REFERENCES

- Java API Specifications

  http://www.oracle.com/technetwork/java/api-141528.html

- My Java programs that I use in my Java classes located at robinson.cs.fiu.edu

//END CHAPTER 4: BUILDING A HOUSE

if Commands

if Command

In my opinion the most used command in programming is the "if" command. In programming we are always making decisions, always asking what if?

The great thing about the implementation of the "if" command is that it is almost identical in every programming language.

Plain if

A plain if is very useful and very easy to implement. The plain if statement has the following structure:

```
if( condition )
{
    commands
}
```

If the condition is TRUE then the commands between the curly brackets will be executed:

```
float temperature = 92.7; //create and load a float variable

if( temperature > 90 )
{
    System.out.println( " Oh man it is hot!!" );
}
```

< 97 >

Your output (results) will look like this:

```
Oh man it is hot!!
```

Let's examine this code:

We create a variable called temperature of primitive data type float and assign the value 92.7 to it:

```
float temperature = 92.7; //create and load a float variable
```

Using the if statement we check to see if the value of temperature is greater than 90. Since this is true then we execute the commands inside the { } brackets, which in this case is to print the phrase: Oh man it is hot!!

```
if( temperature > 90 )
{
    System.out.println( " Oh man it is hot!!" );
}
```

Other Plain if Example

```
/*
   Author  : Michael Robinson
   Program : ifs.java
   Purpose : To show how Java processes the
             plain single if statements
             one set after the other

   Updated : April 26, 2099
*/

public class ifs
{
    public static void if_if( int grade )
    {
        if( grade  >= 95 )
        {
            System.out.println( "Your grade is >= A was " + grade );
        }
        if( grade  >= 90 )
        {
            System.out.println( "Your grade is >= A- was " + grade );
        }
```

```java
    if( grade  >= 87 )
    {
        System.out.println( "Your grade is >= B+ was " + grade );
    }
    if( grade  >= 83 )
    {
        System.out.println( "Your grade is >= B was " + grade );
    }
    if( grade  >= 80 )
    {
        System.out.println( "Your grade is >= B- was " + grade);
    }
    if( grade  >= 76 )
    {
        System.out.println( "Your grade is >= C+ was " + grade );
    }
    if( grade  >= 70 )
    {
        System.out.println( "Your grade is >= C was " + grade );
    }
    if( grade  >= 66 )
    {
        System.out.println( "Your grade is >= C- was " + grade );
    }
    if( grade  >= 60 )
    {
        System.out.println( "Your grade is >= D+ was " + grade );
    }
    if( grade  >= 56 )
    {
        System.out.println( "Your grade is >= D was " + grade );
    }
    if( grade  >= 51 )
    {
        System.out.println( "Your grade is D- was " + grade );
    }
    if( grade  <= 50 )
    {
        System.out.println( "Your grade is >= F was " + grade );
    }

}//end if_if()
```

```
    public static void main( String arg[] )
    {
        if_if( 71 );

    }//end public static void main( String arg[] )

}//end public class ifs
```

If the grade passed to this method was 71, the output is:

```
Your grade is >= C was 71
Your grade is >= C- was 71
Your grade is >= D+ was 71
Your grade is >= D was 71
Your grade is D- was 71
```

because the grade 71 meets all the following conditions:

```
        if( grade   >= 70 )
        if( grade   >= 66 )
        if( grade   >= 60 )
        if( grade   >= 56 )
        if( grade   >= 51 )
```

if_else

The if statement has a sidekick called else, they work very well together, their structure is:

```
    if( condition )
    {
        commands
    }
    else
    {
        commands
    }
```

If the "if" condition is NOT true then else takes charge and its commands are executed:

```
/*
  Author  : Michael Robinson
  Program : if_else.java
```

```
   Purpose : To show how Java processes the
             if else statements

   Updated : April 26, 2099
*/


public class if_else
{
    public static void testIfElse( float temperature )
    {
        if( temperature > 80 )
        {
            System.out.println( " Oh man it is hot!!" );
        }
        else
        {
            System.out.println( " Summer time is gone!!" );
        }

    }//end public static void testIfElse( float temperature )


    public static void main( String arg[] )
    {
        testIfElse( 71 );

    }//end public static void main( String arg[] )

}//end public class if_else
```

Your output (results) will look like this:

```
 Summer time is gone!!
```

Let's examine this code:

We examined this line of code:

```
        if( temperature > 80 )
```

and found out that it is not true, therefore we executed:

```
    else
    {
        System.out.println( " Summer time is gone!!" );
    }
```

Now it gets better, there is another sidekick called "else if"

if else if

There are times that the if and else combination is not enough, then we use the "if else if" combination:

```
/*
  Author   : Michael Robinson
  Program  : if_else_if.java
  Purpose  : To show how Java processes the
             if else if statements

  Updated  : April 26, 2099
*/


public class if_else_if
{
    public static void testIt( double temperature )
    {
        if( temperature > 80 )
        {
            System.out.println( " Oh man it is hot!!" );
        }
        else if( temperature > 32 )
        {
            System.out.println( " Summer time is gone!!" );
        }
        else
        {
            System.out.println( " Oh man it is freezing!!" );
        }

    }//end public static void testIt( float temperature )
```

```
public static void main( String arg[] )
{
    testIt( 31.9 );

}//end public static void main( String arg[] )

}//end public class if_else_if
```

Your output (results) will look like this:

Oh man it is freezing!!

Let's examine this code:

We passed the value 31.9 to the testIt method. This method checked the temperature value, since it was not > 80 the else if section checked to see if temperature was > 32, at this point this condition is still false so it executed the final else executing its contents: Oh man it is freezing!!

```
public static void testIt( double temperature )
{
    if( temperature > 80 )
    {
        System.out.println( " Oh man it is hot!!" );
    }
    else if( temperature > 32 )
    {
        System.out.println( " Summer time is gone!!" );
    }
    else
    {
        System.out.println( " Oh man it is freezing!!" );
    }
```

The key here is that every "else if" and "else" belongs to the closest previous "if" command.

Nested if

The nested if is very powerful and sometimes complex, this is an example:

```java
/*

  Author  : Michael Robinson
  Program : nestedIf.java
  Purpose : To show how Java processes the
            nested if statements
  Updated : April 26, 2099
*/


public class nestedIf
{
    public static void ifNested( int number )
    {
        //at this place number == 20
        if( number > -1 ) //outer if
        {
            if( number > 1 ) //inner if
            {
                number++;    //at this place number == 21

                if( number < 1 ) //inner inner if
                {
                    System.out.println( number );
                }
                else
                {
                    System.out.println( "number is > 1 == " +
                                        number );
                }
            }
            else
            {
                System.out.println( "the number is < 1 == " +
                                    number );
            }
        }
        else
        {
```

```
            System.out.println( "the value of number is == " +
                                 number );
        }

    }//end public static void ifNested()


    public static void main( String arg[] )
    {
        ifNested( 20 );

    }//end public static void main( String arg[] )

}//end public class nestedIf
```

Your output (results) will look like this:

```
number is > 1 == 21
```

Let's examine this code:

```
//from main assign the value 20 to the variable number
number = 20;

//since number > -1 we follow this if
if( number > -1 )
{
    //here number is still > 1, so follow this if
    if( number > 1 )
    {
        //add one to variable number, now it is 21
        number++;

        //this if fails because number is > 1
        if( number < 1 )
        {
            System.out.println( number );
        }
        //so we follow this else,
        //since this else is true we terminate the entire
        //logic at this location and print this result
        else
        {
```

```java
            System.out.println( "number is > 1 == " + number );
        }
    }
    else
    {
        System.out.println( "the number is < 1 == " + number );
    }
}
else
{
    System.out.println( "the value of number is == " + number );
}

}//end public static void ifNested()
```

Ternary if

The ternary (three way) "if" replaces some implementations of if else if statements

```java
expression1 ? expression2 : expression3

if   expression1 is true
then expression2 is selected
else expression3 is selected
```

another way to look at it is:

```java
condition ? value_if_true : value_if_false
```

```java
/*

  Author  : Michael Robinson
  Program : ternaryIf.java
  Purpose : To show how Java processes the
            ternaryIf statements
  Updated : April 26, 2099
*/
```

```
public class ternaryIf
{

    public static void testTernaryIf( int grade )
    {

        System.out.println(
                "Grade: " + (grade < 70 ? "Fail" : "Pass" ) );

    }//end public static void testTernaryIf( int grade )

    public static void main( String arg[] )
    {

        testTernaryIf( 96 );
    }
//end public static void main( String arg[] )
}//end public class ternaryIf
```

Your output (results) will look like this:

Grade: Pass

Let's examine this code:

```
        ( grade < 70 ?  "Fail."  :  "Pass." )

        if grade < 70
                        Fail is printed
        else
                        Pass is printed
```

Summary

In programming the statement that is used the most is the "if" statement, and it has multiple forms and usages. The simplest form is when we are asking if some condition happens, whatever that condition is, it must be true for the if to be true.

We also have the "if else" form, if the if condition is false then the else gets executed. The "if else if else", "nested if" and "ternary if" are also other forms of if statements.

The combination of these statements allows us to be very creative and develop very powerful programs.

Key Terms

if Command	In my opinion the most used command in programming is the "if" command. In programming we are always making decisions, always asking what if?
	The great thing about the implementation of the "if" command is that it is almost identical in every programming language.
	A plain if is very useful and very easy to implement. The plain if statement has the following structure:
	if(condition)
	{
	commands
	}
	If the condition is TRUE then the commands between the curly brackets will be executed:
	float temperature = 92.7; //create and load a float variable
	if(temperature > 90)
	{
	System.out.println(" Oh man it is hot!!");
	}
if else if	There are times that the if and else combination is not enough, then we use the "if else if" combination:
	Please see program if_else_if.java
if_else	The if statement has a sidekick called else, they work very well together, their structure is:
	if(condition)
	{
	commands
	}
	else
	{
	commands
	}
	If the "if" condition is NOT true then else takes charge and its commands are executed.

if. nested if	The nested if is very powerful and sometimes complex.
	Please see program nestedIf.java
if. ternary If	The ternary (three way) "if" replaces some implementations of if else if statements
	expression1 ? expression2 : expression3
	if expression1 is true
	then expression2 is selected
	else expression3 is selected
	other way to look at it is:
	condition ? value_if_true : value_if_false
	Please see program ternaryIf.java

Exercises

1. Write a method that will find which number of two is the lowest.

2. Write a method that will find which number of two is the highest.

3. Write a method that will find which number of two is less or equal.

4. Write a method that will find which number of two is greater or equal.

5. Write a method that will find a number modules 5 that equals 0.

6. What is the purpose of if statement _____ (Select all that apply)
   a. To create Java programs
   b. To call the import classes into Java
   c. To make mathematical and/or logical decisions
   d. To use the System.out.printf class

7. Show multiple if statements _____ (Select all that apply)
   a. if, for , while
   b. if, if else, else if, if
   c. for, if, while
   d. if, if else, else if

8. What is the value of a ? show all a, b, c, d results
   ____ int a = (100 % 5 == 1) ? 10 : 5;
   ____ int a = (100 % 5 == 0) ? 10 : 5;
   ____ int a = (100 % 5 = 1) ? 10 : 5;
   ____ int a = (100) ? 10 : 5;

9. How many parts does the ternary if have _____ (Select all that apply)
   a. One, ternary If (condition)
   b. Two, true and false
   c. Three, condition, false and true
   d. Three, condition, true and false

REFERENCES

- Java API Specifications

 http://www.oracle.com/technetwork/java/api-141528.html

- My Java programs that I use in my Java classes located at robinson.cs.fiu.edu

//END CHAPTER 5: IF COMMANDS

Loops

chapter **6**

Loops

In Java we have three types of loops: for, while, and do while loops.

for Loops

There are two types of for loops in Java, the standard for loop which has three parts and the enhanced for loop (see Enhanced For Loops at the end of the arrays section in Chapter 7: Data Structures - Arrays).

The standard for loop looks as follows:

```
for( start ; stop condition ; step )
{
    commands
}
```

The for loop requires a counter variable, in most cases the int x variable is selected.

The start section determines the beginning of the loop, the loop can start at any location, 0, the end value, or any value in between.

```
int x = 0;
for( x = 0;
for( x = lastValue;
for( x = lastValue/2;
```

< 113 >

The stop condition section tells the loop that when such condition is met to terminate the loop:

```
        start    stop
    for( x = 0; x <= 5
```

The step section tells the for loop that every time it does a loop, execute whatever command is in the step:

```
        start    stop    step
    for( x = 0; x <= 5; x++ )
```

x++ means add one to the current value of x.

Notice that we must place a ; after the first and second conditions.

Now that we have the heading or control line of the "for loop," we add its body:

```
/*
   Author  : Michael Robinson
   Program : forLoop.java
   Purpose : To present three samples
             of the for loop

   Updated : Jan 29, 2099
*/


public class forLoop
{
    public static void main( String arg[] )
    {
        int x = 0;

        for( x = 0; x <= 5; x++ )
        {
            System.out.print( x + " " );
        }

        System.out.println();

        for( x = 0; x < 6; x++ )
        {
            System.out.print( x + " " );
        }
```

```
        System.out.println();

        for( x = 5; x > -1; x--)
        {
            System.out.print( x + " " );
        }

        System.out.println();

    }//end public static void main( String arg[] )

}//end public class forLoop
```

Your output (results) will look like this:

```
0 1 2 3 4 5
0 1 2 3 4 5
5 4 3 2 1 0
```

Let's examine this code:

This for loop starts by assigning 0 to the x variable. Condition: as long as the value of x is less than or equal to 5 the loop continues, once the value of x becomes 6 the for loop terminates. Step: every time the program goes thru a loop it adds 1 to its current value.

```
for( x = 0; x <= 5; x++ )
{
    System.out.print( x + " " );
}
```

Notice that the program is checking if x < 5 and then if x = 5, so it is executing two instructions every time it does a loop, we can reduce the amount of instructions to half by modifying the for loop header as follows:

```
for( x = 0; x < 6; x++ )
{
    System.out.print( x + " " );
}
```

by making this modification the loop only executes one instruction x < 6, giving us the same result as checking for <= 5 in half the time.

The following code show us how we can print the data backwards:

```
for( x = 5; x > -1; x--)
```

```
{
    System.out.print( x + " " );
}
```

Note that we can applied any operator we want to the step section:

```
x+=3, x-=1, x*=2, x/=2, x%=2, etc.
```

while Loops

The while loop looks like this:

```
while( condition )
{
    commands
}
```

When we compare the while loop with the for loop, what goes between the () in the while is the looping condition, same purpose but more flexible than in the for loop.

Assume we have variables that control the temperature, humidity, and altitude and we want to do a task while these three conditions meet some values.

```
int temperature = 50;
int humidity    = 10;
int altitude    = 0;

while( ( (temperature > 0) && (humidity<100) && (altitude>0) )||
       ( (temperature < 100) && (humidity>0) && (altitude>0) )
     )
{
    //fly away
}
```

In this case we are evaluating if:

```
( (temperature > 0) && (humidity < 100) && (altitude > 0) )
||
( (temperature < 100) && (humidity > 0) && (altitude > 0) )
```

as long as either one of these group of conditions is true the while loop will continue. The moment that either one is NOT true the loop will terminate.

As we have seen here, we can have as multiple conditions inside the () as needed.

Boolean Conditions in while Loops Program

When we studied the primitive data type in Chapter 3, we learned about the boolean data type. While loops use boolean values by checking if their values are true or false, as follow:

```java
/*
  Author   : Michael Robinson
  Program  : whileLoop.java
  Purpose  : To present the while loop

  Updated  : Jan 29, 2099
*/


public class whileLoop
{
    public static void theWhileLoop( int temperature )
    {
        boolean x = false;

        System.out.print( "Temperature is normal" );

        while( x != true )
        {
            System.out.print( "." );

            if( temperature  >= 99 )
            {
                System.out.println(
                     "\nTemperature is > 99 degrees" );

                System.out.println( "Turning computer off ....." );

                x = true; //reset condition to true & terminate loop
            }
```

```
        temperature++; //increasing temperature by one degree

    }//end while( x != true )

}//end public static void theWhileLoop()


public static void main( String arg[] )
{
    theWhileLoop( 60 );

}//end public static void main( String arg[] )

}//end public class whileLoop
```

Your output (results) will look like this:

```
Temperature is normal.......................................
Temperature is > 99 degrees
Turning computer off .....
```

Let's examine this code:

We create the variable x and set it to false.

```
boolean x = false;
```

Now we start a while loop that will allow us at least one loop, since the condition is correct:

```
while( x != true )
```

Once we process the commands inside the last statement sets the condition to true:

```
x = true; //will reset condition to true & terminate loop
```

forcing the while loop to terminate.

Endless while Loop

We use the endless loop when we do not know when the ending condition will be reached.

The following program shows us a simple example:

```java
/*
  Author   : Michael Robinson
  Program  : whileLoopEndless.java
  Purpose  : To present the while loop

  Updated  : Jan 29, 2099
*/

public class whileLoopEndless
{
    public static void endLessLoop()
    {
        int counter = 0;

        while( true )
        {
            if( counter > Math.pow( 10.0, 2.0 ) )
            {
                System.out.println(
                "\nCounter is > Math.pow( 10.0, 2.0 ) = " +
                  counter );

                break; //terminate while loop
            }

            counter++;

        }//end while( true )

    }//end public static void endLessLoop()

    public static void main( String arg[] )
    {
        endLessLoop();

    }//end public static void main( String arg[] )

}//end public class whileLoopEndless
```

The break command terminates any type of loop.

Your output (results) will look like this:

```
Counter is > Math.pow( 10.0, 2.0 ) = 101
```

Let's examine this code:

```java
while( true ) //this is the endless condition
{
    if( counter > Math.pow( 10.0, 2.0 ) )
    {
        System.out.println(
        "\nCounter is > Math.pow( 10.0, 2.0 ) = " +
          counter );

        break; //this terminates the while loop
    }

    counter++;

}//end while( true )
```

As we see the endless while loop is very simple to implement, the true condition inside the while statement means to execute the loop as long as it is true. The easiest manner to terminate the loop is that when a specific situation happens we need to execute the break statement which terminates the loop by jumping to the line of code after the while loop.

do while Loops

The do while loops are different from the while loops in that they will be executed at least once.

The do while loop looks like this:

```java
/*
  Author   : Michael Robinson
  Program  : whileLoopDO.java
  Purpose  : To present the do while loop

  Updated  : Jan 29, 2099
*/
```

```java
public class whileLoopDO
{
    public static void doWhileLoop()
    {
        int temperature = 50;
        int humidity    = 10;
        int altitude    = -5;

        do
        {
            System.out.println( "this line prints at least ONCE" );
            System.out.println( "altitude is " + altitude );
        }

        while(
        ((temperature > 0) && (humidity < 100) && (altitude > 0))||
        ((temperature < 100) && (humidity > 0) && (altitude > 0))
            );
    }//end public static void theWhileLoop()


    public static void main( String arg[] )
    {
        doWhileLoop();

    }//end public static void main( String arg[] )

}//end public class whileLoop
```

The difference between the while and the do while loop is that in the do while loop the process between the { } gets done at least once, while the regular while(condition) loop gets executed only if the condition is met, in other words "while the condition is true."

Your output (results) will look like this:

this line has to print at least ONCE

altitude is -5

Let's examine this code:

the loop begin with the statement `do`:

```
do
{
    System.out.println( "this line prints at least ONCE" );
    System.out.println( "altitude is " + altitude );
}

while(
((temperature > 0) && (humidity < 100) && (altitude > 0))||
((temperature < 100) && (humidity > 0) && (altitude > 0))
    );
```

then it processes anything between the **{ }** before evaluating the condition statement between the while()
statement.

Enhanced for Loops (Summary)

These loops will be described in Chapter 7. We need to know about Arrays to easier understand these type
of loops.

switch Command

Limitations of the switch Command

I look at the switch statement as a variation of the if statement. The limitations of the switch class is that
it only accepts integers or characters as input, while the "if" command accepts any type and amount of
conditions. Also, the switch command does not allow for comparison statements as follows:

evaluations (=, >=, ,=, etc).

switch Command Using int as Input

The following example will show us how to use int as input data:

```
/*
  Author  : Michael Robinson
  Program : swithClass.java
```

```
  Purpose : To present the switch statement using int
            as data input.
            NOTE:
            switch does not allow for comparision
            evaluations ( =, >=, ,=, etc)

  Updated : Jan 29, 2099
*/


import java.util.Scanner;


public class switchClass
{
    public static void switchOne()
    {
        String label = "\n Enter your grade (70, 80, 90" +
                       " to pass the class or 0 to exit) : ";

        int grade = 999;

        System.out.print( label );

        //request input from user
        Scanner keyboard = new Scanner( System.in );

        //convert input to int data type
        grade = (int)keyboard.nextInt();

        while( grade != 0 )
        {
            switch( grade ) //execute switch using the grade entered
            {
                case 90:  //if grade = 90
                        System.out.println( "\n You obtained " +
                                                "grade, A range" );
                        break; //terminate loop

                case 80:  //if grade = 80
                        System.out.println( "\n You obtained " +
                                                "grade, B range" );
                        break; //terminate loop
```

```java
          case 70:   //if grade = 70
                     System.out.println( "\n You obtained " +
                                              "grade, C range" );
                     break; //terminate loop

          default:   //else
                     System.out.print( "\n Enter grade" );
          }//end switch

          System.out.print( label );

          //convert input to int data type
          grade = (int)keyboard.nextInt();

       }//end while(grade !=0)

    }//end public static void switchOne()


    public static void main( String arg[] )
    {
        switchOne();

        System.out.println( "\n\tEnd of Program" );

    }//end public static void main( String arg[] )

}//end public class switchClass
```

Your output (results) will look like this:

```
Enter your grade (70, 80, 90 to pass the class or 0 to exit) : 90
You obtained grade, A range

Enter your grade (70, 80, 90 to pass the class or 0 to exit) : 80
You obtained grade, B range

Enter your grade (70, 80, 90 to pass the class or 0 to exit) : 70
You obtained grade, C range

Enter your grade (70, 80, 90 to pass the class or 0 to exit) : -5
Please re-enter grade
```

```
Enter your grade (70, 80, 90 to pass the class or 0 to exit) : 80
You obtained grade, B range

Enter your grade (70, 80, 90 to pass the class or 0 to exit) : 0

    End of Program
```

Let's examine this code:

From the main method we call the switchOne() method. In this method we see the statement switch(grade). Assume the value of grade is 90, so when we read the statement case 90: we will execute all statements belonging to this case. In switch, case is equivalent to a regular if statement.

```java
while( grade != 0 )
{
    switch( grade ) //execute switch using the grade entered
    {
        case 90:   //if grade = 90
                System.out.println( "\n You obtained " +
                                    "grade, A range" );
                break; //terminate switch loop

        case 80:   //if grade = 80
                System.out.println( "\n You obtained " +
                                    "grade, B range" );
                break; //terminate switch loop

        case 70:   //if grade = 70
                System.out.println( "\n You obtained " +
                                    "grade, C range" );
                break; //terminate switch loop

        default:   //else
                System.out.print( "\n Enter grade" );
    }//end switch

    System.out.print( label );

    //convert input to int data type
    grade = (int)keyboard.nextInt();

}//end while(grade !=0)
```

switch Command Using char as Input

The following example will show how to use char as input data:

```
/*

    Author  : Michael Robinson
    Program : swithClassChar.java
    Purpose : To present the switch statement using char
              as data input and add char input using +=.
              NOTE:
              switch does not allow for comparision
              evaluations ( =, >=, ,=, etc)

    Updated : Jan 29, 2099
*/



import java.util.Scanner;



public class switchClassChar
{
    public static void switchTwo()
    {
        //using chars, leaving break out until the last case to show
        //what happens
        Scanner sc = new Scanner(System.in);

        System.out.print( "Enter your program grade: " );
        String s = sc.next();   //request input from user
        char    p = s.charAt(0); //convert input to char data type

        String details = "";

        switch(p)
        {
            case 'F':  //if p == 'F'
            case 'f':  //if p == 'f'
                        details += "F";
                        break;  //terminate loop
```

```java
        case 'D':    //if p == 'D'
        case 'd':    //if p == 'd'
                    details += "D";
                    break;  //terminate loop

        case 'C':    //if p == 'C'
        case 'c':    //if p == 'c'
                    details += "C";
                    break;  //terminate loop

        case 'B':    //if p == 'B'
        case 'b':    //if p == 'b'
                    details += "B";
                    break;  //terminate loop

        case 'A':    //if p == 'A'
        case 'a':    //if p == 'a'
                    details += "A";
                    break;  //terminate loop

        default:    details = s;
                    break;  //terminate loop
        }

    System.out.println( "\nNice work on getting " + details +
                        " on your First program" );

    }//end public static void switchTwo()


    public static void main( String arg[] )
    {
        switchTwo();

        System.out.println( "\n\tEnd of Program" );

    }//end public static void main( String arg[] )

}//end public class switchClassChar
```

Your output (results) will look like this:

Enter your program grade: d

Nice work on getting D on your First program

       End of Program

Enter your program grade: c

Nice work on getting C on your First program

       End of Program

Enter your program grade: a

Nice work on getting A on your First program

       End of Program

Let's examine this code:

From the main method we call the switchOne() method. In this method we see the statement switch(p). Assume the value of p is a, so when we read the statement case a: we will execute all statements belonging the this case. In switch, case is equivalent to a regular if statement.

```
switch (p)
{
    case 'A':  //if p == 'A'
    case 'a':  //if p == 'a'
            details += "A";
            break;  //terminate loop
```

Once we find the above code, we assign the value A to the variable details and terminate the switch statement using break, then we execute the following code:

```
System.out.println( "\nNice work on getting " + details +
                " on your First program" );
```

Finally, in the main menu we find and execute:

```
System.out.println( "\n\tEnd of Program" );
```

```
which is executed after the program command comes back to main.
```

Summary

If we were comparing 1 million different items we can do it using the if statement. However if we just use the if statement we will need at least 1 million if statements. Fortunately we have several statements that are part of a group of statements called "loops." Java has several types of loops such as: the regular for loop and the enhanced for loop. The while loop and the do while are another two forms of loops.

The code inside the loops gets executed multiple times based on the conditions given to the loop.

Key Terms

for Loops	There are two types of for loops in Java, the standard for loop which has three parts and the enhanced for loop (see Enhanced For Loops at the end of the arrays section in Chapter 7 - Data Structures - Arrays).
	
	The standard for loop looks as follows:
	`for( start ;  stop condition ;  step )`
	`{`
	`    commands`
	`}`
	
	The for loop requires a counter variable, in most cases the int x variable is selected.
	
	The start section determines the beginning of the loop, the loop can start at any location, 0, the end value, or any value in between.
	
	`int  x = 0;`
	`for( x = 0;`
	`for( x = lastValue;`
	`for( x = lastValue/2;`
	
	The stop condition section tells the loop that when such condition is met to terminate the loop:
	
	`    start    stop`
	`for( x = 0;  x <= 5`
	
	The step section tells the for loop that every time it does a loop, execute whatever command is in the step:
	
	`    start    stop    step`
	`for( x = 0;  x <= 5;  x++ )`
	
	x++ means add one to the current value of x.

Loops	In Java we have three types of loops: for, while, and do while loops.

switch Command	Limitations of the switch command:
	I look at the switch statement as a variation of the if statement.
	The limitations of the switch class is that it only accepts integers or characters as input, while the "if" command accepts any type and amount of conditions. Also, the switch command does not allow for comparison statements as follows:
	evaluations (=, >=, ,=, etc).
	Please see program swithClass.java.
while Loop, endless	We use the endless loop when we do not know when the ending condition will be reached.
	The whileLoopEndless.java program shows us a simple example.
while Loops	The while loop looks like this:

	while(condition)
	{
	 commands
	}

	When we compare the while loop with the for loop, what goes between the () in the while is the looping condition, same purpose but more flexible than in the for loop.
	Assume we have variables that control the temperature, humidity, and altitude and we want to do a task while these three conditions meet some values:

	int temperature = 50;
	int humidity = 10;
	int altitude = 0;
	
	while(((temperature > 0) &&
	 (humidity<100) && (altitude>0)) ||
	 ((temperature < 100) &&
	 (humidity>0) && (altitude>0)
	))
	{
	 //fly away
	}

While. do while Loops	The do while loops are different from the while loops in that they will be executed at least once.
	Please see program whileLoopDO.java

Exercises

1. Using a regular for loop that will process numbers from 1 to 100, create a program that will find the results of calculating each number from (1 to 100 mod 5) + 3.

   After the for loop ends, display the average for all previous results.

2. Using a while loop write your name forwards.

3. Divide by Zero. Implement division by 0, with error trapping, using if and while statements as follows:
   a. Using two variables: FirstNumber and LastNumber, use a while loop.
   b. Ask the user to enter the first number.
   c. Ask the user to enter the second number.
   d. If the user enters the value 99 for the first or the second number, you must exit the while loop immediately.
   e. If the second number is ZERO inform the user that you CANNOT divide by ZERO, and ask for a correct second number. If the second number is NOT a zero or 99, do the division and using labels display all numbers for this computation. Example: 4 divided by 1 = 4.

4. Using a for loop write your name backwards.

5. Using a for loop write your name forwards in ASCII.

6. How many sections does the regular for loop has _____ (Select all that apply)
   a. Three (start, step, stop condition)
   b. Three (start, stop condition, step)
   c. Three (start, increment, stop condition)
   d. Three (start, stop condition, decrement)

7. How many sections does the while loop has _____ (Select all that apply)
   a. Three (start, stop condition, step)
   b. Two (start, stop condition)
   c. One (stop condition)
   d. None

8. What is a nested for loop _____ (Select all that apply)
   a. A loop that has loops inside loops
   b. It does not exist
   c. A loop that has multiple for loops inside while loops ONLY
   d. A loop that has multiple while loops inside for loops ONLY

9. Can we mix for loops with while loops _____ (Select all that apply)
   a. No because the program will get confused
   b. Yes, but not while loops inside for loops
   c. Yes, either one can be the inner or outer loop
   d. Yes, but not for loops inside for loops

10. Can the switch statements do all that the if statement does? (T=true F=false)
    ___ The switch statements is as powerful as the if statement
    ___ The switch statement is more powerful than the if statement
    ___ The switch statement is a loop that has a case statement which acts as
        a simple if statement
    ___ The switch statement does not exist in Java.

REFERENCES

- Java API Specifications

  http://www.oracle.com/technetwork/java/api-141528.html

- My Java programs that I use in my Java classes located at robinson.cs.fiu.edu

//END CHAPTER 6: LOOPS

Data
Structures-
Arrays

chapter

7

Data Structures

As we know data comes in many forms such as int, float, strings, etc. Data needs to be placed inside specific structures called Data structures. Once in there we can use the data as needed. One of the most used data structures in computer science is the array.

Arrays

Arrays are data structures that group data items of the same data type. Arrays can contain data of one data type at the same time such as int, char, float, double or any other primitive data type, but we cannot mix data types in the same array. We can also declare arrays of wrapper data types such as Integer, Character, Float, Double, etc., or string data type. Arrays of objects is a special case that will be addressed in Chapter 8.

Arrays can be of one or multiple dimensions. Every location in an array is called an index. Arrays are very useful, but they have two short comings. First, arrays can not have mixed data types, and once declared, their size can not be changed. Secondly, we can not add or delete indexes, however the data inside each index can be changed.

One Dimension Array

A one dimension array contains one row and one or more columns. We refer to a location in an array as "the index" and we always name the row first then the column. If the data is in row 0 and column 3, we say that the data is at index location 0,3. "Red Cross" will help us remember R,C for Row,Column. We can also use

< 137 >

"RC Cola," a soda found in parts of the United States or "RiCola" (RC), a famous medication of unique delicious taste for soothing of the mouth and throat. Always place the "row" before the "column," if we place the column before the row we will have unpredictable results.

The following array has only one row which is row 0, and five columns as follow:

	Col 0	Col 1	Col 2	Col 3	Col 4
Row 0	132	115	165	103	176
Index	0,0	0,1	0,2	0,3	0,4
Contains	132	115	165	103	176

This could be a row of stores on a one story tall strip mall.

We can also look at this array as follows:

row	col	contains
0	0	132
0	1	115
0	2	165
0	3	103
0	4	176

Declaring/Creating One Dimension Arrays

Now lets create one dimensional arrays:

```
int     arrayOne[];      //creates the array arrayOne to hold ints
float   arrayTwo[];      //creates the array arrayTwo to hold floats
double  arrayThree[];    //creates the array arrayThree to hold doubles
String arrayFour[];      //creates the array arrayFour to hold Strings
```

Allocating Space to Declared Arrays

When we declare an array as above, we create it, but we do not allocate space for it in RAM memory. The size of an array is specified when we allocate space for it, as follows:

```
arrayOne[]   = new int[ 3 ];    //creates space for 3 elements
arrayTwo[]   = new float[ 2 ];   //creates space for 2 elements
arrayThree[] = new double[ 4 ]; //creates space for 4 elements
arrayFour[]  = new String[ 2 ]; //creates space for 2 elements
```

Declare and Allocate at the Same Time

We can also declare (create) an array and assign it space at the same time as follows:

```
int    arrayOne[]   = new int[ 3 ];
float  arrayTwo[]   = new float[ 2 ];
double arrayThree[] = new double[ 4 ];
String arrayFour[]  = new String[ 2 ];
```

When we have an array with 4 indexes

```
double arrayThree[] = new double[ 4 ];
```

we say that its length is 4, with indexes 0, 1, 2, and 3, therefore the indexes go from 0 to length-1.

One of the most common mistakes when accessing an array is trying to access an index at location "length." This will give us the error "index out of range." We must remember that indexes begin at location 0 and end at location "length − 1," always!

Create, Allocate and Load Data into Arrays

```
   int    arrayOne[]   = { 43,235,101 };
or int    arrayOne[ 3 ] = { 43,235,101 };
```

creates a single dimension array named arrayOne of int data type placing the values 43 at index 0, 235 at index 1, and 101 at index 2, again the length of arrayOne is 3 with indexes 0, 1, and 2.

If you declare the array as arrayOne[] and assign values to it, it knows how many indexes to create. You can also create the array giving it a size : arrayOne[3]

The previous rules apply to the following arrays:

```
     float    arrayTwo[]       = { 12.54,4.23 };
or   float    arrayTwo[ 2 ]    = { 12.54,4.23 };


     double arrayThree[]       = { 2.33,2.31,9.0,7.12 };
or   double arrayThree[ 4 ] = { 2.33,2.31,9.0,7.12 };


     String arrayFour[]        = { "Joe", "Smith" };
or   String arrayFour[2]       = { "Joe", "Smith" };
```

Load Data to a Declared Array

We can also load data directly into each index as follows:

```
arrayOne[ 0 ] =   43;
arrayOne[ 1 ] = 235;
arrayOne[ 3 ] = 101;

arrayTwo[ 0 ] = 12.54;
arrayTwo[ 1 ] =  4.23;

arrayThree[ 0 ] = 2.33;
arrayThree[ 1 ] = 2.31;
arrayThree[ 2 ] = 9.0;
arrayThree[ 3 ] = 7.12;

arrayFour[ 0 ]  =  { "Joe" };
arrayFour[ 1 ]  =  { "Smith" };
```

Note: String arrays are themselves arrays of characters

arrayFour[0] contains an array of 3 characters = Joe

If we wanted to load an array of length 1,000,000 with the value of its corresponding location values, e.g. array[55] = 55; we will need 1,000,000 lines of code if we follow the above manual samples, but thanks to the for loop we only need 3 lines of code.

```
int x;
for( x = 0; x < 1,000,000; x++ )
{
    array[x] = x;
}
```

Printing all Values Inside this Array

```
for( x = 0; x < 1,000,000; x++ )
{
    System.out.printf( "%d\n", array[x] );
}
```

Multi Dimensional Arrays

Arrays of two or more dimensions are called Multidimensional Arrays. Humans can visualize three dimension arrays. After that it is very difficult for us. But using computer programing I have been able to create an array of 21 dimensions, until the computer froze.

Two Dimension Arrays

A two dimensional array is a group of one dimension arrays and they look like this:

	Col 0	Col 1	Col 2	Col 3	Col 4
Row 0	0,0	0,1	0,2	0,3	0,4
Row 1	1,0	1,1	1,2	1,3	1,4
Row 2	2,0	2,1	2,2	2,3	2,4
Row 3	3,0	3,1	3,2	3,3	3,4
Row 4	4,0	4,1	4,2	4,3	4,4

In this graph we have a 5 x 5 array that has 5 rows and 5 columns, from 0 to 4 each. Each location is called the index of the array.

In computer science we always start counting at 0. Here indexes 0 to 4 contain 5 indexes, therefore the size of this array is 5x5.

Again, every location is referred by the row,col location, Red Cross, RC cola, and RiCola are words that I have used in class to help remember that the ROW always comes before the COLUMN.

The r,c left to right diagonal locations in a 5x5 array from 0,0 to 4,4 are:

r,c	r,c	r,c	r,c	r,c
0,0	1,1	2,2	3,3	4,4
0,0				
	1,1			
		2,2		
			3,3	
				4,4

The r,c right left diagonal locations in a 5x5 array from 0,4 to 4,0 are:

r,c	r,c	r,c	r,c	r,c
0,4	3,1	2,2	1,3	4,0
				4,0
			1,3	
		2,2		
	3,1			
0,4				

When dealing with data we always need to analyze the meaning of such data. In this example, if we analyze the r,c of diagonal indexes from left,top to bottom,right locations we see that the rows == cols.

The indexes of the other diagonal indexes (top,right to bottom,left) when we add the row+col of each index the totals are always 4.

Why is this important? In computer science there is a discipline called algorithms. The difference of a working program and a very efficient program is that the efficient program is done with efficient algorithms. So if we learn to analyze the data we are using, it will help us to come up with very efficient algorithms.

The following code will declare a two dimensional int array named numbers2d as well as two variables, row and col.

Using a for loop we will load into each array location the addition of its row + col location.

Two Dimensional int Arrays

Again, a two dimensional array is a group of one dimension arrays. The following is a sample program of a two dimensional array of int data type, how to create it , pass it to another method, load it with data, and display it.

```java
/*
  Author   : Michael Robinson
  Program  : array2dimensions.java
  Purpose  : To present a two dimension array
             of int data type

  Updated  : Jan 29, 2099
*/

public class array2dimensions
{
    public static void process2dArray( int numbers2d[][], int row,
                                        int col, int x, int y )
    {
        //Load two dimensional array with each location's row+col
        System.out.println( "\nLoading two dimensional array" );

        for( x = 0; x < row; x++ ) //process rows
        {
            for( y = 0; y < col; y++ ) //process columns
            {
                numbers2d[x][y] = x+y; //load up array with data
            }
        }

        //Display the contents of the two dimensional array
        System.out.println( "  \nTwo dimensional array contents" );

        for( x = 0; x < row; x++ ) //process rows
        {
            for( y = 0; y < col; y++ ) //process columns
            {
                if( (x+y) < col ) //test for variable width
                {
                    System.out.print( " " ); //display space
                }
                //display data inside each array index
                System.out.print( " " + numbers2d[x][y] );
```

```
            }
            System.out.println(); //display a line feed
        }

    }//end public static void process( int numbers2d )


    public static void main( String arg[] )
    {
        //Declare and initialize local variables
        //you can create multiple variables of the same type on
        //the same line
        int row = 10, col = 10;
        int x = 0, y = 0;

        //declares a 10x10 two dimensional array
        int numbers2d[][] = new int[ row ][ col ];

        process2dArray( numbers2d, row, col, x, y );

    }//end public static void main( String arg[] )

}//end public class array2dimensions
```

Your output (results) will look like this:

Loading two dimensional array

```
                Two dimensional array contents
                0  1  2  3  4  5  6  7  8  9
                1  2  3  4  5  6  7  8  9 10
                2  3  4  5  6  7  8  9 10 11
                3  4  5  6  7  8  9 10 11 12
                4  5  6  7  8  9 10 11 12 13
                5  6  7  8  9 10 11 12 13 14
                6  7  8  9 10 11 12 13 14 15
                7  8  9 10 11 12 13 14 15 16
                8  9 10 11 12 13 14 15 16 17
                9 10 11 12 13 14 15 16 17 18
```

Notice that the following results can be obtained from this array. These are the answers for one of the exercises requested at the end of this chapter:

The diagonal on previous page values from locations 0,0 to 9,9 are:

0 2 4 6 8 10 12 14 16 18 = 90

The diagonal on the previous page values from locations 0,9 to 9,0 are:

9 9 9 9 9 9 9 9 9 = 90

Let's examine this code:

I documented basically every line of code in the above program. Please review it in detail. In addition I would like to explain two items:

- In the main method I assigned 10 to the row and column variables. The entire program depends on these two values. If we want to create a larger or smaller size array we can do it by changing those two values. The entire program will adjust to any new two values. Multidimensional arrays do not need to be perfect squares such as previously shown. They can have a different amount of rows and columns. Improvements can be made to the display spacing. I am leaving this as an exercise.
- In arrays, following the graphical norms in math, I use the variable x for rows and y for columns. For three dimensional arrays I use x, y and z. Some people prefer other variables such as I and J.

To manually load data into a multidimensional array is a little tricky:

```
//declares and initializes a 10x10 two dimensional array
int numbers2d[][] = {  //each {} section represents a row
            { 0,  1,  2,  3,  4,  5,  6,  7,  8,  9 },
            { 1,  2,  3,  4,  5,  6,  7,  8,  9, 10 },
            { 2,  3,  4,  5,  6,  7,  8,  9, 10, 11 },
            { 3,  4,  5,  6,  7,  8,  9, 10, 11, 12 },
            { 4,  5,  6,  7,  8,  9, 10, 11, 12, 13 },
            { 5,  6,  7,  8,  9, 10, 11, 12, 13, 14 },
            { 6,  7,  8,  9, 10, 11, 12, 13, 14, 15 },
            { 7,  8,  9, 10, 11, 12, 13, 14, 15, 16 },
            { 8,  9, 10, 11, 12, 13, 14, 15, 16, 17 },
            { 9, 10, 11, 12, 13, 14, 15, 16, 17, 18 }
        };
```

It is doable but using loops makes life a lot easier.

Two Dimensional String Arrays (Using Array's Length)

Again, a two dimensional array is a group of one dimension arrays. There are times when we receive an array and we do not know its length. Arrays have many methods, and in this case we will use the array.length method to find the array's length.

```java
/*
  Author   : Michael Robinson
  Program  : array2dimLength.java
  Purpose  : To present a two dimension array
             of int data type

  Updated  : Jan 29, 2099
*/


public class array2dimLength
{
    public static void stringLoadDisplay2d()
    {
        //load 2D array with strings
        String names[][] = {   { "Joe", "Smith" },
                               { "Maria", "Perez" },
                               { "James", "Einstein" }
                           };
        int x = 0;
        int y = 0;

        System.out.println(
                " names.length = " + names.length + "\n" );

        //process rows based on array's length
        for( x = 0; x < names.length; x++ )
        {
            for( y = 0; y < 2; y++ ) //process columns
            {
                System.out.print( " " + names[x][y] ); //display data
            }
            System.out.println(); //display a line feed
        }

    }//end public static void stringLoadDisplay2d()
```

```
public static void main( String arg[] )
{
    stringLoadDisplay2d();

}//end public static void main( String arg[] )

}//end public class array2dimLength
```

Your output (results) will look like this:

```
names.length = 3

Joe Smith
Maria Perez
James Einstein
```

Let's examine this code:

I documented basically every line of code in the above program. Please review it in detail. In addition I would like to explain the following:

The names.length command gives us the length of the current row in the array. In this case it is three. Now we are going to cover three dimensional arrays.

Three Multidimensional Arrays

A three dimensional array is a group of two dimension arrays. I think that one of the best ways to explain what a three dimensional array is, to use the representation of an apartment building, everybody knows what they look like:

```
/*
  Author  : Michael Robinson
  Program : array3d.java
  Purpose : To present the three dimensional arrays


  Updated : Jan 29, 2099
*/
```

```java
public class array3d
{

    public static void DisplayStatistics(
                    int floors, int rows, int columns )
    {
        System.out.println( "\n This is a building with:" );
        System.out.printf(  " %3d Floors \n", floors );
        System.out.printf(  " %3d Rows    \n", rows    );
        System.out.printf(  " %3d Columns\n", columns );
        System.out.printf(  " %3d Total Amount of Apartments\n",
                    ( floors * rows * columns ) );
        System.out.println(
                    " Created using a 3 Dimensional Array\n" );

    }//end public static void DisplayStatistics( int floors,
     //int rows, int columns )


    public static void cubeBuilding( int floors, int rows,
                                int columns )
    {

        //create a three dimensional array of String data type
        String array3D[][][] = new String[floors] [rows][columns];

        int x=0; //create and initialize variable x for floors
        int y=0; //create and initialize variable y for rows
        int z=0; //create and initialize variable z for columns

        int units=0; //create and initialize variable units

        DisplayStatistics( floors, rows, columns );

        //load data into array
        for( x=0; x<floors; x++ )  //controls the floors
        {
            for( y=0; y<rows; y++ )  //controls the rows
            {
                for( z=0; z<columns; z++ )  //controls the columns
                {
                    //creates the apartment number into temp variable
                    String temp = "" + (x+1) + y + z;
```

```java
            // count the amount of apartments created
            units++;

            //load array with apartment number
            array3D[x][y][z] = temp;

            System.out.print( "\n Apartment number " +
                              array3D[x][y][z] + " -> " );

            System.out.print( " Floor = " + (x+1) +
                              " Row = " + y + " Col = " + z );

        }//end for( z=0; z<columns; z++ )

      }//end for( y=0; y<rows; y++ )

      System.out.println( "\n" );

    }//end for( x=0; x<floors; x++ )



    System.out.print( " Total Amount of Apartments = " + units );
    System.out.println();

    DisplayStatistics( floors, rows, columns );

  }//public static void cubeBuilding( int floors, int rows,
   //int columns )


  public static void main( String args[] )
  {
      int floors  = 4; //floors
      int rows    = 2; //rows
      int columns = 10; //columns

      //call method passing data variables
      cubeBuilding( floors, rows, columns );

  }//end public static void main(String[] args)

}//end public class array3d
```

Your output (results) will look like this:

This is a building with:
```
   4 Floors
   2 Rows
  10 Columns
  80 Total Amount of Apartments
Created using a 3 Dimensional Array
```

```
Apartment number 100 ->   Floor = 1 Row = 0 Col = 0
Apartment number 101 ->   Floor = 1 Row = 0 Col = 1
Apartment number 102 ->   Floor = 1 Row = 0 Col = 2
Apartment number 103 ->   Floor = 1 Row = 0 Col = 3
Apartment number 104 ->   Floor = 1 Row = 0 Col = 4
Apartment number 105 ->   Floor = 1 Row = 0 Col = 5
Apartment number 106 ->   Floor = 1 Row = 0 Col = 6
Apartment number 107 ->   Floor = 1 Row = 0 Col = 7
Apartment number 108 ->   Floor = 1 Row = 0 Col = 8
Apartment number 109 ->   Floor = 1 Row = 0 Col = 9
Apartment number 110 ->   Floor = 1 Row = 1 Col = 0
Apartment number 111 ->   Floor = 1 Row = 1 Col = 1
Apartment number 112 ->   Floor = 1 Row = 1 Col = 2

Apartment number 113 ->   Floor = 1 Row = 1 Col = 3
Apartment number 114 ->   Floor = 1 Row = 1 Col = 4
Apartment number 115 ->   Floor = 1 Row = 1 Col = 5
Apartment number 116 ->   Floor = 1 Row = 1 Col = 6
Apartment number 117 ->   Floor = 1 Row = 1 Col = 7
Apartment number 118 ->   Floor = 1 Row = 1 Col = 8
Apartment number 119 ->   Floor = 1 Row = 1 Col = 9

Apartment number 200 ->   Floor = 2 Row = 0 Col = 0
Apartment number 201 ->   Floor = 2 Row = 0 Col = 1
Apartment number 202 ->   Floor = 2 Row = 0 Col = 2
Apartment number 203 ->   Floor = 2 Row = 0 Col = 3
Apartment number 204 ->   Floor = 2 Row = 0 Col = 4
Apartment number 205 ->   Floor = 2 Row = 0 Col = 5
Apartment number 206 ->   Floor = 2 Row = 0 Col = 6
Apartment number 207 ->   Floor = 2 Row = 0 Col = 7
Apartment number 208 ->   Floor = 2 Row = 0 Col = 8
Apartment number 209 ->   Floor = 2 Row = 0 Col = 9
Apartment number 210 ->   Floor = 2 Row = 1 Col = 0
Apartment number 211 ->   Floor = 2 Row = 1 Col = 1
Apartment number 212 ->   Floor = 2 Row = 1 Col = 2
```

```
Apartment number 213 ->    Floor = 2 Row = 1 Col = 3
Apartment number 214 ->    Floor = 2 Row = 1 Col = 4
Apartment number 215 ->    Floor = 2 Row = 1 Col = 5
Apartment number 216 ->    Floor = 2 Row = 1 Col = 6
Apartment number 217 ->    Floor = 2 Row = 1 Col = 7
Apartment number 218 ->    Floor = 2 Row = 1 Col = 8
Apartment number 219 ->    Floor = 2 Row = 1 Col = 9

Apartment number 300 ->    Floor = 3 Row = 0 Col = 0
Apartment number 301 ->    Floor = 3 Row = 0 Col = 1
Apartment number 302 ->    Floor = 3 Row = 0 Col = 2
Apartment number 303 ->    Floor = 3 Row = 0 Col = 3
Apartment number 304 ->    Floor = 3 Row = 0 Col = 4
Apartment number 305 ->    Floor = 3 Row = 0 Col = 5
Apartment number 306 ->    Floor = 3 Row = 0 Col = 6
Apartment number 307 ->    Floor = 3 Row = 0 Col = 7
Apartment number 308 ->    Floor = 3 Row = 0 Col = 8
Apartment number 309 ->    Floor = 3 Row = 0 Col = 9
Apartment number 310 ->    Floor = 3 Row = 1 Col = 0
Apartment number 311 ->    Floor = 3 Row = 1 Col = 1
Apartment number 312 ->    Floor = 3 Row = 1 Col = 2
Apartment number 313 ->    Floor = 3 Row = 1 Col = 3
Apartment number 314 ->    Floor = 3 Row = 1 Col = 4
Apartment number 315 ->    Floor = 3 Row = 1 Col = 5
Apartment number 316 ->    Floor = 3 Row = 1 Col = 6
Apartment number 317 ->    Floor = 3 Row = 1 Col = 7
Apartment number 318 ->    Floor = 3 Row = 1 Col = 8
Apartment number 319 ->    Floor = 3 Row = 1 Col = 9

Apartment number 400 ->    Floor = 4 Row = 0 Col = 0
Apartment number 401 ->    Floor = 4 Row = 0 Col = 1
Apartment number 402 ->    Floor = 4 Row = 0 Col = 2
Apartment number 403 ->    Floor = 4 Row = 0 Col = 3
Apartment number 404 ->    Floor = 4 Row = 0 Col = 4
Apartment number 405 ->    Floor = 4 Row = 0 Col = 5
Apartment number 406 ->    Floor = 4 Row = 0 Col = 6
Apartment number 407 ->    Floor = 4 Row = 0 Col = 7
Apartment number 408 ->    Floor = 4 Row = 0 Col = 8
Apartment number 409 ->    Floor = 4 Row = 0 Col = 9
Apartment number 410 ->    Floor = 4 Row = 1 Col = 0
Apartment number 411 ->    Floor = 4 Row = 1 Col = 1
Apartment number 412 ->    Floor = 4 Row = 1 Col = 2
Apartment number 413 ->    Floor = 4 Row = 1 Col = 3
Apartment number 414 ->    Floor = 4 Row = 1 Col = 4
```

```
Apartment number 415 ->   Floor = 4 Row = 1 Col = 5
Apartment number 416 ->   Floor = 4 Row = 1 Col = 6
Apartment number 417 ->   Floor = 4 Row = 1 Col = 7
Apartment number 418 ->   Floor = 4 Row = 1 Col = 8
Apartment number 419 ->   Floor = 4 Row = 1 Col = 9

Total Amount of Apartments = 80

This is a building with:
   4 Floors
   2 Rows
  10 Columns
  80 Total Amount of Apartments
Created using a 3 Dimensional Array
```

Let's examine this code:

I documented basically every line of code in the above program. Please review it in detail. Three dimensional arrays are cubes, again a building is a cube and a three dimensional array. We need three variables and I use the math variables of a cube: x, y and z, however you can use any variables you want. Also remember that a three dimensional array is a group of two dimension arrays.

Parallel Arrays

Parallel arrays are used to combine multiple one dimensional arrays that might contain different data types, but each row in each array is related to each other:

```
int    studentID[]      = { 50102, 23908, 12098 };
String studentName[]    = { "Joe Ho", "Ann Paz", "Mo Sy" };
double studentBalance[] = { 10.00, 23.78, 1.07 };
```

Here we have three arrays, each containing three items, and each array holds different type of data, int, String and double.

The following program creates a report showing the student's name, id and current balance owed. To create this report we use what is called parallel arrays. The only requirement is that all arrays must have the same amount of rows. In this case there are three rows in each array.

This is the sample program:

```java
/*
   Author   : Michael Robinson
   Program  : arraysParallel.java
   Purpose  : To present a parallel arrays
              example.

   Updated  : Jan 29, 2099
*/


public class arraysParallel
{
    public static void parallel()
    {
        int      studentID[]      =
                    { 50102, 23908, 12098 }; //id array

        String studentName[]     =
                    { "Joe Ho", "Ann Paz", "Mo Sy" }; //names array

        double studentBalance[] =
                    { 10.00, 23.78, 1.07 }; //amounts due

        for( int x = 0; x < studentID.length; x++ )
        {
            System.out.println( studentName[x] + "\t" +
                                studentID[x]   + "\t" +
                                studentBalance[x]
                              );
        }

    }//end public static void parallel()


    public static void main(String[] args)
    {
        parallel();

    }//end public static void main(String[] args)

}//end public class arraysParallel
```

Your output (results) will look like this:

```
Joe  Ho     50102    10.0
Ann  Paz    23908    23.78
Mo   Sy     12098    1.07
```

You can use as many arrays as needed to produce parallel arrays.

Let's examine this code:

We simply have multiple arrays with the same amount of rows and we use them as if each array was a data file where each row/record in each file, corresponds to the same person.

Enhanced for Loops

Now that we know how arrays work, lets see what "enhanced for loops" are. Enhanced for loops are a variation of the "for loop" that is used with arrays and other data structure called ArrayList which we will see in Chapter 8, this is an example:

```java
/*
  Author   : Michael Robinson
  Program  : enhancedForLoops.java
  Purpose  : To present the
             enhanced for loop

  Updated  : Jan 29, 2099
*/


public class enhancedForLoops
{
    public static void process( String arrayOne[] )
    {
        //search the above array and display one index at the time
        for( String elements : arrayOne )
        {
            //display all indexes
            System.out.printf( " %s\n", elements );
        }

    }//end public static void process()
```

```java
public static void main( String args[] )
{
    //create an array of String data type
    String arrayOne[] =
            { "one", "two", "three", "four", "five" };

    process( arrayOne );

}//end public static void main( String args[] )

}//end public class array3d
```

Your output (results) will look like this:

one
two
three
four
five

Let's examine this code:

Inside the parenthesis of the enhanced for loops:

```java
for( String elements : arrayOne )
```

we create a string variable, in this case I call it "elements." Then we place the : symbol between elements and the name of the array that we want to process, in this case arrayOne.

This line of code iterates through the array, sequentially, from the beginning to the end. We do not need to know the length of the array. The value of each index in the array is then assigned to the variable "element."

The disadvantage of enhanced for loops is that we process them from beginning to end, we can not select a specific beginning or end.

Advantages are that we do not need to know the length of the array and that we are guaranteed that all indexes will be processed.

String Tokenizer

When analyzing data, lets say the contents of a book, we need to be able to split the entire book into words. The string tokenizer is what we use to do so. This is a simple but clear program that does just that.

```java
/*
  Author  : Michael Robinson
  Program : tokenizer.java
  Purpose : To present String tokenizer class
            and some of its methods using the
            enhanced for loop

  Updated : April 26, 2099
*/

public class tokenizer
{
    public static void split1()
    {
        // Create a string to be tokenized.
        String str = "one two three four";

        //display heading with the String str values
        System.out.println(
        "\n\nSplitting  " + str + " delimited by ' '" );

        //here we display the str string
        System.out.println( "\t    " + str );

        //Using the split method of the String class,
        //place each word in str separated by one space
        //into their own index inside an array called tokens
        String tokens[] = str.split( " " );

        //here we display each word in the tokens array
        for ( String s : tokens )
        {
            System.out.println( "\t    " + s );

        }//end for ( String s : tokens )

    }//end public static void split1()
```

```java
public static void split2()
{
    // Create a string to tokenized.
    String str = "one and two and three and four";

    //display heading with the String str values
    System.out.println(
    "\n\nSplitting  " + str + " delimited by ' and '" );

    //here we display the str string
    System.out.println( "\t   " + str );

    //Using the split method of the String class,
    //place each word in str separated by " and "
    //into their own index inside an array called tokens
    String tokens[] = str.split( " and " );

    //here we display each word in the tokens array
    for ( String s : tokens )
    {
        System.out.println( "\t   " + s );

    }//end for (String s : tokens)

}//end public static void split2()


public static void split3()
{
    // Create a string to tokenized.
    String str = "joe@gaddisbooks.com";

    //display heading with the String str values
    System.out.println(
    "\n\nSplitting  " + str + " delimited by @." );

    //here we display the str string
    System.out.println( "\t   " + str );

    //Using the split method of the String class,
    //place each word in str separated by any of the
    //following variables inside the "" of: "[@.]"
    //into their own index inside an array called tokens
    String tokens[] = str.split( "[@.]" );
```

```java
        //here we display each word in the tokens array
        for ( String s : tokens )
        {
            System.out.println( "\t    " + s );

        }//end for ( String s : tokens )

    }//end public static void split3()


    public static void split4()
    {
        // Create a string to tokenized.
        String str = "Jill$Billy%Becky*Tara&Mary";

        //display heading with the String str values
        System.out.println(
        "\n\nSplitting  " + str + " delimited by [$%*&]");

        //here we display the str string
        System.out.println( "\t    " + str );

        //Using the split method of the String class,
        //place each word in str separated by any of the
        //following variables inside the "" of: "[$%*&]"
        //into their own index inside an array called tokens
        String tokens[] = str.split( "[$%*&]" );

        //here we display each word in the tokens array
        for ( String s : tokens )
        {
            System.out.println( "\t    " + s );

        }//end for ( String s : tokens )

    }//end public static void split4()


    public static void main( String[] args )
    {
        split1();
        split2();
        split3();
```

```
        split4();
        System.out.println( "\nEnd of program" );

    }//end public static void main( String[] args )

}//end public class tokenizer
```

Your output (results) will look like this:

```
Splitting   one two three four delimited by ' '
            one two three four
            one
            two
            three
            four

Splitting   one and two and three and four delimited by ' and '
            one and two and three and four
            one
            two
            three
            four

Splitting   joe@gaddisbooks.com delimited by @.
            joe@gaddisbooks.com
            joe
            gaddisbooks
            com

Splitting   Jill$Billy%Becky*Tara&Mary delimited by [$%*&]
            Jill$Billy%Becky*Tara&Mary
            Jill
            Billy
            Becky
            Tara
            Mary

End of program
```

Let's examine this code:

This program was highly documented, basically every line of code is documented in great detail. Please review line by line.

Summary

This "arrays" chapter is very important. A lot of students have difficulty learning about arrays. I have provided are vast amount of examples and detailed documentation to this topic. Arrays are very powerful programming data structures that work exactly the same way in all languages. In the computer science data structure classes, arrays are studied in detail. I recommend that you conquer this chapter completely. It will help you greatly in your future classes.

To the program, `array2dimensions.java` in this chapter, add the code to find the diagonal values from locations 0,0 to 9,9 and the diagonal values from locations 0,9 to 9,0. Also improve the code that displays spacing.

Key Terms

Arrays	Arrays are data structures that group data items of the same data type. Arrays can contain data of one data type at the same time such as int, char, float, double or any other primitive data type, but we can not mix data types in the same array. We can also declare arrays of wrapper data types such as Integer, Character, Float, Double, or String data type. Arrays of objects is a special case which will be addressed in Chapter 8. Arrays can be of one or multiple dimensions. Every location in an array is called an index. Arrays are very useful, but they have two short comings. First arrays can not have mixed data types, and once declared, their size can not be changed. Secondly, we can not add or delete indexes, however the data inside each index can be changed.

**Arrays.
Allocating Space
to Declared
Arrays**
	When we declare an array as above, we create it, but we do not allocate space for it in RAM memory.
	
	The size of an array is specified when we allocate space for it, as follows:
	
	//creates space for 3 ints
	arrayOne[] = new int[3];
	
	//creates space for 2 floats
	arrayTwo[] = new float[2];
	
	//creates space for 4 doubles
	arrayThree[] = new double[4];
	
	//creates space for 2 Strings
	arrayFour[] = new String[2];

Arrays. Declare and Allocate at the Same Time	We can also declare (create) an array and assign it space at the same time as follows:
	
	int arrayOne[] = new int[3];
	float arrayTwo[] = new float[2];
	double arrayThree[] = new double[4];
	String arrayFour[] = new String[2];
	
	When we have an array with 4 indexes:
	double arrayThree[] = new double[4];
	
	We say that this array is of length 4, and we know that is has indexes 0, 1, 2, and 3, therefore the indexes go from 0 to length-1.
	
	One of the most common mistakes when accessing an array is trying to access an index at location "length." This will give us the error "index out of range." We must remember that indexes begin at location 0 and end at location "length − 1," always!

Arrays. Declaring/ Creating One Dimension Arrays	Creating one dimensional arrays:
	
	//creates the array arrayOne to hold ints
	
	int arrayOne[];
	
	//creates the array arrayTwo to hold floats
	
	float arrayTwo[];
	
	//creates the array arrayThree to hold doubles
	
	double arrayThree[];
	
	//creates the array arrayFour to hold Strings
	
	String arrayFour[];

Arrays.
Load Data to a
Declared Array
	We can also load data directly into each index as follows:
	arrayOne[0] = 43;
	arrayOne[1] = 235;
	arrayOne[3] = 101;
	
	arrayTwo[0] = 12.54;
	arrayTwo[1] = 4.23;
	
	arrayThree[0] = 2.33;
	arrayThree[1] = 2.31;
	arrayThree[2] = 9.0;
	arrayThree[3] = 7.12;
	
	arrayFour[0] = { "Joe" };
	arrayFour[1] = { "Smith" };

Arrays. **One Dimension** **Array**	A one dimension array contains one row and one or more columns. We refer to a location in an array as "the index" and we always name the row first then the column. If the data is in row 0 and column 3, we say that the data is at index location 0,3. "Red Cross" will help us remember R,C for Row,Column. We can also use "RC Cola," a soda found in parts of the United States or "RiCola" (RC), a famous medication of unique delicious taste for soothing of the mouth and throat. Always place the "row" before the "column," if we place the column before the row we will have unpredictable results.
Arrays. **Parallel Arrays**	Parallel arrays are used to combine multiple one dimensional arrays that might contain different data types, but each row in each array is related to each other: int studentID[] = { 50102, 23908, 12098 }; String studentName[] = { "Joe Ho", "Ann", "Mo" }; double studentBalance[] = { 10.00, 23.78, 1.07 }; Here we have three arrays, each containing three items, and each array holds a different type of data, int, string and double. Program arraysParallel.java creates a report showing the student's name, id and current balance owed. To create this report we use what is called parallel arrays. The only requirement is that all arrays must have the same amount of rows, in this case there are three rows in each array.

Arrays. **Printing All Values** **Inside this Array**	```java for(x = 0; x < 1,000,000; x++) { System.out.printf("%d\n", array[x]); } ```
Arrays. **Three** **Multidimensional** **Arrays**	A three dimensional array is a group of two dimension arrays. I think that one of the best ways to explain what a three dimensional array is, is to use the representation of an apartment building, everybody knows what they look like. Please see program array3d.java
For. Enhanced for **Loops**	Now that we know how arrays work, lets see what "enhanced for loops" are. Enhanced for loops are a variation of the "for loop" that is used with arrays and other data structure called ArrayList which we will see in Chapter 8. enhancedForLoops.java
String Tokenizer	When analyzing data, lets say the contents of a book, we need to be able to split the entire book into words. The string tokenizer is what we use to do so. Please see program tokenizer.java

Exercises

1. Create a one dimensional array of int data type.

2. Create a two dimensional array of string data type.

3. Create a three dimensional array of double data type.

4. Create a parallel array using three one dimensional arrays of int data type.

5. Using question one here, create a program using an enhanced for loop.

6. Tokenize a string delimited by '& and $@!'.

7. To the above program, `array2dimensions.java` **in this chapter,** add the code to find the diagonal values from locations 0,0 to 9,9 and the diagonal values from locations 0,9 to 9,0. Also improve the code that displays spacing.

8. What is a string _____ (Select all that apply)
   a. A single dimension array of char data type
   b. A primitive data type
   c. A tokenizer
   d. An enhanced for loop

9. What is a two dimensional array _____ (Select all that apply)
   a. A group of data containing multiple data types
   b. A data structure the contain one specific data type
   c. A data structure that once created can not be expanded
   d. A data structure that can be reduce in size at any time

10. What is a three dimensional array _____ (Select all that apply)
    a. Is a group of two dimensional arrays
    b. Is a group of one dimensional arrays
    c. A data structure of enhanced for loops
    d. Does not exist

11. What is tokenizing _____ (Select all that apply)
    a. To split words separated by specific values
    b. Is a term in math to find the modulus of integers
    c. To concatenate ASCII numbers into words

REFERENCES

- Java API Specifications

    http://www.oracle.com/technetwork/java/api-141528.html

- My Java programs that I use in my Java classes located at robinson.cs.fiu.edu

//END CHAPTER 7: DATA STRUCTURES - ARRAYS

Data Structures – ArrayList

ArrayList

Array data structures have a size limitation, once an array declares its size it can not be modified. We can not add or delete rows or columns to/from it.

ArrayLists are the solution. ArrayLists are another type of data structure; we can modify the ArrayList's size at any time, and we can add or delete indexes from any location. ArrayLists are dynamic.

Let's create an ArrayList containing string type data as follows:

```
ArrayList<String> arrayList = new ArrayList<String>();
```

Now we create an ArrayList containing integer type data as follows:

```
ArrayList<Integer> arrayList = new ArrayList<Integer>();
```

Notice the type of data in the second ArrayList is <Integer> instead of <int>, the reason is that ArrayLists require data type with methods and the primitive data types DO NOT have methods so we need to use the wrappers data types which DO have methods. We studied wrappers in chapter three.

This is an ArrayList using for loops:

```
/*
  Author  : Michael Robinson
  Program : arrayListSimpleClass.java
  Purpose : How to create a Java ArrayList using for loops.
            Shows how to add elements to an ArrayList
            How to delete items
```

< 167 >

```
                How to get and print data items using for loops.

    Updated : June 29th, 2099
*/


import java.util.ArrayList;


public class arrayListSimpleClass
{
    static String lines =
                "-------------------------------------------";

    public static void alphaArrayList()
    {
        System.out.println( lines );
        System.out.println( " Processing ArrayList of String Data" +
                        " Type" );
        System.out.println( "                    Using for Loops" );
        System.out.println( lines );
        System.out.println( " Creating ArrayList..." );

        //create an ArrayList object
        ArrayList<String> arrayList = new ArrayList<String>();

        System.out.println( " Adding data elements to the" +
                        " ArrayList..." );

        //data is always added at the end of the Array List
        arrayList.add( "a" ); //adding a to Array List arrayList
        arrayList.add( "b" ); //adding b to Array List arrayList
        arrayList.add( "c" ); //adding c to Array List arrayList
        arrayList.add( "d" ); //adding d to Array List arrayList
        arrayList.add( "e" ); //adding e to Array List arrayList
        arrayList.add( "f" ); //adding fa to Array List arrayList

        System.out.println( "\n Getting data elements from " +
                        "the ArrayList" );

        //Use get method of ArrayList class to retrieve an element.
        //get( index ) returns element at the index in the ArrayList.
        //Notice that the command to retrieve an element/index from
        //and Array List is: arrayListName.get( location )
        for( int x = 0; x < arrayList.size(); x++ )
        {
            System.out.print( " " + arrayList.get(x) );
        }
```

```java
        //now remove elements !!! always remove from the highest" +
        //to the lowest location
        System.out.println( "\n\n Removing data elements from the " +
                            "ArrayList on index 3 = " +
                             arrayList.get(3) +
                            "\n and index 1 = " + arrayList.get(1) );


        arrayList.remove(3); //always remove highest location first
        arrayList.remove(1);

        System.out.println( "\n Getting data elements from" +
                            " ArrayList after removing" );

        //arrayList.size() is equivalent to array.length in arrays
        for( int x = 0; x < arrayList.size(); x++ )
        {
            System.out.print( " " + ArrayList.get(x) );
        }
        System.out.println( "\n" );

}//end public static void alphaArrayList()


public static void numericArrayList()
{
    System.out.println( lines );
    System.out.println( " Processing ArrayList of Integer Data" +
                        " Type" );
    System.out.println( "                Using for Loops" );
    System.out.println( lines );
    System.out.println( " Creating ArrayList..." );

    //create an ArrayList object
    ArrayList<Integer> arrayList = new ArrayList<Integer>();

    System.out.println( " Adding data elements to the" +
                        " ArrayList..." );

    //data is always added at the end of the ArrayList
    arrayList.add( 1100 ); //adding 1100 to ArrayList arrayList
    arrayList.add( 2100 ); //adding 2100 to ArrayList arrayList
    arrayList.add( 3100 ); //adding 3100 to ArrayList arrayList
    arrayList.add( 4100 ); //adding 4100 to ArrayList arrayList
    arrayList.add( 5100 ); //adding 5100 to ArrayList arrayList
    arrayList.add( 6100 ); //adding 6100 to ArrayList arrayList
```

```java
        System.out.println( "\n Getting data elements in the" +
                            " ArrayList" );

        //Use get method of ArrayList class to retrieve an element.
        //get( index ) returns element at the index in the ArrayList.
        //Notice that the command to retrieve an element/index from
        //and ArrayList is: arrayListName.get( location )
        for( int x = 0; x < arrayList.size(); x++ )
        {
            System.out.print( " " + arrayList.get(x) );
        }

        System.out.println( "\n\n Removing data elements from the" +
                            " ArrayList on index 3 = " +
                                arrayList.get(3) +
                            "\n and index 1 = " + arrayList.get(1) );

        //now remove some !!! always remove from the height to
        //the lowest location
        arrayList.remove(3); //always remove highest location first
        arrayList.remove(1);

        System.out.println( "\n Getting data elements from" +
                            "  ArrayList after remove" );

        //arrayList.size() is equivalent to array.length in arrays
        for( int x = 0; x < arrayList.size(); x++ )
        {
            System.out.print( " " + arrayList.get(x) );
        }

        System.out.println( "\n" );

    }//end public static void numericArrayList()


    public static void main( String arg[] )
    {
        alphaArrayList();

        numericArrayList();

    }//end public static void main( String arg[] )

}//end public class arrayListSimpleClass
```

Your output (results) will look like this:

```
---------------------------------------------

 Processing ArrayList of String Data Type
             Using for Loops

---------------------------------------------

 Creating ArrayList...
 Adding data elements to the ArrayList...

 Getting data elements from the ArrayList
 a b c d e f

 Removing data elements from the ArrayList on index 3 = d
 and index 1 = b

 Getting data elements from ArrayList after removing
 a  c  e  f


---------------------------------------------

 Processing ArrayList of Integer Data Type
             Using for Loops

---------------------------------------------

 Creating ArrayList...
 Adding data elements to the ArrayList...

 Getting data elements in the ArrayList
 1100 2100 3100 4100 5100 6100

 Removing data elements from the ArrayList on index 3 = 4100
 and index 1 = 2100

 Getting data elements from  ArrayList after remove
 1100 3100 5100 6100
```

Let's examine this code:

This program was highly documented, basically every line of code is documented in great detail. Please review program line by line.

Iterator

The iterator class is very powerful, in a way it is similar to the for loop. It allows us to see if we have data/ elements in a data structure, it moves forward element by element, and remove any element in the data structure. Iterator exists in several data structures, among them the ArrayList and the list.

We use an iterator to go through a data structure, the items inside the structure are called elements. This is how an iterator is created and used:

First we need to create an instance of the iterator, in this case we will call it itr:

```
//create an Iterator object using Iterator.
Iterator<Integer> itr = arrayList.iterator();
```

Here we created the "itr" iterator for the ArrayList called arrayList that we created in the previous ArrayList section.

Java iterators have three methods: hasNext, next and remove

hasNext returns a boolean primitive data type. If it returns the boolean true, the iteration has found an element inside the data structure. If it returns false it means that it is at the end of the data structure and there are no more elements in it:

```
//use hasNext() to iterate through the elements
System.out.println( "Iterating through ArrayList elements..." );
while( itr.hasNext() )
{
    commands;
}
```

If the command "itr.hasNext()" returns true, we have determined that the data structure has data elements in it. Now we can extract those elements, one by one, and use them as follows:

```
//use hasNext() and next() methods of Iterator
//to iterate through the elements
System.out.println( "Iterating through ArrayList elements..." );
while( itr.hasNext() )
{
    System.out.print( " " + itr.next() );
}
```

next(). Here the line "System.out.print(" " + itr.next()); uses the next() method of the iterator "itr", itr. next() to extract the next element in the data structure and print it.

Using Iterator in an ArrayList

The following program, IteratorsAddNextRemove.java, shows us in detail how to use iterators in an ArrayList with examples on how to create an ArrayList, add data/elements into it, print all elements using the iterator class, find out if the ArrayList has elements, go to the next element and display it, remove the elements and print an empty ArrayList:

```java
/*
  Author   : Michael Robinson
  Program  : IteratorsAddNextRemove.java
  Purpose  : How to create a Java ArrayList using Iterators.
             Shows how to add elements to an ArrayList
             How to use itr.hasNext(), itr.next(), itr.remove()
             How to get and print data items using for loops.

  Updated : July 2nd, 2099
*/



import java.util.ArrayList;
import java.util.Iterator;


public class IteratorsAddNextRemove
{
    public static String label =
            "-----------------------------------------";
    public static void alphaArrayList()
    {
        System.out.println( label );
        System.out.println( " Processing ArrayList of String" +
                            " data type " );
        System.out.println( "             using ITERATORS        " );
        System.out.println( label );
        System.out.println( " Creating ArrayList..." );

        //create an ArrayList object
        ArrayList<String> arrayList = new ArrayList<String>();

        System.out.println( " Adding data elements to the" +
                            " ArrayList..." );

        //Add and displaying elements to ArrayList using:
        arrayList.add( "a" );
```

```java
System.out.println( " arrayList.add( \"a\" )" );
arrayList.add( "b" );
System.out.println( " arrayList.add( \"b\" )" );
arrayList.add( "c" );
System.out.println( " arrayList.add( \"c\" )" );
arrayList.add( "d" );
System.out.println( " arrayList.add( \"d\" )" );
arrayList.add( "e" );
System.out.println( " arrayList.add( \"e\" )" );
arrayList.add( "f" );
System.out.println( " arrayList.add( \"f\" )" );

System.out.println( "\n Getting data elements from the" +
                    " ArrayList" );

System.out.println( " Iterating through ArrayList " +
                    " elements..." );

//This is a loop type class which allows to loop thru
//the ArrayList

Iterator<String> itr = arrayList.iterator();

//use hasNext() and next() methods of Iterator to
//iterate through the ArrayList
while( itr.hasNext() )
{
    System.out.print( " " + itr.next() );

}//end while( itr.hasNext() )

//now remove elements !!! always remove from the highest
//to the lowest location
System.out.println( "\n\n Removing data elements from " +
                    "the ArrayList on index 3 = " +
                    arrayList.get(3) +
        "\n                                and" +
                    " index 1 = " + arrayList.get(1) );

arrayList.remove(3);
arrayList.remove(1);

System.out.println();
System.out.println( " Getting data elements from the " +
                    "  ArrayList after removing" );
```

```java
        System.out.println( " Iterating through ArrayList " +
                            " elements..." );

        //reset iterator to beginning of ArrayList
        itr = arrayList.iterator();

        //use hasNext() and next() methods of Iterator to iterate
        //through the ArrayList
        while( itr.hasNext() )
        {
            System.out.print( " " + itr.next() );

        }//end while( itr.hasNext() )

        System.out.println( "\n\n" );

    }//end public static void alphaArrayList()


    public static void numericArrayList()
    {
        System.out.println( label );

        System.out.println( " Processing ArrayList of Integer " +
                            " data type" );
        System.out.println( "              using ITERATORS" );
        System.out.println( label );

        System.out.println( " Creating ArrayList..." );
        //create an ArrayList object
        ArrayList<Integer> arrayList = new ArrayList<Integer>();

        System.out.println( " Adding data elements to the" +
                            " ArrayList..." );

        //Add elements to Arraylist using
        arrayList.add( 1100 );
        System.out.println( " arrayList.add( \"1100\" )" );
        arrayList.add( 2100 );
        System.out.println( " arrayList.add( \"2100\" )" );
        arrayList.add( 3100 );
        System.out.println( " arrayList.add( \"3100\" )" );
        arrayList.add( 4100 );
        System.out.println( " arrayList.add( \"4100\" )" );
```

```java
arrayList.add( 5100 );
System.out.println( " arrayList.add( \"5100\" )" );
arrayList.add( 6100 );
System.out.println( " arrayList.add( \"6100\" )" );

System.out.println( "\n Getting data elements in the" +
                    "ArrayList" );

System.out.println( " Iterating through ArrayList" +
                    " elements..." );

//This is a loop type class which allows to loop
//thru the ArrayList
Iterator<Integer> itr = arrayList.iterator();

//use hasNext() and next() methods of Iterator to
//iterate through the ArrayList

while( itr.hasNext() )
{
    System.out.print( " " + itr.next());

}//end while( itr.hasNext() )


System.out.println( "\n\n Removing data elements from " +
                    "the ArrayList on index 3 = " +
                     arrayList.get(3) + "\n" +
        "                                          " +
                    " and index 1 = " + arrayList.get(1) );

//now remove some !!! always remove from the height to
//the lowest
arrayList.remove(3);
arrayList.remove(1);

System.out.println( "\n Getting data elements from the " +
                    "ArrayList after removing" );

System.out.println( " Iterating through ArrayList" +
                    " elements..." );

//reset iterator to beginning of ArrayList
itr = arrayList.iterator();
```

```java
        //use hasNext() and next() methods of Iterator to iterate
        //through the ArrayList
        while( itr.hasNext() )
        {
            System.out.print( " " + itr.next() );

        }//end while( itr.hasNext() )

        System.out.println();

    }//end public static void numericArrayList()


    public static void addNextRemoveIterator()
    {
        System.out.println( label );
        System.out.println( " Processing ArrayList of String data" +
                            " type " );
        System.out.println( "            using ITERATORS" );

        System.out.println( label );
        System.out.println( " Creating ArrayList..." );

        //create an ArrayList object
        ArrayList<String> arrayList = new ArrayList<String>();

        System.out.println( " Adding data elements to the" +
                            " ArrayList..." );

        //Add elements to Arraylist using
        arrayList.add( "A" );
        System.out.println( " arrayList.add( \"A\" )" );
        arrayList.add( "B" );
        System.out.println( " arrayList.add( \"B\" )" );
        arrayList.add( "C" );
        System.out.println( " arrayList.add( \"C\" )" );
        arrayList.add( "D" );
        System.out.println( " arrayList.add( \"D\" )" );
        arrayList.add( "E" );
        System.out.println( " arrayList.add( \"E\" )" );
        arrayList.add( "F" );
        System.out.println( " arrayList.add( \"F\" )" );
```

```java
System.out.println( "\n Getting data elements from the" +
                    "ArrayList" );

System.out.println( " Iterating through ArrayList " +
                    " elements..." );

//This is a loop type class which allows to loop thru
//the ArrayList
Iterator<String> itr = arrayList.iterator();

String temp = "";
//use hasNext() and next() methods of Iterator to iterate
//through the ArrayLis
while( itr.hasNext() )
{
    if( itr.hasNext() )
    {
        System.out.println( "\n\n itr.hasNext() = " +
                            itr.hasNext() );

        temp = itr.next();
        System.out.println( " itr.next() = " + temp );
        System.out.println( " removing =    " + temp );
        itr.remove();

    }
    else
    {
        System.out.println( "\n The Arraylist is empty" +
                            "itr.hasNext() = [" +
                            itr.hasNext() + "]" );

    }//end if( itr.hasNext() )

}//end while( itr.hasNext() )


if( itr.hasNext() )
{
    System.out.println( "\n itr.hasNext() = " +
                        itr.hasNext() );
}
else
{
    System.out.println( "\n itr.hasNext() = [" +
                        itr.hasNext() + "]" );
```

```java
        System.out.println( " The Arraylist is empty" +
                            " itr.hasNext() = [" +
                            itr.hasNext() + "]" );

    }//end if( itr.hasNext() )

    System.out.println();
    System.out.println( " Getting data elements from the " +
                        " ArrayList after removing" );
    System.out.println( " Iterating through ArrayList " +
                        " elements" );

    //reset iterator to beginning of ArrayList
    itr = arrayList.iterator();

    System.out.print( " [" );

    //use hasNext() and next() methods of Iterator to iterate
    //through the ArrayList
    while( itr.hasNext() )
    {
        System.out.print( " " + itr.next() );

    }//end while( itr.hasNext() )

    System.out.print( "]\n\n" );

}//end public static void addNextRemoveIterator()


public static void main(String[] args)
{
    alphaArrayList();
    numericArrayList();
    addNextRemoveIterator();

}//end public static void main(String[] args)

}//end public class IteratorsAddNextRemove
```

Your output (results) will look like this:

```
-------------------------------------------

Processing ArrayList of String data type

            using ITERATORS

-------------------------------------------

Creating ArrayList...

Adding data elements to the ArrayList...
arrayList.add( "a" )
arrayList.add( "b" )
arrayList.add( "c" )
arrayList.add( "d" )
arrayList.add( "e" )
arrayList.add( "f" )

Getting data elements from the ArrayList
Iterating through ArrayList  elements...
a  b  c  d  e  f

Removing data elements from the ArrayList on index 3 = d
                                  and index 1 = b

Getting data elements from the ArrayList after removing
Iterating through ArrayList elements...
a  c  f


-------------------------------------------
Processing ArrayList of Integer  data type
          using ITERATORS
-------------------------------------------

Creating ArrayList...
Adding data elements to the ArrayList...
arrayList.add( "1100" )
arrayList.add( "2100" )
arrayList.add( "3100" )
arrayList.add( "4100" )
arrayList.add( "5100" )
arrayList.add( "6100" )
```

```
Getting data elements in theArrayList
Iterating through ArrayList elements...
1100 2100 3100 4100 5100 6100

Removing data elements from the ArrayList on index 3 = 4100
                                        and index 1 = 2100

Getting data elements from the ArrayList after removing
Iterating through ArrayList elements...
1100 3100 5100 6100


--------------------------------------------
Processing ArrayList of String data type
            using ITERATORS
--------------------------------------------


Creating ArrayList...
Adding data elements to the ArrayList...
arrayList.add( "A" )
arrayList.add( "B" )
arrayList.add( "C" )
arrayList.add( "D" )
arrayList.add( "E" )
arrayList.add( "F" )

Getting data elements from theArrayList
Iterating through ArrayList  elements...

itr.hasNext() = true
itr.next() = A
removing =    A

itr.hasNext() = true
itr.next() = B
removing =    B

itr.hasNext() = true
itr.next() = C
removing =    C

itr.hasNext() = true
itr.next() = D
removing =    D
```

```
itr.hasNext() = true
itr.next() = E
removing =   E

itr.hasNext() = true
itr.next() = F
removing =   F

itr.hasNext() = [false]
The Arraylist is empty itr.hasNext() = [false]

Getting data elements from the  ArrayList after removing
Iterating through ArrayList  elements
[]
```

Let's examine this code:

This program was highly documented, basically every line of code is documented in great detail. Please review program line by line. Also at the beginning of this section I explain in detail the methods of the iterator class.

Copying Arrays into an ArrayList Modify and Back

Remember that arrays have two shortcomings. An array contains only one type of data at the time: int, float, String, etc. and also once we declare an array we can not modify its size. Fortunately we can use ArrayList to modify any array's size. By moving the array's data into an ArrayList, then we can modify the size of the ArrayList by adding or removing elements in it. Then once we get the new required size we copy the ArrayList data back into one or multiple new arrays.

The following program show us how to do this by creating multiple arrays, one ArrayList, Iterators, and the enhanced for loops.

```
/*
  Author  : Michael Robinson
  Program : arrayToArrayListAndBack.java
  Purpose : How to copy Array's data to an ArrayList
            Modify the ArrayList
            Copy ArrayList data to a new Array

  Updated : December 10, 2099
*/
```

```java
import java.util.ArrayList;
import java.util.Iterator;


public class arrayToArrayListAndBack
{
    public static void arraysToListAndBack()
    {
        //create Array array1
        System.out.println( "-Creating Array array1" );
        String array1[] = { "one ","square","two ", "three", "cube",
                            "seven" };

        //create an ArrayList object
        System.out.println("-Creating ArrayList list1");
        ArrayList<String> list1 = new ArrayList<String>();

        //add Array array1 to ArrayList list1
        System.out.println( "\n-Copying Array array1 to" +
                            " ArrayList list" );

        for( String elements : array1 )
        {
            list1.add( elements );
            System.out.printf( " %s", elements );
        }

        //create another Array array2
        System.out.println( "-Creating Array array2" );
        String array2[] = { "four", "triangle", "five", "cone",
                            "six", "eight" };

        //add Array array2 to ArrayList list1
        System.out.println( "\n-Copying Array array2 to " +
                            "ArrayList list" );

        for( String elements : array2 )
        {
            list1.add( elements );
            System.out.printf( " %s", elements );
        }
        System.out.println( "\n" );

        //create Iterator itr to travel through the Arraylist
```

```java
//list
System.out.println( "-Create Iterator itr to " +
                    "travel through the ArrayList list" );


Iterator<String> itr = list1.iterator();



//use hasNext() and next() methods of Iterator to
//iterate through the elements
System.out.println( "-Iterating through ArrayList " +
                    "list1 elements..." );


while( itr.hasNext() )
{
    System.out.print( " " + itr.next() );
}
System.out.println( "\n" );


System.out.println( "- Using the new Iterator itr2 we copy" +
                    " the elements in the even locations " +
                    "\n to a new array of length 10 called" +
                    "array3, and the elements in the odd " +
                    "locations to a new array of length 10" +
                    " called array4" );


System.out.println( "\n- Create Iterator itr2 to travel" +
                    " thru the Arraylist list." +
                    "\n In Java Iterators can NOT be reset" +
                    " to the beginning of the list " +
                    "\n to travel the list again we must " +
                    "create a new Iterator." );


//create a new iterator itr2 to copy element to new bigger
//arrays
Iterator<String> itr2 = list1.iterator();


System.out.println( "\n-Creating two new arrays of length" +
                    " 10 each. array3 and array4" );
//create two arrays of size 10 each
String array3[] = new String[ 10 ];
String array4[] = new String[ 10 ];


System.out.println( "\n-Copying even elements in list1 to" +
                    " array3 and odd elements to array4" );
```

```java
    //copy even elements in list1 to array3 and odd elements
    //to array4
    int x = 0;
    int y = 0;
    int z = 0;

while( itr2.hasNext() )
{
    //copy even elements in list to array3
    if( ( x % 2 ) == 0 )
    {
        array3[z] =  itr2.next();
        System.out.print( "  array3[" + z + "] = " +
        array3[z] + "\t" );

        z++;
    }
    else //copy odd elements in list to array4
    {
        array4[y] =  itr2.next();
        System.out.println( "array4[" + y + "] = " +
                            array4[y]);
        y++;
    }
    x++;

}//end while( itr2.hasNext() )

z = 0;
System.out.println( "\n-Displaying the elements in list1" +
                    " of length " + list1.size() );

for( x = 0; x < list1.size(); x++ )
{
    System.out.print( " " + list1.get(x) + "\t" );
    z++;
    if( z == 2 )
    {
        System.out.println();
        z = 0;
    }

}//end for( x = 0; x < list1.size(); x++ )
```

```java
        z = 0;
        System.out.println( "\n-Displaying the elements in array3" +
                            " of length " + array3.length);

        for( x = 0; x < array3.length; x++ )
        {
            System.out.print( " " + array3[x] + "\t" );
            z++;

            if( z == 2 )
            {
                System.out.println();
                z = 0;
            }

        }//end for( x = 0; x < array3.length; x++ )

        z = 0;

        System.out.println( "\n-Displaying the elements in array4" );

        for( x = 0; x < array4.length; x++ )
        {
            System.out.print( " " + array4[x] + "\t" );
            z++;

            if( z == 2 )
            {
                System.out.println();
                z = 0;
            }

        }//end for( x = 0; x < array4.length; x++ )

        System.out.println( "\n" );

    }//end arraysToListAndBack()


    public static void main( String arg[] )
    {
        arraysToListAndBack();
    }

}//end public class arrayToArrayListAndBack
```

Your output (results) will look like this:

```
- Creating Array array1
- Creating ArrayList list1

- Copying Array array1 to ArrayList list
  one   square two   three cube seven-Creating Array array2

- Copying Array array2 to ArrayList list
  four triangle five cone six eight

- Create Iterator itr to travel through the Arraylist list
- Iterating through ArrayList list1 elements...
  one   square two   three cube seven four triangle five cone six eight

- Using the new Iterator itr2 we copy the elements in the even
  lo cations to a new array of length 10 calledarray3, and the
  elements in the odd locations to a new array of length 10 called
  array4.

- Create Iterator itr2 to travel thru the Arraylist list.
  In Java Iterators can NOT be reset to the beginning of the list
  to travel the list again we must create a new Iterator.

- Creating two new arrays of length 10 each. array3 and array4

- Copying even elements in list1 to array3 and odd elements to array4
  array3[0] = one      array4[0] = square
  array3[1] = two      array4[1] = three
  array3[2] = cube     array4[2] = seven
  array3[3] = four     array4[3] = triangle
  array3[4] = five     array4[4] = cone
  array3[5] = six      array4[5] = eight

- Displaying the elements in list1 of length 12
  one         square
  two         three
  cube        seven
  four        triangle
  five        cone
  six         eight

- Displaying the elements in array3 of length 10
  one         two
  cube        four
```

```
    five        six
    null        null
    null        null

-   Displaying the elements in array4
    square      three
    seven       triangle
    cone        eight
    null        null
    null        null
```

Notice that in array3 and array4 the last four indexes/locations contain the word null, this means that those locations are not initialize/used, they were created when we created them.

Let's examine this code:

This program was highly documented, basically every line of code is documented in great detail. Please review program line by line. Also at the beginning of this section I explained in detail how we can change the size of an array. Java does not have a class for this purpose so we have to create a program to do this. This program shows how to change the size of an array.

Object Data Types

We have been using primitive, wrappers and string data types from the beginning. In this chapter we used them to populate arrays and ArrayLists. Now that we are experts in using these data types, we are going to learn about another data type called Objects (notice here Objects are written with uppercase O). Remember that when we create an object of a class we refer to this using the lowercase o. Objects and objects are two different things. An object of a class is an identical copy of a class. I like to refer to objects of a class as clones, simply because they are exact clone copies of a class. In this section we are going to learn about Object data types.

An Object data type allows us to create data structures like arrays to accept data of multiple data types. Up to now, when we create an array or an ArrayList we make them to accept only one type of data. This new data type called Object data type allows us to accept the mixture of all previous learned data types into an array or ArrayList.

The following program will teach us how to use Object data type.

```
/*
    Author  : Michael Robinson
    Program : ObjectsArraysArrayLists.java
    Purpose : - To create an Array of Objects and
```

```
                    copy it into an ArrayList of Objects
              - From a text file load Objects into an Array
                and display them

    Updated : July 3rd, 2099
*/


import java.util.ArrayList;


public class ObjectsArraysArrayLists
{
    public static void arrayListObjects( Object arrayObjects[] )
    {
        //notice that we have accepted and array of Object data
        //type containing multiple data types
        System.out.println( "\n Copying an array of Objects into" +
                            " an ArrayList of Objects" );

        //create an ArrayList of Objects data type
        ArrayList<Object> arrayListObjects = new ArrayList<Object>();

        //copy the elements in an array of Objects to an ArraList of
        //Objects and display them
        int x = 0;

        for( x = 0; x < arrayObjects.length; x++ )
        {
            arrayListObjects.add( arrayObjects[x] );
            System.out.println( " arrayListObjects( " + x + " ) = "+
                                arrayListObjects.get(x) );
        }

    }//end public static void arrayListObjects(Object arrayObjects[])


    public static void arrayOfObjects()
    {
        System.out.println( "\n Processing an array of Objects" );

        //create an array of Objects. Notice that they are made with
        //multiple data types
        Object arrayObjects[] =
```

```
                    { 1, "one", 1.4, 0.25, "COP2250", "Java Language", 100 };

            //display elements in an array to Objects
            for( int x = 0; x < arrayObjects.length ; x++ )
            {
                System.out.println( " arrayObjects[" + x + "] = " +
                                        arrayObjects[x] );
            }

            //call a method passing an array of Objects
            arrayListObjects( arrayObjects );

    }//end public static void arrayOfObjects()


        public static void main( String arg[] )
        {
            arrayOfObjects();

        }//end public static void main( String arg[] )

}//end public class ObjectsArraysArrayLists
```

Your output (results) will look like this:

```
Processing an array of Objects
arrayObjects[0] = 1
arrayObjects[1] = one
arrayObjects[2] = 1.4
arrayObjects[3] = 0.25
arrayObjects[4] = COP2250
arrayObjects[5] = Java Language
arrayObjects[6] = 100


Copying an array of Objects into an ArrayList of Objects

arrayListObjects( 0 ) = 1
arrayListObjects( 1 ) = one
arrayListObjects( 2 ) = 1.4
arrayListObjects( 3 ) = 0.25
arrayListObjects( 4 ) = COP2250
arrayListObjects( 5 ) = Java Language
arrayListObjects( 6 ) = 100
```

Let's examine this code:

This program was highly documented, basically every line of code is documented in great detail. Please review program line by line. Notice how we can create ArrayLists containing data of multiple data types.

Summary

This chapter presents ArrayList, the data structure that solves the expansion and reduction in size problem that we encounter in the Arrays. In the data structures courses you will find that ArrayLists have several benefits over arrays and at the same time arrays have benefits over arrayLists. When creating an ArrayList we do not need to select a size, the default size is 20 and when it reaches it limits it doubles the current size automatically. When creating arrays we must describe the size and it can not be changed after it is created.

Iterator is a class that can be used with ArrayList and it is similar to for loops in that it allows us to transverse the data structure forward and backwards.

We also learned how to manually expand arrays using ArrayLists. There are times when we need need to do this.

Finally, we saw how to use Object data type to create data structures like arrays to accept data of multiple data types.

Key Terms

ArrayList	Array data structures have a size limitation, once an array declares its size it can not be modified. We can not add or delete rows or columns to/from it.
	ArrayLists are the solution. ArrayLists are another type of data structure; we can modify the ArrayList's size at any time, we can add or delete indexes from any location, ArrayLists are dynamic.
	Let's create an ArrayList containing string type data as follows:
	ArrayList<String> arrayList = new ArrayList<String>();
	We create an ArrayList containing integer type data as follows:
	ArrayList<Integer> arrayList = new ArrayList<Integer>();
Arrays. **Copying Arrays** **into an ArrayList** **Modify and Back**	Remember that arrays have two shortcomings, an array contains only one type of data at the time: int, float, string, etc. and also once we declare an array we can not modify its size.
	Fortunately we can use ArrayList to modify any array's size, by moving the array's data into an ArrayList, then we can modify the size of the ArrayList by adding or removing elements in it. Once we get the new required size we copy the ArrayList data back into one or multiple new arrays.
	The program arrayToArrayListAndBack.java shows us how to do this by creating multiple arrays, an ArrayList, Iterators, and one enhanced for loop.

Data Types. Object Data Types	We have been using primitive, wrappers and string data types from the beginning. In this chapter we used them to populate arrays and ArrayLists.

Now that we are experts in using these data types, we are going to learn about another data type called Objects (notice here Objects are written with uppercase O). Remember that when we create an object of a class we refer to this using the lowercase o.

Objects and objects are two different things. An object of a class is an identical copy of a class. I like to refer to objects of a class as clones, simply because they are exact clone copies of a class.

In this section we learn about Object data types.

An Object data type allows us to create data structures like arrays to accept data of multiple data types. Up to now, when we create an array or an ArrayList we make them to accept only one type of data. This new data type called Object data type allows us to accept the mixture of all previously learned data types into an array or ArrayList.

Please see program ObjectsArraysArrayLists.java |
| Iterator | The iterator class is very powerful, in a way it is similar to the for loop. It allows us to see if we have data/elements in a data structure, it moves forwards element by element, and remove any element in the data structure. Iterator exists in several data structures, among them the ArrayList and the List.

We use an iterator to go through a data structure. The items inside the structure are called elements. This is how an iterator is created and used:

First we need to create an instance of the iterator, in this case we will call it itr:

//create an Iterator object using Iterator.
Iterator<Integer> itr = arrayList.iterator();

Here we created the "itr" iterator for the ArrayList called arrayList that we created in the previous ArrayList section.

Java iterators have three methods: hasNext, next and remove |
| Using Iterator in an ArrayList | IteratorsAddNextRemove.java, shows us, in detail, how to use iterators in an ArrayList with multiple examples about how to create an ArrayList, add data/elements into it, print all elements using the iterator class, find out if the ArrayList has elements, go to the next element and display it, remove the elements and print an empty Array List. |

Exercises

1. Create an ArrayList of Integer data types.

2. Modify the ArrayList created in question 1 to display all values using an enhanced for loop.

3. Modify the ArrayList created in question 1 to display all values using the iterator class.

4. Create an Object data type array of size 10, then double its size.

5. Write a method that will create an Object data structure containing Integer, Double, and String data fields.

6. What is an ArrayList _____ (Select all that apply)
   a. A list of Arrays.
   b. The forward display of the data contained in an array of Objects.
   c. An array of Object data types.
   d. A data structure that its size can be changed.

7. What is an Iterator _____ (Select all that apply)
   a. A class that is used in while loops.
   b. A class that is used in ArrayLists.
   c. All of the above.
   d. None of the above.

8. What is an Object data type _____ (Select all that apply)
   a. It allows to have data structures of multiple data types.
   b. Use to create objects of a class.
   c. Use to create an instance of a class.
   d. They do not exist.

9. In iterators what does the delete command do _____ (Select all that apply)
   a. It erases data from arrays.
   b. It deletes data from ArrayLists.
   c. Both in 1 and 2.
   d. None of the above.

10. Can we use ArrayLists to change an array size _____ (Select all that apply)
    a. Array size can not be changed.
    b. Only increase, they can not be reduced.
    c. Yes.
    d. No.

REFERENCES

- Java API Specifications

  http://www.oracle.com/technetwork/java/api-141528.html

- My Java programs that I use in my Java classes located at robinson.cs.fiu.edu

//END CHAPTER 8: DATA STRUCTURES - ARRAYLIST

Data Structures— Files

chapter

9

What is a File?

Files are data structures that are used to store data. Basically there are two types of data files, binary and text files. Text files are usually created using text editors. We can also use operating systems commands to create text files. See details in the *Operating Systems for IT* book by Michael Robinson, published by Kendall-Hunt. Text files can be accessed with any text editor or any program that can access binary files.

Binary files is the name given to any file that is not a text file and requires its corresponding program to access the data. Text editors can not access binary files.

The Windows operating system uses a text editor named Notepad. There are other third-party editors such as Notepad++ and EditPro that work in Windows. Linux has many text editors, among them Gedit, Nano, Pico, VM, VIM and many others. We also have IDEs (Integrated Development Environment) systems like NetBeans and Eclipse that allows us to write programs. IDEs have build in text editors. All the Java source code (programs) presented in this book were created using Gedit in Ubuntu Linux operating system.

When we create a Java program with a text editor, we write lines of code and of course every line is made with characters. Any program can be viewed as a two dimensional array. It has rows and columns, every line of code is a row, and every character is a column. Files are exactly the same. In files, every line/row is called a record. Every column is called a field.

< 197 >

What is a Record?

In Chapter 6: Data Structures – Arrays, we learned what arrays are. We can say that a text file with one record is a single dimensional array, and that a text file with more than one record is a two dimensional array. In other words, a record is a line of text in a data structure such as a file or an array.

Records such as: Joe Smith CS

are composed of the following segments: Joe, Smith, and CS. Each of these segments are called fields and each field is given a unique name. The field name for Joe could be First Name, for Smith Last Name, and for CS could be School. Records are separated (delimited) in many different forms, for instance spreadsheets use the tab symbol to delimit their fields, the above record example (Joe Smith CS) is delimited by the space symbol.

A file can contain thousands of records, and a record can contain thousands of fields. It is limited by the type of data structure, the operating system, and the Java file management class we use.

With today's technologies we have text files that can contain terabytes of records, therefore, it is very important to select the appropriate file class for the job. Java has multiple classes that we can use to work with files. In this chapter I am presenting the following file classes: FileWriter, PrintWriter, FileReader, BufferedReader, File, Formatter, Scanner, FileInputStream, DataInputStream, FileOutputStream and DataOutputStream, and my favorite which allows us to process files larger than 2 gigabytes. BufferedWriter bw = new BufferedWriter(new FileWriter(filename)).

Catching Errors Exceptions In Data Files

When we create Java programs we create at least three different types of errors, the most common is called "Syntax error" which is a typographical error. For instance, instead of writing print we write frint. Next we can have "logical errors" in which we are telling the computer to do one thing when we think we are telling something else, and also errors called "runtime errors" which only happens when we run a program and try, for instance, to open a file that does not exist.

In Java, errors are called exceptions. As we will see in the following sections, every method that deals with files must have in their headings the command:

throws IOException

This command will take care of any type of error that has to do with files.

If we try to open a file that does not exist we will get an error like this:

```
At 4 - addAllValuesInFile() : Exception in thread "main"
 java.io.FileNotFoundException: customer.txt (No such file or directory)
     at java.io.FileInputStream.open(Native Method)
     at java.io.FileInputStream.<init>(FileInputStream.java:137)
     at java.io.FileInputStream.<init>(FileInputStream.java:96)
     at java.io.FileReader.<init>(FileReader.java:58)
     at filesBasicClass.addAllValuesInFile(filesBasicClass.java:96)
     at filesBasicClass.main(filesBasicClass.java:152)
```

When we encounter this type of errors the program terminates/stops which is not always a desired result.

Java gives us ways to handle errors like this without terminating/stopping the program. Ahead in this chapter we have a section called Exceptions Handling, which explains how to implement this process.

Text Files

In this section we will see several text and binary files program examples that demonstrate the following classes used in Java:

- FileWriter, PrintWriter
- FileReader, BufferedReader
- Formatter
- Scanner
- FileOutputStream, DataOutputStream
- BufferedWriter bw = new BufferedWriter (new FileWriter(filename))

Text Files Using:

FileWriter, PrintWriter, FileReader and BufferedReader

```
/*
  Author  : Michael Robinson
  Program : filesBasicClass.java
  Purpose : Create new text file & write data into file
            Read and process data from text file
            Open existing text file, write and read data into/from
            file
```

```
              Also converts String to double and String to integer

   To Create and write to a new file;
   FileWriter        customers = new FileWriter("customers.txt");
   PrintWriter       output    = new PrintWriter( customers );

   To Open an existing text file and append data to it;
   FileWriter        customers = new FileWriter("customers.txt", true);
   PrintWriter       output    = new PrintWriter( customers );

   To open and read and existing text file:
   FileReader        customers = new FileReader("customers.txt");
   BufferedReader  inputFile = new BufferedReader( customers );

   Updated : May 4, 2099
*/


import java.io.*;
import java.util.Scanner;


public class filesBasicClass
{
    // To Create and write to a new file;
    public static void openWriteNewFile() throws IOException
    {
        System.out.println( "\n At 1 - openWriteNewFile()" +
                        " creating new file and adding: " );

        //customers.txt is the name of the file to be written
        //to the secondary storage (hard disk, CD, etc)
        FileWriter  customers = new FileWriter( "customers.txt" );

        //customers is the FileWriter class which has all the
        //the information about customers.txt the file to be
        //written to secondary storage (cd, hard disk etc)
        PrintWriter output    = new PrintWriter( customers );

        //write the numbers from 10 to 0 to the output file
        //and display them to the screen
        for( int x = 10; x >= 0; x-- )
```

```java
    {
        output.println( x );
        System.out.print( " " + x );
    }

    output.close(); //closes the file
    System.out.println( "<---eof" );

}//end public static void openWriteNewFile() throws IOException


public static void openWriteExistingFile() throws IOException
{
    System.out.print( "\n At 2 - openWriteExistingFile() " +
                    "Appending data: " );

    //customers is the FileWriter class which has all the
    //the information about the customers.txt file

    FileWriter  customers =
            new FileWriter( "customers.txt", true );

    //output is the PrintWriter Class that has all the
    //information about the customers object of the
    //FileWriter class
    PrintWriter output = new PrintWriter( customers );

    //write the numbers from 10 to 15 to the output file
    //and display them to the screen
    for( int x = 10; x < 16; x++ )
    {
        output.println( x );
        System.out.print( " " + x );
    }

    output.close();
    System.out.println( "<---eof" );

}//end public static void openWriteExistingFile()


//To open and read and existing text file:
public static void openReadExistingFile() throws IOException
```

```java
{
    System.out.print( "\n At 3 - openReadExistingFile() : " );

    //customers is the FileReader class which has all the
    //the information about customers.txt which is the file
    //to be read from secondary storage (cd, hard disk etc)
    FileReader      customers = new FileReader( "customers.txt" );

    //inputFile is the BufferedReader class which buffers the
    //data read by the customers object of the FileReader class
    BufferedReader inputFile = new BufferedReader( customers );

    //to store data read from customers.txt text file
    String inputFileRecord;

    //reads one record from customers.txt text file
    inputFileRecord = inputFile.readLine();

    //field to append all records read from customers.txt file
    String temp="";

    //read all records found in customers.txt file until it finds
    //the null character indicating EOF (end of file)
    while( inputFileRecord != null)
    {
        temp = temp + inputFileRecord;              //append records
        System.out.print( "[" + temp + "]" );
        inputFileRecord = inputFile.readLine(); //read record
    }

    inputFile.close();
    System.out.println( "<---eof" );

}//end public static void openReadExistingFile()


public static void addAllValuesInFile() throws IOException
{
    System.out.print( "\n At 4 - addAllValuesInFile() : " );

    //customers is the FileReader class which has all the
    //the information about customers.txt which is the file
    //to be read from secondary storage (cd, hard disk etc)
    FileReader      customers = new FileReader( "customers.txt" );
```

```java
        //inputFile is the BufferedReader class which buffers the
        //data read by the customers object of the FileReader class
        BufferedReader inputFile = new BufferedReader( customers );


        //to store data read from customers.txt text file
        String inputFileRecord;

        //reads one record from customers.txt text file
        inputFileRecord    = inputFile.readLine();


        //to do calculations with the data from the above files
        double sumDouble  = 0;
        int    sumInteger = 0;

        //read all records found in customers.txt file until it finds
        //the null character indicating EOF (end of file)
        while( inputFileRecord != null )
        {
            //converts String to Double
            sumDouble =
                sumDouble + Double.parseDouble(inputFileRecord);

            //converts String to int
            sumInteger =
                sumInteger + Integer.parseInt(inputFileRecord);
            System.out.print( " " + inputFileRecord );
            inputFileRecord = inputFile.readLine();   //read record
        }

        inputFile.close();
        System.out.printf(
            " = Total Double = %.2f  Total Integer = %d",
        sumDouble, sumInteger);

    }//end public static void addAllValuesInFile()



    public static int menu()
    {
```

```java
        System.out.print(
                "\n\t*********************************\n\t" +
                "*          Enter file mode        *\n\t" +
                "*    1 - openWriteNewFile          *\n\t" +
                "*    2 - openWriteExistingFile     *\n\t" +
                "*    3 - openReadExistingFile      *\n\t" +
                "*    4 - addAllValuesInFile        *\n\t");

        System.out.print( "\n\t  Enter  1, 2, 3, or 0 to exit: " );

        //read the keyboard
        Scanner keyboard = new Scanner( System.in );

        int fileType = keyboard.nextInt();

        return( fileType);

}//end public static int menu()


public static void main( String arg[] )   throws IOException
{

        System.out.println( "\n Working with files - basic" );

        int fileType = menu();

        while( fileType != 0 )
        {
            switch( fileType )
            {
                case 0  : break;
                case 1  : openWriteNewFile(); break;
                case 2  : openWriteExistingFile(); break;
                case 3  : openReadExistingFile(); break;
                case 4  : addAllValuesInFile(); break;
                default : System.out.println( "\tPlease Enter " +
                                        "1, 2, 3, or 0 to exit" );

            }

            fileType = menu();

        }//end while( fileType != 0 )
```

```
            System.out.println( "\n\t End Of Program" );

        }//end public static void main( String arg[] )

}//end public class filesBasicClass
```

Your output (results) will look like this:

```
  Working with files - basic


        * * * * * * * * * * * * * * * * * * * * * * * * * * *
        *          Enter file mode          *
        *    1 - openWriteNewFile           *
        *    2 - openWriteExistingFile      *
        *    3 - openReadExistingFile       *
        •  4 - addAllValuesInFile        *
        •

        Enter  1, 2, 3, or 0 to exit: 1


  At 1 - openWriteNewFile() creating new file and adding:
  10 9 8 7 6 5 4 3 2 1 0<---eof



        * * * * * * * * * * * * * * * * * * * * * * * * * * *
        *          Enter file mode          *
        *    1 - openWriteNewFile           *
        *    2 - openWriteExistingFile      *
        *    3 - openReadExistingFile       *
        *    4 - addAllValuesInFile         *

        Enter  1, 2, 3, or 0 to exit: 2

  At 2 - openWriteExistingFile() Appending data:   10 11 12 13 14 15<---
  eof
```

```
********************************
*        Enter file mode       *
*    1 - openWriteNewFile       *
*    2 - openWriteExistingFile  *
*    3 - openReadExistingFile   *
*    4 - addAllValuesInFile     *

    Enter  1, 2, 3, or 0 to exit: 3

At 3 - openReadExistingFile() :
[10][109][1098][10987][109876][1098765][10987654][109876543]
[1098765432][10987654321][109876543210][10987654321010]
[1098765432101011][1098765432101011112][10987654321010111213]
[1098765432101011121314][10987654321010111213141 5]<---eof


********************************
*        Enter file mode       *
*    1 - openWriteNewFile       *
*    2 - openWriteExistingFile  *
*    3 - openReadExistingFile   *
*    4 - addAllValuesInFile     *

    Enter  1, 2, 3, or 0 to exit: 4


At 4 - addAllValuesInFile() :   10 9 8 7 6 5 4 3 2 1 0 10 11 12 13 14
15 = Total Double = 130.00   Total Integer = 130


********************************
*        Enter file mode       *
*    1 - openWriteNewFile       *
*    2 - openWriteExistingFile  *
*    3 - openReadExistingFile   *
*    4 - addAllValuesInFile     *

    Enter  1, 2, 3, or 0 to exit: 0


    End Of Program
```

Let's examine this code:

This program is highly documented, every line of code is documented in great detail. Please review program line by line. Also I encourage you to modify the code to see what happens when you change the values. Programming is like driving a car, you can not just read about it, you need to do it.

Text Files Using the File Class

Java uses the file class in java.io.File to obtain information about files and directories. The file class does not create files or allows us to make input or obtain output to/from files. Here are some of the methods that we can use with the file class:

```java
/*
  Author  : Michael Robinson
  Program : filesFile.java
  Purpose : Checks the status of a  file

  Updated : Dec 15, 2099
*/



import java.io.*;


public class filesFile
{
    public static void processFile() throws IOException
    {
        //creates the object myFile of the File class
        File myFile = new File( "1200.dna" );

        //displays the name of the myFile object
        System.out.print( myFile.getName() );

        //self explanatory
        if( !myFile.exists() )
        {
            System.out.println( " Does NOT exist" + "\n" );
        }
        else
        {
            //the following lines execute the methods
```

```java
      //of the myFile object of the File class:
      //canExecute, canRead, canWrite and others
      System.out.println( " exists"\n" );
       System.out.println( "canExecute()         = " +
                           myFile.canExecute() );
       System.out.println( "canRead()            = " +
                           myFile.canRead() );
       System.out.println( "canWrite()           = " +
                           myFile.canWrite() );
       System.out.println( "createNewFile()      = " +
                           myFile.createNewFile() );

      //if you remove the // in the next two lines
      //the 1200.dna file will be removed
      //System.out.println( "delete()            = "+
      //                   myFile.delete() );

      System.out.println( "exists()              = " +
                          myFile.exists() );
       System.out.println( "getClass()           = " +
                           myFile.getClass() );
       System.out.println( "getFreeSpace()       = " +
                           myFile.getFreeSpace() );
       System.out.println( "getName()            = " +
                           myFile.getName() );
       System.out.println( "getParent()          = " +
                           myFile.getParent() );
       System.out.println( "getParentFile()      = " +
                           myFile.getParentFile() );
       System.out.println( "getPath()            = " +
                           myFile.getPath() );
       System.out.println( "getTotalSpace()      = " +
                           myFile.getTotalSpace() );
       System.out.println( "getAbsoluteFile()    = " +
                           myFile.getAbsoluteFile() );
       System.out.println( "getAbsolutePath()    = " +
                           myFile.getAbsolutePath() );

   }//end if( !myFile.exists() )

}//end public static void processFile()


public static void main( String arg[] ) throws IOException
```

```
    {
        processFile();

    }//end public static void main( String arg[] )

}//end public class filesFile
```

Your output (results) will look like this:

```
1200.dna exists


canExecute()        = false
canRead()           = true
canWrite()          = true
createNewFile()     = false
exists()            = true
getClass()          = class java.io.File
getFreeSpace()      = 61239652352
getName()           = 1200.dna
getParent()         = null
getParentFile()     = null
getPath()           = 1200.dna
getTotalSpace()     = 488448720896
getAbsoluteFile()   = /home/mr/Kendall_Hunt/Java/programs/1200.dna
getAbsolutePath()   = /home/mr/Kendall_Hunt/Java/programs/1200.dna
```

Let's examine this code:

The line

```
        File myFile = new
        File( "1200.dna" );
```

checks the current directory for the file called 1200.dna, if it does not exist the program displays "1200.dna Does NOT exist" and terminates, else the program will process multiple methods of the file class, applied to the 1200.dna file, such as:

```
        //the following lines execute the methods
        //of the myFile object of the File class:
        //canExecute, canRead, canWrite and others
```

```
System.out.println( " exists"\n" );
System.out.println( "canExecute()           = " +
                    myFile.canExecute() );
System.out.println( "canRead()              = " +
                    myFile.canRead() );

//System.out.println( "delete()             = " +
//                    myFile.delete() );
```

Notice that I placed remarks // at this line:

```
//System.out.println( "delete() = " + myFile.delete());
```

This line will delete the 1200.dna file if the remarks // are removed. There are more methods than these in the file class, please experiment using the other methods. This file class is very useful.

Exceptions Handling

In Java errors are called exceptions. There are a large amount of classes that handle errors, allowing us to maintain control of the program. For a detailed explanation of exceptions see Appendix IV.

To handle an exception, or control an error, Java requires the following:

import in the java.util.* package

```
import java.util.*;
```

A typical code for exceptions handling looks like this:

```
try
{
    String s = "";

    BufferedWriter bw = new BufferedWriter( new
                FileWriter( "/home/mr/Bigtest" ) );

    BufferedReader br = new BufferedReader( new
                FileReader( "/home/mr/Bigtest" ) );
```

```java
        String sc = "12230381 Vallicos Inc";

            s = sc;

        int x = 0;

        while( x < 99999999 )
        {
            s = br.readLine();
            bw.write( s + "\n" );
            x++;
        }

        bw.close();

    }

catch( Exception e )
{
    e.printStackTrace();

}
```

Notice that we write all the code we want tested inside the try section

```java
    try
    {

    }
```

If Java finds any errors in the try section, in the catch section we tell Java what to do.

```java
    Catch( Exception e )  //catches ALL errors, can print e
    {

    }
```

As we see in the catch section we find (Exception e). This is the default Exception Handler which can handle any error. Java writes the error inside the variable e, which can then be printed.

Finally, the optional section can be used for any purpose.

```java
finally
{
    System.out.println( "At finally, catch terminates here\n" );
}
```

In the following program we will see a simple implementation. In the following sections in this chapter you will find additions exception implementations.

```java
/*

   Author  : Michael Robinson
   Program : exceptions.java
   Purpose : Checks the status of a  file

   Updated : Dec 15, 2099
*/



import java.util.*;


public class exceptions
{

    public static void process()
    {
        Scanner input = new Scanner( System.in );
        int x  = 1; //to handle the do while
        int fn = 0;
        int sn = 0;

        do   //this is do while loop
        {
            try
            {
                System.out.println( " Enter first number : " );
                fn = input.nextInt();

                System.out.println( " Enter second number : " );
                sn = input.nextInt();

                //if divide by zero occurs, Java jumps to catch
                int result = fn/sn;

                //if divide by zero occurs this line does NOT execute
                x = 2;
            }
            catch(Exception e) //catches ALL errors, can print e
            {
```

```java
                System.out.print(" Division by zero NOT possible");
                System.out.print(" Error = " + e.getMessage() );
            }
            finally
            {
                System.out.println( " At finally. The try catch" +
                                    " terminates here\n" );
            }

        } while( x == 1 ); //go back to the beginning of do loop

        //only if NOT divide by zero error
        float result2 = (float)fn/sn;

        System.out.printf( " %d / %d = %.2f", fn, sn, result2 );

        System.out.println( "\n\nEnd Exception e sample" );

    }//end public static void process()


    public static void main( String arg[] )
    {
        process();

    }//end public static void main( String arg[] )

}//end public class exceptions
```

Your output (results) will look like this:

```
Enter first number  : 4
Enter second number : 0
Division by zero NOT possible
Error = / by zero
At finally. The try catch terminates here


Enter first number  : 4
Enter second number : 2
At finally. The try catch terminates here

4 / 2 = 2.00

End Exception e sample
```

We must have one try section, and as many catch sections as needed. The finally section is optional.

Let's examine this code:

Under the heading Exceptions Handling and inside the above sample and full program, you will find very detailed instructions and comments describing this section.

Text Files Using The Formatter Class

In Java there are several ways to create files, and using the formatter class is probably the easiest and fastest way to create a file. Formatter also allows us to write data into the file. However make sure this file does NOT exist otherwise it will overwrite it (deletes it and re-creates it).

```
/*
   Author  : Michael Robinson
   Program : filesFormatter.java
   Purpose : This program uses the Formatter class
             this is a very quick way
             to create the file called fileone then we
             write data into into and finally
             close it.

   Updated : Jan 29, 2099
*/


import java.util.*;


public class filesFormatter
{
    //creating a private global variable
    private static Formatter fileName;


    public static void createAfile()
    {

        try
```

```java
        {
            //make sure this file does NOT exist
            //otherwise it will overwrite it (delete and re-create)
            fileName = new Formatter( "fileOne" );

            System.out.println( "I have created fileOne" );
        }
        catch(Exception e)
        {
            System.out.println( "fileOne was not created ERROR!!" );

        }

}//end public static void createAfile()


public static void writeDataToFile(
                                String fn, String ln, String major)
{
    try
    {
        //exactly as using printf
        //write data into file fileOne
        fileName.format( "%s %s %s\n", fn, ln, major);
        System.out.println( "Inserted record : " +
                                fn + " " + ln + " " + major );
    }
    catch(Exception e)
    {
        System.out.println( "fileOne was not created ERROR!!" );
    }

}//end public static void writeDataToFile()


public static void closeFile()
{
    fileName.close();
    System.out.println( "File has been closed" );

}//end public static void closeFile()


public static void main( String arg[] )
```

```
    {
        createAfile(); //creates a file

        //writes the following data to the file
        writeDataToFile( "Joe", "Smith", "CS" );
        writeDataToFile( "Tom", "Richards", "IT" );
        writeDataToFile( "Daniel", "Thomason", "Math" );
        writeDataToFile( "Robert", "Lambert", "EE" );
        writeDataToFile( "Miguel", "Gonzalez", "CS" );

        closeFile();

    }//end public static void main( String arg[] )

}//end public class filesFormatter
```

Your output (results) will look like this:

```
I have created fileOne

Inserted record : Joe Smith CS
Inserted record : Tom Richards IT
Inserted record : Daniel Thomason Math
Inserted record : Robert Lambert EE
Inserted record : Miguel Gonzalez CS


File has been closed
```

Let's examine this code:

As we can see, to create a file using the formatter class all we need to do is create a final formatter object

```
        final Formatter fileName;
```

and then give it the name of the file that will be created in the secondary storage (hard disk/cd/tape/flash/ etc):

```
        fileName = new Formatter( "fileOne" );
```

When we write data to the file we use the object name for the file (fileName) and its method format. This method is used exactly in the same manner we use the printf method:

```
        fileName.format( "%s %s %s\n", fn, ln, major );
```

This section can be used in combination with any other files classes, for instance, now we are going to use the Scanner class to read the data in the file we just created.

Text Files Using the Scanner Class

The scanner class is usually used to obtain data from the keyboard. Here we will see we can also use it to open text files and process them.

For the following program, we use the previous text file called fileOne which contains the following data:

```
Joe Smith CS
Tom Richards IT
Daniel Thomason Math
Robert Lambert EE
Miguel Gonzalez CS
```

```java
/*
  Author  : Michael Robinson
  Program : filesScanner.java
  Purpose : This program uses the Scanner class this is a
            very quick way to read data from a text file.
            Data can be read one record at the time, or
            one String at the time separated by a space.

  Updated : August 26th, 2099
*/


import java.io.*;
import java.util.*;


public class filesScanner
{
    //create a private global variable of Scanner type
    private static Scanner inputFile;

    //create a public global variable of String type
    public static String fileName = "fileOne";


    public static void openFile( String fileName )
    {
        try
```

```java
    {
        //open fileOne text file using the Scanner class
        inputFile = new Scanner( new File( fileName ) );
    }
    catch( Exception e )
    {
        System.out.println( "Could not open file" );
    }

}//end public static void openFile()


public static void readStringFromFile( String fileName )
{
    try
    {
        int recordNum = 0; //create a counter variable

        System.out.println();

        //read records from the fileOne text file
        while( inputFile.hasNext() )
        {
            recordNum++;
            String fn    = inputFile.next(); //reads one field
            String ln    = inputFile.next(); //reads one field
            String major = inputFile.next(); //reads one field

            System.out.printf( " %s %s %s\n", fn, ln, major );

        }//end while( inputFile.hasNext() )
    }
    catch( Exception e )
    {
        System.out.println( "Could not read file " + fileName );
    }

}//end public static void readStringFromFile( String fileName )


public static void readLineFromFile( String fileName )
{
    try
```

```java
        {
            System.out.println();
            int recordNum = 0;

            //read records from the fileOne text file
            while( inputFile.hasNext() )
            {
                recordNum++;

                //reads one full record/row
                String recordLine = inputFile.nextLine();
                System.out.printf( "[ %d %s ]\n",
                                    recordNum, recordLine );

            }//end while( inputFile.hasNext() )
        }
        catch(Exception e)
        {
            System.out.println( "Could not read file " + fileName );
        }

}//end public static void readLineFromFile( String fileName )


public static void closeFile( String fileName )
{
    try
    {
        inputFile.close();
    }
    catch( Exception e)
    {
        System.out.println( "Could not close file " + fileName );
    }
}

}//end public static void closeFile( String fileName )


public static void main( String arg[] )
{
    openFile( fileName );
    readStringFromFile( fileName );
    closeFile( fileName );
```

```
        openFile( fileName );
        readLineFromFile( fileName );
        closeFile( fileName );

   }//end public static void main( String arg[] )

}//end public class filesScanner
```

Your output (results) will look like this:

```
Joe Smith CS
Tom Richards IT
Daniel Thomason Math
Robert Lambert EE
Miguel Gonzalez CS

[ 1 Joe Smith CS ]
[ 2 Tom Richards IT ]
[ 3 Daniel Thomason Math ]
[ 4 Robert Lambert EE ]
[ 5 Miguel Gonzalez CS ]
```

Let's examine this code:

This is how we opened the file using the scanner class

```
inputFile = new Scanner( new File( fileName ) );
```

To read each string from the file we used:

```
inputFile.next();
```

And to read each record (line of data in the file) we used:

```
inputFile.nextLine();
```

To close the file we used:

```
inputFile.close();
```

The rest of the logic commands used are standard.

Large Files. Writing and Reading

Last but not least, I recommend to make sure that all students learn how to use the classes in the following program. These classes allow us to write, faster than the other above classes, files above the 2gig limit. Unfortunately the above classes in Java do not allow us to write files greater than 2 gigs, and worse than that, it does not give us any errors or warning when we try.

In the following program I also implement, from the string class, the substring,   toUpperCase() and compareTo methods, as well as the Scanner(System.in) class to be able to read from the keyboard.

```java
/*
   Author   : Michael Robinson
   Program  : filesLargeSize.java
   Purpose  : This program uses the Formatter class
              this is a very quick way
              to create the file called fileone then we
              write data into into and finally
              close it.

              ************* WARNING *****************
              this program will produce a text file
              of size close to three gigabytes

   Updated : Jan 29, 2099
*/


import java.util.*;
import java.io.*;
import java.text.DecimalFormat;


public class filesLargeSize
{

    //create the public global object recordsFormat of class
    //DecimalFormat

    public static DecimalFormat recordsFormat =
                        new DecimalFormat( " #,###" );

    public static void writeFile()
    {
        System.out.println(
            "\n  Writing records into the text LargeFile" );

        try
```

```java
    {
        //creates the bufferedWrite object of BufferedWriter
        //class to write data into the LargeFile text file.
        //This class allows us to write very large
        //files limited by the storage available
        BufferedWriter bufferedWrite =
            new BufferedWriter( new FileWriter( "LargeFile" ) );


        String record =
            "Java uses the File class in java.io.File";

        int x = 0;

        while( x < 69999999 )
        {
            //write record to file
            bufferedWrite.write( record + "\n" );
            x++;
        }

        bufferedWrite.close();

        System.out.println(
            "\n  Records written = " + recordsFormat.format(x) );
    }
    catch( Exception e )
    {
        e.printStackTrace();
    }

}//end public static void writeFile()


public static void readFile()
{

    System.out.println(
        "\n  Reading records from the text LargeFile" );

    try
    {
        //creates the bufferedReader object of BufferedReader
        //class to read data from the LargeFile text file.
        //This class allows us to read from very large files
        BufferedReader bufferedReader =
            new BufferedReader( new FileReader( "LargeFile" ) );
        //read record from file
        String record = bufferedReader.readLine();

        int x = 1;
```

```java
        while( record != null )
        {
            //read record from file
            record = bufferedReader.readLine();
            x++;
        }

        bufferedReader.close();

        System.out.println( "  Records read = " +
                    recordsFormat.format(x-1)  + "\n\n" );
    }
    catch( Exception e )
    {
        e.printStackTrace();
    }

}//end public static void readFile()


public static void main( String args[] )
{
    Scanner kb = new Scanner( System.in );

    System.out.println(
            "\n\n\n*********** WARNING *****************" );
    System.out.println(
            "  this program will produce a text file" );
    System.out.println( "    of size close to three gigabytes" );
    System.out.print(
            "\n      Do you want to continue (Y/N): " );


    //read the keyboard and assign value entered to the keyboard
    //String variable
    String keyboard = kb.nextLine();

    //extract the first character of the keyboard String and
    //assign it to the String letter
    String letter = keyboard.substring(0,1).toUpperCase();

    //displays the distance from Y's ASCII code. 0 means that the
    //letter entered was Y
    System.out.println( "\n      ASCII distance from Y to " +
                letter + " = " + letter.compareTo( "Y" )   );

    if( letter.compareTo( "Y" ) != 0 )
    {
        System.out.print( "\n   I received " + letter +
                        " Exiting program, Thank You\n\n\n" );
```

```
            //exit/terminate this program at this point
            System.exit(0);
        }

        writeFile();    //call this method
        readFile();     //call this method

    }//end public static void main( String args[] )

}//end public class filesLargeSize
```

Your output (results) will look like this:

```
************* WARNING *****************
   this program will produce a text file
     of size close to three gigabytes


      Do you want to continue (Y/N): y

      ASCII distance from Y to Y = 0

   Writing records into the text LargeFile
   Records written =  69,999,999

   Reading records from the text LargeFile
   Records read =  69,999,999

or

************* WARNING *****************
   this program will produce a text file
     of size close to three gigabytes

      Do you want to continue (Y/N): n

      ASCII distance from Y to N = -11

   I received N Exiting program, Thank You
```

Let's examine this code:

This program is highly documented, every line of code is documented in great detail. Please review program line by line. Also I encourage you to modify the code to see what happens when you change the values. Programming is like driving a car, you can not just read about it, you need to do it. Please also see the comments at the beginning of this topic.

Printing Numbers Using Decimal Format

Now that we have learned how to work with files, we need to learn to print numeric data in with dollar signs, numbers separated with commas and periods, and multiple decimal numbers. For this Java has a class called DecimalFormat.

```java
/*
  Author   : Michael Robinson
  Program  : decimalFormatClass.java
  Purpose  : How to print numbers with decimal formats

  Updated  : Jan 29, 2099
*/


import java.text.DecimalFormat;
import java.util.Scanner;


public class decimalFormatClass
{

    public static void process()
    {
        int x = 0;
        double amount = 1000;

        //creates the moneyFormat object used to describe how numbers
        //are to be displayed
        DecimalFormat moneyFormat = new DecimalFormat("$ #,###.000");

        for( x = 10; x < 15; x++ )
        {
            amount = amount + ( .005 * x );
            System.out.println( "\nOriginal : " + amount );
```

```
        //using moneyFormat.format to display numbers
        System.out.println( "Formatted: US " +
                            moneyFormat.format( amount ) );

    }//end for loop

}//end public static void process()


public static void main( String arg[] )
{
    process();

}//end public static void main( String arg[] )

}//end class decimalFormatClass
```

Your output (results) will look like this:

```
Original : 1000.05
Formatted: US $ 1,000.050

Original : 1000.1049999999999
Formatted: US $ 1,000.105

Original : 1000.1649999999998
Formatted: US $ 1,000.165

Original : 1000.2299999999999
Formatted: US $ 1,000.230

Original : 1000.3
Formatted: US $ 1,000.300
```

Let's examine this code:

First we need to import the class:

```
import java.text.DecimalFormat;
```

To create the numerical format to be used we need:

```
DecimalFormat moneyFormat = new DecimalFormat( "$ #,###.000" );
```

DecimalFormat is the class to be used
moneyFormat   is the name of the object we are creating
$ #,###.000   is the format we want. This means:

1. Place a $ leaving a space before the number
2. #,###.000 write the number using this format
3. Using commas as needed, and a period for decimals
4. If there are no decimals, place up to three zeros
5. Always display no more than three decimals using ceiling

To print use the object moneyFormat.format(amount) as follows:

```
System.out.println( "Formatted: US " +
                        moneyFormat.format(amount) );
```

Modifications of this format are allowed, using different currency symbols and amount of whole numbers and/or decimals.

This program is very short and it is explained in detailed using internal comment lines.

Test this program by using other formats, for instance, the $ can be replaced with any other currency symbol, also in other countries the commas are replaced by periods and vice-versa.

Binary Files

Binary files can only be seen by binary editors and usually they are compiled programs.

This is how Java handles binary Files:

```
/*
  Author  : Michael Robinson
  Program : FilesBinary.java
  Purpose : This program
            creates a binary files
            writes data to it
```

```
            closes file and then
            opens the binary file,
            reads and displays the contents.

   Updated : Jan 29, 2099
*/


import java.io.DataInputStream;
import java.io.DataOutputStream;
import java.io.EOFException;
import java.io.FileInputStream;
import java.io.FileOutputStream;
import java.io.IOException;


public class filesBinary
{
    //create numbers.dat binary file if it does not exist
    public static void createBinaryFile( int numbers[] )
                        throws IOException
    {
        //accepted array to be written to a file:
        //int numbers[] = { 2, 4, 6, 8, 10, 12, 14 };

        //create the binary outputBinary object
        //if file exists it appends data to it
        //else creates a new file, done by true parameter.
        FileOutputStream outputBinary = new
                    FileOutputStream( "numbers.dat", true );

        //creates the outputBinFile object to write data into
        //the numbers.dat binary file
        DataOutputStream outputBinFile = new
                    DataOutputStream( outputBinary );

        System.out.println( "Writing the numbers to the file..." );

        //write the array elements into the numbers.dat binary file
        for( int i = 0; i < numbers.length; i++ )
        {
            outputBinFile.writeInt( numbers[i] );
            System.out.print( numbers[i] + " " );
        }
```

```java
        //outputBinFile.writeChars("\n");
        System.out.println( "\nDone." );

        //close the file.
        outputBinFile.close();

}//end public static void createBinaryFile()


//opens and reads all records in numbers.dat binary file
public static void openReadBinaryFile( int numbersLength )
                throws IOException
{
    int number = 0;                   //number read from the file
    boolean endOfFile = false;   //EOF flag

    //Create the inputBinary object to help in reading the
    //numbers.dat binary file
    FileInputStream inputBinary = new
                FileInputStream( "numbers.dat" );

    //Create the inputBFile object to be able to use the previous
    //inputBinary object to read the numbers.dat binary file
    DataInputStream inputBFile = new
                DataInputStream( inputBinary );

    System.out.println( "\nReading numbers from Binary file:" );

    //read and display all the records in the numbers.dat file.
    while( !endOfFile )
    {
        try
        {
            for( int x = 0; x < numbersLength; x++ )
            {
                //read record
                number = inputBFile.readInt();


                //display record

                System.out.printf( "%d ", number );
            }
            System.out.println();
```

```
                }
                catch ( EOFException e )
                {
                    endOfFile = true;
                }

        }//end public static void openReadBinaryFile( int
         //numbersLength ) throws IOException

        System.out.println( "\nDone." );

        //close the file
        inputBFile.close();

    }//end public static void openReadBinaryFile() throws IOException


    public static void main( String args[] ) throws IOException
    {
        //create array to be written into numbers.dat binary file
        int numbers[] = { 2, 4, 6, 8, 10, 12, 14 };

        //create numbers.dat binary file and write array data into it
        createBinaryFile( numbers );

        //open, read and display all data in numbers.dat binary file
        openReadBinaryFile( numbers.length );

    }//end public static void main(String[] args) throws IOException

}//end public class filesBinary
```

Your output (results) will look like this:

Writing the numbers to the file...

2 4 6 8 10 12 14

Done.

Reading numbers from binary file:

2 4 6 8 10 12 14

Done.

Let's examine this code:

This program is highly documented, every line of code is documented in great detail. Please review program line by line. Also I encourage you to modify the code to see what happens when you change the values. Programming is like driving a car, you can not just read about it, you need to do it.

Regularly the data contents in text files you can be seen with any editor or with terminal mode or command line commands. Binary files can only be seen with the software that it was created or special programs that can read binary.

Summary

In this chapter we learned about text and binary files as well as records. We studied the different classes that Java uses to create and manage files as well as the exception handlers which help us to trap errors.

We see classes such as FileWriter, PrintWriter, FileReader, BufferedReader, File, Formatter, Scanner, FileInputStream, DataInputStream, FileOutputStream and DataOutputStream. Finally we learned to use the DecimalFormat class to help us display numeric data in proper formats.

In the last topic of this chapter (Large Files. Writing and Reading) I demonstrate how to write files greater than 2 gigs. I also implemented, from the string class, the substring, toUpperCase() and compareTo methods. The Scanner(System.in) class was also implemented to learn how to read from the keyboard.

Key Terms

Binary Files	Binary files can only be seen with binary editors and usually they are compiled programs.
	To see how we handle binary files in Java, please see program FilesBinary.java
Catching Errors Exceptions In Data Files	When we write Java programs we create at least three different types of errors:
	The most common is called "syntax error" which is a typographical error, for instance, instead of writing print we write frint.
	We can also have "logical errors" in which we are telling the computer to do one thing, when we think we are telling it to do something else.
	Lastly there are other errors called "runtime errors" that only happen when we run a program. For instance when we try to open a file that does not exist.
	In Java, errors are called exceptions. As we will see in the following sections, every method that deals with files must have in their headings the command: throws IOException
	This command will take care of any type of error that has to do with files.
	If we try to open a file that does not exist we will get an error like this:
	At 4 - addAllValuesInFile() : Exception in thread "main" java. io.FileNotFoundException: customer.txt (No such file or directory) at java.io.FileInputStream.open(Native Method) at java. io.FileInputStream.<init>(
	FileInputStream.java:137)
Decimal Format. **Printing Numbers.**	Now that we have learned how to work with files, we need to learn to print numeric data in with dollar signs, numbers separated with commas and periods, and multiple decimal numbers. For this, Java has a class called DecimalFormat.
	Please see program decimalFormatClass.java

Exceptions Handling	In Java errors are called exceptions. There are a large amount of classes that handle errors, allowing us to maintain control of the program.
	To handle an exception, or control an error, Java requires the following import in the java.util.* package:
	import java.util.*;
	This is a typical code for exceptions handling:

```
try
{
    BufferedWriter bw = new BufferedWriter(
        new FileWriter( "/home/mr/Bigtest" ) );

    BufferedReader br = new BufferedReader(
        new FileReader( "/home/mr/Bigtest" ) );

        String sc = "12230381 Vallicos Inc";
        int x = 0;
        while( x < 99999999 )
        {
            sc = br.readLine();
            bw.write( sc + "\n" );
            x++;
        }
        bw.close();
}
catch( Exception e )
{
    e.printStackTrace();
}
```

In the catch section we find (Exception e), this is the default exception handler which can handle any error. Java writes the error inside the variable e, which can then be printed.

File. **What is a file?**	Files are data structures that are used to store data. Basically there are two types of data files, binary and text files. Text files are usually created using text editors. We can use operating systems commands to create text files. See details in the *Operating Systems for IT* book by Michael Robinson, published by Kendall-Hunt. Text files can be accessed with any text editor or any program that can access binary files. Binary files is the name given to any file that is not a text file and requires its corresponding program to access the data. Text editors can not access binary files. The Windows operating system uses a text editor named Notepad. There are other third party editors such as Notepad++ and EditPro that work in Windows. The Linux operating system has many text editors, among them Gedit, Nano, Pico, VM, VIM and many others. We also have IDEs (Integrated Development Environment) systems like NetBeans and Eclipse that allows us to write programs. IDEs have build in text editors. All the Java source code (programs) presented in this book were create using Gedit in Ubuntu Linux operating system. When we create a Java program with a text editor, we write lines of code and of course every line is made with characters. Any program can be viewed as a two dimensional array, it has rows and columns, every line of code is a row and every character is a column. Files are exactly the same. In files, every line/row is called a record. Every column is called a field.
Files. **Large Files.** **Writing and** **Reading**	I recommend to make sure that all students learn how to use all the classes in program filesLargeSize.java. These classes allow us to write, faster than the other above classes, files above the 2gig limit. In the filesLargeSize.java program, using the string class, we implement the substring, toUpperCase() and compareTo methods, as well as the Scanner(System.in) class to be able to read from the keyboard.

Files.
Text Files
	In this section we see several text and binary files program examples that demonstrate the following classes used in Java:
	
	FileWriter, PrintWriter
	FileReader, BufferedReader
	Formatter
	Scanner
	FileOutputStream, DataOutputStream
	BufferedWriter bw = new
	     BufferedWriter(new
	
	       FileWriter(filename))

Files. **Text Files using** **the File Class**	Java uses the file class in java.io.File to obtain information about files and directories. The file class does not create files or allows us to make input or obtain output to/from files. Please see program filesFile.java
Files. **Text Files using** **the Formatter** **Class**	In Java there are several ways to create files, and using the formatter class is probably the easiest and fastest way to create a file. Formatter also allows us to write data into the file, however, make sure this file does NOT exist otherwise it will overwrite it (deletes it and re-creates it). Please see program filesFormatter.java
Files. **Text Files** **using the** **Scanner Class**	The scanner class is usually used to obtain data from the keyboard. Here we will see we can also use it to open text files and process them. For the program filesScanner.java, we use a text file called fileOne which contains the following data: Joe Smith CS Tom Richards IT Daniel Thomason Math Robert Lambert EE Miguel Gonzalez CS
Files. **Text Files** **using:** **FileWriter,** **PrintWriter,** **FileReader and** **BufferedReader**	Please see the appropiate programs in Chapter 9 for each type of the following text files: FileWriter PrintWriter FileReader BufferedReader

Exercises

1. Write a program that creates a file to add and display with 5 records using the scanner class, and error trapping and DecimalFormat.

2. Write a program that creates a file to add and display with 5 records using the formatter class, and error trapping and DecimalFormat.

3. Write a program that creates a file to add and display with 5 records using the FileReader and File-Writer classes, and error trapping and DecimalFormat.

4. Write a program that creates a file to add and display with 5 records using FileInputStream, DataInputStream, FileOutputStream, DataOutputStream classes, and error trapping and DecimalFormat.

5. Explain the difference in reading the text versus the binary data files.

Select all that apply for the following questions:

6. What is the name of the data file type created in question 4?

   a. Text files
   b. Dynamic files
   c. Binary files
   d. Java files

7. What is the DecimalFormat class used for?

   a. To write binary files to secondary storage
   b. To write text files to secondary storage
   c. To display alphabetical data in proper manner
   d. To display numeric data in proper manner

8. Can I create a file containing text and binary data?

   a. Yes
   b. No
   c. Only if the binary data is less than the text data
   d. Only if the text data is less than the binary data

9. When creating a new file using the following line:

   ```
   FileOutputStream( "numbers.dat", true );
   ```

   what will happen if the file already exists?

   a. It will display an error
   b. It will erase the current file and create a new one
   c. It appends data to it
   d. None of the above

REFERENCES

- Java API Specifications
    http://www.oracle.com/technetwork/java/api-141528.html

- My Java programs that I use in my Java classes located at robinson.cs.fiu.edu

//END CHAPTER 9: DATA STRUCTURES – FILES

External Classes, Methods, This, Constructors

chapter 10

External Classes

Up to this moment we have worked under the assumption that all Java programs must have one "public static void main(String args[])" method.

If we go back to all the programs we have written so far, we can see that the word "class" is on the headings of all our programs, therefore all of our programs are "classes." We need to recognize that just like the Java classes that we used in our programs, such as string, scanner, etc., the programs we have written so far are also classes. They are classes that we wrote.

Now it is time to learn how to create "external classes" which do NOT have the "public static void main(String args[])" method. These external classes only have variables and regular methods which can be used as additional classes, by any other program/class or external class. This means that we are extending the capabilities of the Java language by creating our own additional classes.

External classes, just like methods, give us three great benefits:

1. We can divide a large project into smaller pieces (divide and conquer).
2. When we have an error in a method, we can block that method allowing the rest of the project to continue working.
3. Re-use. This time any other class or method in our projects can re-use any method in any external class. We can also share our own external classes with other teams doing their own projects.

< 239 >

The following simple classes will shows us how to create, implement, and use external classes.

This first program `ExternalClassesCaller.java` calls four methods, `myName()`, `myMajor()`, `setCredits( 92 )` and `getCredits()`, and the variables that are inside an External Class called MyInfo.

```
/*
  Author  : Michael Robinson
  Program : ExternalClassesCaller.java
  Purpose : To call methods in an External Class
            called MyInfo

  Updated : August 16, 2099
*/


public class ExternalClassesCaller
{
    public static void main( String arg[] )
    {
        MyInfo.myName();
        MyInfo.myMajor();
        MyInfo.setCredits( 92 );
        System.out.println( "I have taken " +
                            MyInfo.getCredits() + " credits." );

    }

}//end public class ExternalClassesCaller
```

The following is the MyInfo class:

```
/*
  Author  : Michael Robinson
  Program : MyInfo.java
  Purpose : An External Class
            with variables and methods
            to be used by other classes

  Updated : August 16, 2099
*/
```

```
public class MyInfo
{
    private static int theCredits = 0;

    public static void myName()
    {
        System.out.println( "Hi, my name is Good Looking!!!" );
    }


    public static void myMajor()
    {
        System.out.println( "Well, my major has to" +
                            " do with Science!!!" );
    }


    public static void setCredits( int credits )
    {
        theCredits = credits;
    }


    public static int getCredits()
    {
        return theCredits;
    }

}//end public class MyInfo
```

In the above MyInfo external class we have one private variable called:

```
private static int theCredits = 0;
```

The theCredits variable is declared as private, so only methods in its class (MyInfo) can have access to it.

Then we have four methods:

```
public static void myName()

public static void myMajor()

public static void setCredits( int credits )

public static int getCredits()
```

which are accessed by the ExternalClassesCaller class. Notice that all the methods in the external class MyInfo are declared public, therefore they can be accessed by any other external program/class.

Your output (results) will look like this:

```
Hi, my name is Good Looking!!!

Well, my major has to do with Science!!!

I have taken 92 credits.
```

Let's examine this code:

The MyInfo external class does not have a main method, it only contains one private variable and four public methods. When we compile this class (javac MyInfo.java) it creates the MyInfo.class without any errors.

The ExternalClassesCaller class is a regular program with its own main menu, from where we call the MyInfo external class methods. At the same time we are using the private variable theCredits found in MyInfo class, using its setCredits(int credits) method.

The following section on constructors can make use of external classes, but we choose not to do it at this time, so that we can later concentrate in the multiple issues of constructors. We will come back to external classes in all the following sections starting with Inheritance in Chapter 13.

Final Variables

Sometimes we need a variable to maintain its value throughout the project, making sure that even if its scope is global, its value is not be changed by any method. To do this process is very simple, all we need to do is to declare such variable as final:

```
public final double interestRate = .25;
```

Final variables are known as constant variables in other programming languages. In early Java versions (introduced in Java 1.1) we were allowed to declare a final variable without initializing it, then we could initialize it in a later part of the program. In current versions of Java we must initialize the final variables when we declare them, otherwise we will get errors at compile time. Final variables can not be modified after they are created.

The following is a simple implementation of final variables. In the final methods section below, we will have more challenging examples of final variables.

```
/*
  Author   : Michael Robinson
  Program  : finalStatic.java
  Purpose  : To present the final data type
             once they are declared and a value is assigned
             its value can not be changed

  Updated : May 1, 2099
*/


public class finalStatic
{
    public static final double  MONTHLY_RENT = 950;
    public static final Integer YEARS_LEASED = 30;


    public static void changeLeaseTime( int x )
    {

        try
        {

            YEARS_LEASED = YEARS_LEASED * 1;

        }
        catch( Exception e )
        {

            System.out.println( "YEARS_LEASED is a final variable" +
                                " and can NOT be changed" );
        }


    }//end public static void changeLeaseTime( int x )



    public static void main( String arg[] )
```

```
    {
        System.out.printf( "Montlhy Rent    %.2f\n", MONTHLY_RENT );
        System.out.printf( "Years Leased    %d\n",    YEARS_LEASED );

        System.out.printf( "Total Rent Income :   %.2f \n",
                            ( MONTHLY_RENT * YEARS_LEASED * 12 ) );


        changeLeaseTime( YEARS_LEASED );

    }//end public static void main( String arg[] )

}//end public class finalStatic
```

Your output (results) will look like this:

```
finalStatic.java:22: error: cannot assign a value to final variable YEARS_
LEASED


            YEARS_LEASED = YEARS_LEASED * 1;
            ^
1 error
```

Let's examine this code:

This is how we declare and initialize our final variables:

```
    public static final double   MONTHLY_RENT = 950;
    public static final Integer  YEARS_LEASED = 30;
```

The above error in the "Your output (results) will look like this" paragraph is caused when we try to compile the program by this line of code that tries to change the value of final YEARS_LEASED variable:

```
        YEARS_LEASED = YEARS_LEASED * 1;
```

toString

toString is a Java build-in method which is easy to implement, modify, and it is very useful. The toString method allows us to create an object's string representation.

Here we create a calling program named the_toStringCaller.java, which uses the external class named the-ToStringExternalClass.java that has its own toString method which overrides the Java build-in toString method.

```
/*
  Author  : Michael Robinson
  Program : the_toStringCaller.java
  Purpose : Here we learn to use the Java toString method
            toString is very easy to implement and very useful

  Updated : August 18, 2099
*/



public class the_toStringCaller
{

    public static void main( String arg[] )
    {
        //We create a class called theToStringExternalClass.java
        //in it we have a method called toString() to be used by this
        //program in several ways:

        //First we create an object of class theToStringExternalClass
        //named toStringObj (this class is our own external class)
        theToStringExternalClass toStringObj =
                    new theToStringExternalClass( 8, 3, 2099 );

        //then we can use our toStringObj object as follows:
        System.out.println( "I am using the object's toString" +
                    " method : " + toStringObj );

        //or we can also use it as follows:
        System.out.println( "I am using the object's toString" +
                    " method : " + toStringObj.toString() );

    }//end public static void main( String arg[] )

}//end public class the_toStringCaller
```

Let's examine this code:

toStringObj is an object in our own theToStringExternalClass class. I like to look at objects of a class as clones of a class because they are an exact copy/clone of the original class. Being that the case, our toStringObj clone contains all the functionality of our original class, therefore toStringObj.toString() uses the toString() method in our own theToStringExternalClass class, presented below. Please follow the rest of the documentation in the above program, it is very clear.

The following program creates our class theToStringExternalClass which is being called by the previous program.

```java
/*
  Author  : Michael Robinson
  Program : theToStringExternalClass.java
  Purpose : Learning to use the toString Java method

  Updated : August 18, 2099
*/


public class theToStringExternalClass
{

     private int day;    //this is a global private variable
     private int month;  //this is a global private variable
     private int year;   //this is a global private variable


     public theToStringExternalClass( int d, int m, int y )
     {
          day   = d; //the value of d is assigned to day
          month = m; //the value of m is assigned to month
          year  = y; //the value of y is assigned to year

          //when using the 'this' command below (references the current
          //object) it calls the following toString method
          System.out.println( "The data received by the constructor" +
                          " is : " + this );

     }//end public theToStringExternalClass( int d, int m, int y )


     /*
```

```
    If the toString method is not declared in the class that is
    using the 'this' command to print, Java will NOT give an
    error but it will print the name of the class and its address
*/


public String toString()
{
    //the return can be in any format you want
    return String.format( "%d/%d/%d",  year, month, day );

}//end public String toString()

}//end public class theToStringExternalClass
```

Let's examine this code:

There are several lines of code which were not explained in the previous program, but will be implemented and explained in detail in the coming section. Notice that theToStringExternalClass is the name of the above class and also there is a method with the same name. We will see this in detail in the Constructors section coming after this section, in this chapter.

To execute our external class (theToStringExternalClass), and the previous caller program (the_toString-Caller.java) we need to execute the following compilation process:

Compile the caller program, this process will also compile the external class:

```
javac the_toStringCaller.java
```

Execute the caller program, this process will also execute the external class:

```
java the_toStringCaller
```

Your output (results) will look like this:

```
The data received by the constructor is : 2099/3/8

I am using the object's toString method : 2099/3/8

I am using the object's toString method : 2099/3/8
```

What is 'this'?

The Java 'this' keyword is very useful, and it helps us identify if a variable is of global or local scope. We are going to use it in all the new programs when necessary.

It has many uses allowing us to clarify which variables or objects we are referring to. It sounds complicated but as we start using it, we will see how easy it is to implement it.

In the following program, in the main method, we create an instance of its own class/program named test1. In this section we use local and global variables. Please refer to Chapter 4 for their definition.

```
/*
  Author   : Michael Robinson
  Program  : theThis.java
  Purpose  : To show how to use the "this" command
             to select global and local variables

  Updated  : August 18th, 2099
*/



public class theThis
{

    private int number   = 5;
    private String name   = "Harold";
    private String major = "Computer Science";



    //method test2 accepts variables that have the same name as the
    //above global variables.
    public void test2( int number, String name, String major )
    {
        //the variables with the this command prior to its name is
        //referring to the global variable. The variable without
        //the this command is the local variable accepted by this
        //method.
        System.out.println( this.number + " is not the same as " +
                            number);

        System.out.println( this.name   + " is not the same as " +
                            name);

        System.out.println( this.major  + " is not the same as " +
                            major);
```

```
            System.out.println( "The 'this' variables refer to the" +
                                  " class global variables." );

    }//end public void test2( int number, String name, String major )


    public void test1()
    {
        int number = 4;

        System.out.println( "Local: " + number );
        System.out.println( "Global: " + this.number );

        test2( 22, "Joe", "Computer Engineering" );

    }//end public void test1()


    public static void main( String arg[] )
    {
        //creates an instance of this class/program
        //and calls the test2 method
        new theThis().test1();

    }//end public static void main( String arg[] )

}//end public class theThis
```

Let's examine this code:

This program is highly documented, every line of code is documented in great detail. Please review this program line by line. Also I encourage you to modify the code to see what happens when you change the values. Programming is like driving a car, you can not just read about it, you need to do it.

Your output (results) will look like this:

```
Local: 4
Global: 5
5 is not the same as 22
Harold is not the same as Joe
Computer Science is not the same as Computer Engineering
The 'this' variables refer to the class global variables.
```

What is a Constructor?

A constructor is a class that contains methods with the same names as the class and accepts data with different signatures. Signatures are the data types and variables that are accepted by the methods.

Up to now we have been using classes provided to us by Java, now we are going to learn how to create our own classes using constructors.

Constructors create objects, also called an instance of a class. I also refer to them as clones because every object is an exact clone of its class.

Java names all of its classes using a capital letter at the first character, see examples below, I recommend to follow this custom. However if you place a lowercase letter at the first character of your homemade classes name, Java will NOT complain, but it will be very difficult to differentiate a class from a regular program by its name.

These are examples of some of the Java classes we have used so far.

```
Class                 Object            Data for the Constructor

String                str       = new String( "Hello" );

File                  myFile    = new File( "1200.dna" );

Scanner               keyBoard  = new Scanner( System.in );

FileWriter            customers = new FileWriter( "customers.txt" );

PrintWriter           output    = new PrintWriter( customers );

FileReader            customers = new FileReader( "customers.txt" );

BufferedReader        inputFile = new BufferedReader( customers );

DecimalFormat         moneyFormat = new DecimalFormat( "$ #,###.000" );

ArrayList<String>     arrayList  = new ArrayList<String>();
```

Just like in the above examples we can create our own classes, but in addition we can create classes that accept multiple parameters. For instance, if we create a class called building, which calculates the square area of a room, we can create it so that it can accept different amounts of fields/values, and different data types, e.g.:

```
Building room0 = new Building();          //no variables passed
Building room1 = new Building( 40, 20 );   //pass two ints
Building room2 = new Building( 40.5, 20 ); //pass one double one int
Building room3 = new Building( 4, 20.7 );  //pass one int one double
Building room4 = new Building( 40.5, 19.5 ); //pass two doubles
```

Simple Constructors

Simple constructors have four sections:

1. The global variables
2. The constructors
3. The mutators or setters methods

   Mutator methods are usually named "setSomething," and are used to receive variables from the calling program and assign them to the global variables.

4. The accessors or getters methods

   Accessors methods are usually named "getSomething," and are used to return the global values to the calling program.

So before we can create objects/instance of a class, we need to create the class. The following program is a simple example:

```
/*
  Author  : Michael Robinson modified from book
  Program : Building.java
  Purpose : To present Classes and Objects
            An object is an instance of a class, a clone of a class.
            An object contains methods and data called object's
            fields. Objects are not stand alone programs and can be
            re-used like methods.

  Updated : July 24, 2099
*/



public class Building
{

    private double length; //creates global variable
    private double width;  //creates global variable


    //this first constructor does no accept parameters
    public Building()
    {
        length = 15;
        width  = 15;
    }
```

```java
//this constructor accepts two ints
public Building( int len, int w )
{
    length = len;   //len gets assigned to length
    width  = w;     //w gets assigned to width
}



//this constructor accepts one double and one int
public Building( double length, int width )
{
    //local length gets assigned to the global length
    this.length = length;

    //local width gets assigned to the global width
    this.width  = width;
}



//this constructor accepts one int and one double
public Building( int len, double w )
{
    //local len gets assigned to the global length
    length = len;

    //local w gets assigned to the global width
    width  = w;
}



//this constructor accepts two doubles
public Building( double len, double w )
{
    //local len gets assigned to the global length
    length = len;

    //local w gets assigned to the global width
    width  = w;
}



//Mutators (sets) *************************************
//The setLength method stores a value in the length field.
public void setLength( double len )
```

```
    {
        //local len gets assigned to the global length
        length = len;
    }



    //The setWidth method stores a value in the width field.
    public void setWidth( double w )
    {
        //local w gets assigned to the global width
        width = w;
    }



    //Accessors (gets) ****************************************
    //The getLength method returns a Rectangle object's length.
    public double getLength()
    {
        //return the value of the global length
        return length;
    }



    //The getWidth method returns a Rectangle object's width.
    public double getWidth()
    {
        //return the value of the global width
        return width;
    }



    //The getArea method returns a Rectangle object's area.
    public double getArea()
    {
        //returns the product of length*width.
        return length * width;
    }


}//end public class Building
```

The above program has the following constructors:

```
public Building()

public Building( int len, int w )

public Building( double len, int w )

public Building( int len, double w )

public Building( double len, double w )
```

As we can see, we have created five different types of objects, each receiving different data types.

In addition to standard Java methods such as: equals(), getClass(), hashCode(), notify(), etc., the above constructors will inherit/have access to the following local methods:

```
//Mutators (sets) ****************************************

//change the value of len
public void setLength( double len )

//change the value of w
public void setWidth( double w )


//Accessors (gets) ****************************************

//get the Length value
public double getLength()

//get the Width value
public double getWidth()

//get the Area value
public double getArea()
```

We can have any amount of constructors and methods in each class.

If we compile the above class we will get the following error:

Error: Main method not found in class Building, please define the main method as:

    public static void main(String[] args)

The reason is because this is an external class to be used by other programs and it does not have a main(String args[]) method.

Now we need a program that can make use of our Building.java external class. Here is a small example:

```
/*
  Author  : Michael Robinson
  Program : buildingSamples.java
  Purpose : To present Classes and Objects
            This program create five different objects from
            out own constructor, each object corresponds to
            a different constructor that received different
            data types.

  Updated : December 23, 2099
*/


public class buildingSamples
{

    //this section creates five global objects with different data
    //types no variables passed
    public static Building room0 = new Building();


    //pass two ints
    public static Building room1 = new Building( 40, 20 );


    //pass one double one int
    public static Building room2 = new Building( 40.5, 20 );
```

```java
//pass one int one double
public static Building room3 = new Building( 40, 20.7 );



//pass two doubles
public static Building room4 = new Building( 40.5, 19.5 );



public static void doAccessors()
{
    //these sections obtain the len, width and area of all rooms
    //(objects)

    //Accessors (gets) ****************************************
    System.out.printf( "\nRoom0\n" );

    //display room0's Length
    System.out.printf( "Room0's length is %.2f\n",
                    room0.getLength() );

    //display room0's Width
    System.out.printf( "Room0's width  is %.2f\n",
                    room0.getWidth() );

    //display room0's Area
    System.out.printf( "Room0's area   is %.2f\n",
                    room0.getArea() );

    //display room1's Length
    System.out.printf( "\nRoom1\n" );
    System.out.printf( "Room1's length is %.2f\n",
                    room1.getLength() );


    //display room1's Width
    System.out.printf( "Room1's width  is %.2f\n",
                    room1.getWidth() );

    //display room1's Area
    System.out.printf( "Room1's area   is %.2f\n",
                    room1.getArea() );

    //display room2's Length
    System.out.printf( "\nRoom2\n" );
```

```
        System.out.printf( "Room2's length is %.2f\n",
                        room2.getLength() );

        //display room1's Width
        System.out.printf( "Room2's width  is %.2f\n",
                        room2.getWidth() );

        //display room1's Area
        System.out.printf( "Room2's area   is %.2f\n",
                        room2.getArea() );

        //display room3's Length
        System.out.printf( "\nRoom3\n" );
        System.out.printf( "Room3's length is %.2f\n",
                        room3.getLength() );

        //display room3's Width
        System.out.printf( "Room3's width  is %.2f\n",
                        room3.getWidth() );

        //display room3's Area
        System.out.printf( "Room3's area   is %.2f\n",
                        room3.getArea() );


        //display room4's Length
        System.out.printf( "\nRoom4\n" );
        System.out.printf( "Room4's length is %.2f\n",
                        room4.getLength() );

        //display room4's Width
        System.out.printf( "Room4's width  is %.2f\n",
                        room4.getWidth() );

        //display room4's Area
        System.out.printf( "Room4's area   is %.2f\n",
                        room4.getArea() );

    }//end public static void doAccessors()


    public static void doMutators()
    {
```

```java
        System.out.println( "\nChanging measurements in the new" +
                            " Building..." );

        //now we change measurements in each room (object)

        //mutators (setters)  ***************************************
        room1.setLength( 10 );
        room1.setWidth( 4 );

        room2.setLength( 10.9 );
        room2.setWidth( 7 );

        room3.setLength( 8 );
        room3.setWidth( 14.4 );

        room4.setLength( 10.2 );
        room4.setWidth( 40.1 );

    }//end public static void doMutators()


    public static void main( String arg[] )
    {

        System.out.println( "Finding measurements in the new" +
                            " Building" );

        doAccessors();

        doMutators();

        doAccessors();

    }//end public static void main( String arg[] )

}//end public class buildingSamples
```

Your output (results) will look like this:

```
Finding measurements in the new Building

Room0
Room0's length is 15.00
Room0's width  is 15.00
Room0's area   is 225.00

Room1
Room1's length is 40.00
Room1's width  is 20.00
Room1's area   is 800.00

Room2
Room2's length is 40.50
Room2's width  is 20.00
Room2's area   is 810.00

Room3
Room3's length is 40.00
Room3's width  is 20.70
Room3's area   is 828.00

Room4
Room4's length is 40.50
Room4's width  is 19.50
Room4's area   is 789.75


Changing measurements in the new Building...

Room0
Room0's length is 15.00
Room0's width  is 15.00
Room0's area   is 225.00

Room1
Room1's length is 10.00
Room1's width  is 4.00
Room1's area   is 40.00
```

```
Room2
Room2's length is 10.90
Room2's width  is 7.00
Room2's area   is 76.30

Room3
Room3's length is 8.00
Room3's width  is 14.40
Room3's area   is 115.20

Room4
Room4's length is 10.20
Room4's width  is 40.10
Room4's area   is 409.02
```

Let's examine this code:

As we can see the constructor Building.java that we created above can be used by any program at any location. This class actually has five build-in constructors accepting different sets of data types. We can also build classes that will accept multiple amounts of data types. Think of the class System.out.prinf, how many variations does it have? I do not know, but it would be interesting to study its source code.

Notice that our constructor Building.java does not have the main method, however the calling program buildingSamples being a regular program does have the main method.

In Chapter 12 we will learn to build the bubble sort. We implemented it using constructors that accept arrays of ints and arrays of strings.

What is a Variable-Length Argument List in Methods?

A variable-length argument list passes multiple amount, of data items, usually used in for loops when we need to process records from a file where each record has different amounts of fields or items, e.g.,

```
2,74,6,8,5,60
2,74
2,74,6,8
2,74,6,8,5
2,74,6
```

Here we need to pass each record to a method that adds those items so that we can then obtain an average value. With our current knowledge we would have to create a method for each record passed, based on its amount of fields. However, Java has implemented a way where we only need one method to process the entire file, regardless of the amount of items/fields per record in the file. This is called variable-length argument lists.

The data received by these methods must be of the same type, it could be ints, floats, String, etc, but again, each group must be of the same data type.

The following program shows in detail how to implement this very useful tool.

Notice that the variable that is accepted by the method is automatically converted to a single dimension array. To access each value follow the single dimension array rules. Also notice that to access each value, we can use regular for loops, while loops or enhanced for loop.

```java
/*
  Author  : Michael Robinson
  Program : varLenArgumentsClass.java
  Purpose : To call a method passing VARIABLE AMOUNT OF PARAMETERS.
            Notice that the variable that is accepted by the method
            is automatically converted to an array, so that to access
            each value follow the single dimension array rules.
            To access each value we can use regular for loops, while
            loops or the enhanced for loop.

  Updated : April 6th, 2099
*/


import java.util.*;


public class varLenArgumentsClass
{

    /* Anytime we need to accept variables, and we do not know how
       many are going to be passed we use ( int ... variableName ),
       the three .'s mean that the amount of items we are passing
       could be any amount of unknown ints */


    public static int getIntAverage( int ... numbers )
    {
```

```java
    int total   = 0;
    int counter = 0;

    //accessing and displaying the items passed
    //using the enhanced for loop
    for( int x : numbers )
    {
        System.out.print( x );

        if( counter < numbers.length - 1 )
        {
            System.out.print( " + " );
            counter++;
        }

        total += x;

    }

    System.out.printf( " = %d ", total );

    //return the average value
    return ( total / numbers.length );

}//end public static int getIntAverage( int... numbers )


//accepts unknown amount of floats
public static float getFloatAverage( float ... numbers )
{

    float total = 0;
    int counter = 0;


    //accessing and displaying the items passed
    for( int x = 0; x < numbers.length; x++ )
    {
        System.out.printf( "%.2f" , numbers[x] );

        if( counter < numbers.length - 1 )
        {
            System.out.print( " + " );
            counter++;
```

```java
        }

        total+=x;

    }

    System.out.printf( " = %.2f ", total );


    //return the average value
    return ( total / numbers.length );

}//end public static float getFloatAverage( float... numbers )
 //accepts unknown amount of Strings


public static void printNames( String ... theStrings )
{

    int x = 0;

    //accessing the items passed
    //using a while loop
    while( x < theStrings.length )
    {

        System.out.print( theStrings[x] + " " );
        x++;

    }

    System.out.println( "" );

}//end public static void printNames( String... theStrings )



//************ special data type  ***************
//The Object data type (notice Object with capital O), accepts
//data of all data types such as int, float, double, String, etc
//This method accepts unknown amount of Objects
public static void passingObjects( Object ... args )
{
```

```java
        System.out.println( "\n You have passed in " + args.length +
                            " arguments " );

        for( Object o : args )
        {
            System.out.println( "    " + o );
        }

        System.out.println();

    }//end public static void passingObjects(Object ... args)


    public static ArrayList<Object> ArrayListOfObjects()
    {
        //create ArrayList of Objects named ArrayLobjects
        ArrayList<Object> ArrayLobjects = new ArrayList<Object>();

        //create four wrappers of type Integer
        Integer integer1 = new Integer( 3 );
        Integer integer2 = new Integer( 7 );
        Integer integer3 = new Integer( 11 );
        Integer integer4 = new Integer( 23 );

        //create a variable of data type String
        String food1 = "Tuna Salad";

        //call method passing ArrayList Objects named ArrayLobjects
        ArrayListOfObjectsResults( ArrayLobjects );

        //add two Integer wrapper and one String to the ArrayList
        //ArrayLobjects
        ArrayLobjects.add( integer1 );
        ArrayLobjects.add( integer2 );
        ArrayLobjects.add( food1 );

        //Again call method passing ArrayList of Objects named
        //ArrayLobjects
        ArrayListOfObjectsResults( ArrayLobjects );

        //add four Integer wrappers to the ArrayList
        ArrayLobjects.add( integer1 );
        ArrayLobjects.add( integer2 );
        ArrayLobjects.add( integer3 );
        ArrayLobjects.add( integer4 );
```

```
        //create a new wrapper called integer5
        Integer integer5 = new Integer( 99 );

        //add integer5 wrappers to the ArrayList ArrayLobjects
        ArrayLobjects.add( integer5 );

        //Again call method passing ArrayList of Objects named
        //ArrayLobjects
        ArrayListOfObjectsResults( ArrayLobjects );

        //remove index 3 from the ArrayLobjects
        System.out.printf( "Removing value %s",
                        ArrayLobjects.get( 2 ) + "\n" );

        ArrayLobjects.remove( 2 );

        //copying contents of ArrayLobjects to ArrayLobjects_clone
        System.out.println(
            "Creating ArrayLobjects_clone from ArrayLobjects" );

        Object ArrayLobjects_clone = ArrayLobjects.clone();

        System.out.println( "The clone contains:     " +
                        ArrayLobjects_clone );

        //Again call method passing ArrayList of Objects named
        //ArrayLobjects
        ArrayListOfObjectsResults( ArrayLobjects );

        //returns ArrayLobjects to calling method
        return( ArrayLobjects );

}//end of public static ArrayList ArrayListOfObjects()


public static void ArrayListOfObjectsResults(
                ArrayList<Object> ArrayLobjects )
{

    System.out.println( "ArrayLobjects contains: " +
                    ArrayLobjects);

    System.out.println( "ArrayLobjects size: " +
                    ArrayLobjects.size() + "\n" );
```

```java
}//end of public static void ArrayListOfObjectsResults( ArrayList
//ArrayLobjects)


public static void main( String arg[] )
{

    System.out.println( "\nProcessing ints" );

    //calling getIntAverage() method passing different parameters
    System.out.println( "[  The Average is : " +
                    getIntAverage( 2, 74, 6, 8, 5, 60 ) +
                    "  ]" );

    System.out.println( "[  The Average is : " +
                    getIntAverage( 2, 74, 6, 8, 5 ) +
                    "  ]" );

    System.out.println( "[  The Average is : " +
                    getIntAverage( 2, 74, 6, 8 ) +
                    "  ]" );

    System.out.println( "[  The Average is : " +
                    getIntAverage( 2, 74, 6 ) +
                    "  ]" );

    System.out.println( "[  The Average is : " +
                    getIntAverage( 2, 74 ) + "  ]" );

    System.out.println( "\nProcessing Strings" );


    //calling printNames() method passing different parameters
    printNames( "Pilar", "Mariana", "Mark", "Daniel", "Ivan",
            "Ana Milena", "Sebastian", "Blanca", "Michael");

    printNames( "Pilar", "Ana Milena", "Mariana", "Mark","Ivan",
            "Sebastian", "Daniel", "Blanca" );

    printNames( "Pilar", "Ana Milena", "Mariana", "Mark",
            "Daniel", "Sebastian", "Ivan" );

    printNames( "Pilar", "Ana Milena", "Mariana", "Mark",
            "Daniel","Sebastian" );
```

```
        printNames( "Pilar", "Ana Milena", "Mariana","Mark",
                    "Daniel" );

        System.out.printf( "\n\nProcessing floats\n" );


        //calling getFloatAverage() method passing different
        //parameters
        System.out.printf( "[The Average is : %.2f ]\n",
                        getFloatAverage( 2, 74, 6, 8, 5, 60 ) );

        System.out.printf( "\t  [The Average is : %.2f ]\n",
                        getFloatAverage( 2, 74, 6, 8, 5 )  );

        System.out.printf( "\t\t  [The Average is : %.2f ]\n",
                        getFloatAverage( 2, 74, 6, 8 )  );

        System.out.printf( "\t\t\t  [The Average is : %.2f ]\n",
                        getFloatAverage( 2, 74, 6 )  );

        System.out.printf( "\t\t\t\t  [The Average is : %.2f ]\n",
                        getFloatAverage( 2, 74 )  );

        System.out.println( "\n\nProcessing Objects" );


        //calling passingObjects method passing different parameters
        passingObjects( "This is very interesting..." );

        passingObjects( "very", "flexible", "topic" );

        passingObjects( 5, 3, 7 );

        passingObjects( 5.1, 3, 7, "I can't believe this" );


        //create an ArrayList of Objects
        ArrayList<Object> result = ArrayListOfObjects();

        System.out.println( "The ArrayList of Object = " + result );

    }//end of public static void main( String arg[] )

}//end of public class varLenArgumentsClass
```

Your output (results) will look like this:

```
Processing ints

2 + 74 + 6 + 8 + 5 + 60 = 155 [  The Average is : 25  ]
2 + 74 + 6 + 8 + 5 = 95 [  The Average is : 19  ]
2 + 74 + 6 + 8 = 90 [  The Average is : 22  ]
2 + 74 + 6 = 82 [  The Average is : 27  ]
2 + 74 = 76 [  The Average is : 38  ]


Processing Strings
Pilar Mariana Mark Daniel Ivan Ana Milena Sebastian Blanca Michael
Pilar Ana Milena Mariana Mark Ivan Sebastian Daniel Blanca
Pilar Ana Milena Mariana Mark Daniel Sebastian Ivan
Pilar Ana Milena Mariana Mark Daniel Sebastian
Pilar Ana Milena Mariana Mark Daniel


Processing floats
2.00 + 74.00 + 6.00 + 8.00 + 5.00 + 60.00 = 15.00 [The Average is :
2.50 ]
2.00 + 74.00 + 6.00 + 8.00 + 5.00 = 10.00 [The Average is : 2.00 ]
2.00 + 74.00 + 6.00 + 8.00 = 6.00           [The Average is : 1.50 ]
2.00 + 74.00 + 6.00 = 3.00               [The Average is : 1.00 ]
2.00 + 74.00 = 1.00                      [The Average is : 0.50 ]


Processing Objects

 You have passed in 1 arguments
   This is very interesting...

 You have passed in 3 arguments
   very
   flexible
   topic

 You have passed in 3 arguments
   5
   3
   7
```

```
You have passed in 4 arguments
   5.1
   3
   7
   I can't believe this

ArrayLobjects contains: []
ArrayLobjects size: 0

ArrayLobjects contains: [3, 7, Tuna Salad]
ArrayLobjects size: 3
ArrayLobjects contains: [3, 7, Tuna Salad, 3, 7, 11, 23, 99]
ArrayLobjects size: 8

Removing value Tuna Salad
Creating ArrayLobjects_clone from ArrayLobjects
The clone contains:    [3, 7, 3, 7, 11, 23, 99]
ArrayLobjects contains: [3, 7, 3, 7, 11, 23, 99]
ArrayLobjects size: 7

The ArrayList of Object = [3, 7, 3, 7, 11, 23, 99]
```

Let's examine this code:

```
//method that accepts a Variable Length List of int
public static int getIntAverage( int ... numbers )

//method that accepts a Variable Length List of float
public static float getFloatAverage( float ... numbers )

//method that accepts a Variable Length List of String
public static void printNames( String ... theStrings )
```

The above methods accept unknown amounts of fields therefore these methods can be re-used by any other method, as many times as needed, accepting any amount of items. The only restriction is that the data being passed and received must be of the same data type, e.g. int, float, char, string, arrays, wrappers, etc.

This works because the data being received is accepted by a list variable which is similar to an endless single dimension array, of course this is just a visual representation, lists and arrays have differences. I know this could be confusing because we are used to declaring arrays with the [ ] brackets and in this form the [] brackets are missing.

To process these data items we can use any of the methods used to process arrays such as for, while or enhanced for loops.

In this program, the following method is very special because we are covering a topic that is confusing to some students:

Object Data Types

The Object data type (notice Object with capital O), accepts data of all data types such as int, float, double, string, etc. We can use Object data types in data structures that require data types of only one type such as int, float, double, string, such as arrays and arrayLists. The reason is that the data inside variables of Object data types are exactly that, data of Object data type, therefore Java sees them as one data type. Notice that the name object (with lowercase o) is the name given to objects of a class, also known as instance of a class and clones (this name is used by me) are totally different to Object data types.

The following program shows the implementation of the Object data type:

```
/*
  Author  : Michael Robinson
  Program : theObjectDataType.java
  Purpose : To show the Object data type
            passing multi data type variables to a method that
            accepts and displays them as Object data types and uses
            the Variable Length List and enhanced for loop to process
            them

  Updated : December 23, 2099
*/


public class theObjectDataType
{

    //***************** Object special data type *****************
    //The Object data type (notice Object with capital O), accepts  *
    //all data data types such as int, float, double, String, etc.  *
    //This method accepts unknown amount of Objects                  *
    //***************************************************************

    public static void passingObjects( Object ... args )
    {
```

```java
        System.out.println( " You have passed in " + args.length +
                            " arguments " );

        for( Object o : args )
        {
            System.out.println( "    " + o );
        }

    }//end public static void passingObjects(Object ... args)


    public static void main( String arg[] )
    {
        //calling method passingObjects passing 4 multi data types
        passingObjects( "one", 1, 2.30, "last" );

        //calling method passingObjects passing 5 multi data types
        passingObjects( "hello", 0.23, -2, "bye", 77 );

        //calling method passingObjects passing 6 multi data types
        passingObjects( 99, "one", 6.3210, "nice", 123, -0 );

    }//end public static void main( String arg[] )

}//end public class theObjectDataType
```

Your output (results) will look like this:

```
You have passed in 4 arguments
    one
    1
    2.3
    last

 You have passed in 5 arguments
    hello
    0.23
    -2
    bye
    77

 You have passed in 6 arguments
    99
```

```
one
6.321
nice
123
0
```

Let's examine this code:

When we learned arrays, arrays list and loops, we always studied examples using one single data type. In arrays we learned that two of the shortcomings of arrays are that once arrays are created we can no longer change their size and that all data must be of the same type. Well as we can see using the Object data type, we can have arrays with multiple data types, as far as changing their size, in the array list chapter (Chapter 8), we learned how to expand and reduce the array's size.

This program is highly documented, every line of code is documented in great detail. Please review program line by line. Also I encourage you to modify the code to see what happens when you change the values. Programming is like driving a car, you can not just read about it, you need to do it.

What is the Meaning of main(String arg[])?

Since the beginning of this class we have been using the main method:

```
public static void main( String arg[] )
```

but we have not mentioned what the purpose is of the (String arg[]) in the main method. Well it is similar to the (int ... variable) in the variable-length argument lists methods.

The String arg[] inside the main method is simply a single dimensional array arg of String data type which will accept any amount of items from another program or from the command line. For instance, you have a program written in C which produced multiple output values and it needs the Java program to accept and use these variables in a specific process. So, what we need to do is call the Java program passing these variables to it, and the Java program using the main method will accept them.

The following is a program example when using the command line with the following Java program, will give us an example:

```
/*
  Author  : Michael Robinson
  Program : mainMethod.java
  Purpose : To show how the main( String arg[] ) method works
            To compile enter: javac mainString.java
```

```
            To run enter:     java  mainString  Hello World
            This passes two strings to main, Hello and World

  Updated : April 6th, 2099
*/


import java.util.*;


public class mainMethod
{

    public static void main( String arg[] )
    {
        for( int x = 0; x < arg.length; x++ )
        {
            System.out.print( " [" + arg[x] + "]" );
        }

        System.out.println();

    }//end public static void main( String arg[] )

}//end public class mainString
```

Use this terminal mode command to compile the following program:

```
javac mainMethod.java
```

The following line of code runs the above compiled program passing Hello World to the main method, as follows:

```
java mainMethod Hello World
```

Your output (results) will look like this:

```
[Hello] [World]
```

Let's examine this code:

Remember since String arg[] is an array of string data type of an undefined length, it will accept just about any input. Please review the code in the above program, it is very simple and self-explanatory.

Summary

In this chapter we covered several very important concepts.

External classes is how classes are created in Java providing a lot of flexibility in their developing and implementation. These classes are called/used by other programs.

Final variables allows us to create variables which can be accessed and used but they can not be modified, their initial value is final.

toString is a build-in Java method that allows us to do an object's string representation. This method can be customize by overriding it. We will learn about overriding in later chapters.

this helps us identify if a variable is global or local.

Constructors are classes that contain multiple methods with the same name as the class, each method accepting/or not, different variable names with different data types. Constructors use global variables and they must have a Mutators/Setters and a Accessors/Getters methods that accept changes for the variables values and allows access to those values by other programs. This is a constructor example:

```
public class Building
{
    //constructor does no accept parameters
    public Building() { }

    //constructor accepts two ints
    public Building( int len, int w ){ }

    //constructor accepts one double and one int
    public Building( double length, int width ) { }

    public static void doAccessors() { }

    public static void doMutators()  { }

    public static void main( String arg[] )  { }
}
```

Variable-length argument list is a very useful way of passing lists of variables of multiple lengths. We provide examples on how to use them in for loops.

Object data types allow us to create data structures with multiple data types, such as arrays and arraylists. We also showed programs that combine the above topics, making them very powerful and useful.

Key Terms

Records. What is a Record?	In Chapter 6: Data Structures – Arrays, we learned what arrays are.
	We can say that a text file with one record is a single dimensional array, and that a text file with more than one record is a two dimensional array. In other words, a record is a line of text in a data structure such as a file or an array.
	Records such as: Joe Smith CS are composed of the following segments: Joe, Smith, and CS. Each of these segments are called fields and each field is given a unique name. The field name for Joe could be First Name, for Smith Last Name, and for CS could be School.
	Records are separated (delimited) in many different forms, for instance spreadsheets use the tab symbol to delimit their fields, the above record example (Joe Smith CS) is delimited by the space symbol.
	A file can contain thousands of records, and a record can contain thousands of fields. It is limited by the type of data structure, the operating system, and the Java file management class we use.
	With today's technologies we have text files that can contain terabytes of records, therefore is very important to select the appropriate file class for the job. Java has multiple classes that we can use to work with files.
	In this chapter we are presenting the following file classes: FileWriter, PrintWriter, FileReader, BufferedReader, File, Scanner, FileInputStream, DataInputStream, Formatter, FileOutputStream and DataOutputStream, and my favorite one which allows us to process files larger than 2 gigabytes:

	BufferedWriter bw = new
	    BufferedWriter(new
	
	    FileWriter(filename));

Constructor. What is a Constructor?	A constructor is a class that contains methods with the same names as the class and accepts data with different signatures. Signatures are the data types and variables that are accepted by the methods.
	Up to now we have been using classes provided to us by Java, now we are going to learn how to create our own classes using constructors.
	Constructors create objects, also called an instance of a class. I also refer to them as clones because every object is an exact clone of its class.
	Java names all of its classes using a capital letter at the first character, see examples on page 250, I recommend to follow this custom, however, if you place a lower case letter at the first character of your homemade classes name, Java will NOT complain, but it will be very difficult to differentiate a class from a regular program by its name.
Contructors. Simple Constructors	Simple constructors have four sections:
	• The global variables
	• The constructors Methods with the same name as the class with unique signatures.
	• The mutators/setters methods Mutator methods are usually named "setSomething," and are used to receive variables from the calling program and assign them to the global variables.
	• The accessors/getters methods Accessors methods are usually named "getSomething," and are used to return the global values to the calling program.
	So before we can create objects/instance of aclass, we need to create the class, the Building.java program is a simple example.
Data Types. Object Data Types	The Object data type (notice Object with capital O), accepts data of all data types such as int, float, double, string, etc.
	We can use Object data types in data structures that accept data of only one type as int, float, double or string, such as arrays and arrayLists.
	The theObjectDataType.java program shows the implementation of the Object data type.

External Classes	Up to this moment we have worked under the assumption that all Java programs must have one "public static void main(String args[])" method.
	If we go back to all the programs we have written so far, we can see that the word "class" is on the headings of all our programs, therefore all our programs are "classes."
	We need to recognize that just like the Java classes that we used in our programs, such as string, scanner, etc., the programs we have written so far are also classes. They are classes that we wrote.
	Now it is time to learn how to create "external classes" which do NOT have the "public static void main(String args[])" method. These external classes only have variables and regular methods which can be used as additional classes, by any other program/class or external class. This means that we are extending the capabilities of the Java language by creating our own additional classes.
	External classes, just like methods, gives us three great benefits:
	• We can divide a large project into smaller pieces (divide and conquer).
	• When we have an error in a method, we can block that method allowing the rest of the project to continue working.
	• Re-use. This time any other class or method in our projects can re-use any method in any external class. We can also share our own external classes with other teams doing their own projects.
This. What is this?	The Java 'this' keyword is very useful, it helps us identify if a variable is of global or local scope. We are going to use it in all the new programs when necessary.
	It has many uses allowing us to clarify which variables or objects we are referring to. It sounds complicated but as we start using it, we will see how easy it is to implement it.
	In the This.java program, in the main method, we create an instance of its own class/program named test1. In this section we use local and global variables, please refer to Chapter 4 for their definition.
toString	toString is a Java build-in method which is easy to implement, modify, and it is very useful.
	Here we create a calling program named the_toStringCaller.java, which uses the external class named theToStringExternalClass.java that has its own toString method which overrides the Java build-in toString method.

Variables. **Final Variables**	Sometimes we need a variable to maintain its value throughout the project, making sure that even if its scope is global, its value is not be changed by any method. To do this process is very simple, all we need to do is to declare such variable as final: public final double interestRate = .25; Final variables are known as constant variables in other programming languages.
What is a **Variable-Length** **Argument List in** **Methods?**	A variable-length argument list passes multiple amount of data items, usually used in for loops, when we need to process records from a file where each record has different amounts of fields or items, e.g.: 2,74,6,8,5,60 2,74 2,74,6,8 2,74,6,8,5 2,74,6 Here we pass each record to a method that adds those items so that we can then obtain an average value. With our current knowledge we would have to create a method for each record passed, based on its amount of fields, however, Java has implemented a way where we only need one method to process the entire file, regardless of the amount of items/fields per record in the file. They are called variable-length argument lists. The data received by these methods must be of the same type, it could be ints, floats, string, etc., but again, each group must be of the same data type. Program varLenArgumentsClass.java shows in detail how to implement this very useful tool. Notice that the variable that is accepted by the method is automatically converted to a single dimension array. To access each value follow the single dimension array rules. Also notice that to access each value, we can use regular for loops, while loops, or enhanced for loop.

What is the Meaning of main(String arg[])?	Since the beginning of this class we have been using the main method: public static void main(String arg[]) but we have not mentioned what the purpose is of the (String arg[]) in the main method. Well it is similar to the (int ... variable) in the variable-length argument lists methods listed above. The String arg[] inside the main method is simply a single dimensional array arg of string data type which will accept any amount of items from another program or from the command line. For instance, you have a program written in C which produced multiple output values and it needs the Java program to accept and use these variables in a specific process. So, what we need to do is call the Java program passing these variables to it, and the Java program using the main method will accept them. The mainMethod.java is a program example of using the command line to pass data to a Java program.

Exercises

1. Create a program containing an external class with final variables.

2. Create a program that will use the previous external class using the this command.

3. Create a constructor program with getters, setters and two constructors inside.

4. Create a program that uses variable-length argument list in methods.

5. Create a program that uses Object data types and an object of class example.

Select all that apply for the following questions:

6. What is the difference between Object and object?
   a. There is no difference
   b. Object in Java does not exist, there is only object
   c. Object refers to an Object of a class
   d. Object is a data type and object is a clone of a class

7. What is a variable-length argument list
   a. A string that has multiple lengths
   b. A list that passes multiple amount of data items, usually used in for loops
   c. An ArrayList of Objects
   d. A list of global arguments used in constructors only

8. What is a constructor?
   a. A class that contains methods with the same names as the class and accepts data with different signatures
   b. A method that must have a return
   c. Classes that can not have a main method
   d. None of the above

9. What is the this command used for?
   a. Used to print variables of multiple length
   b. When you want to make sure to process this and not that variable
   c. To refer to local variables
   d. To refer to global variables

10. What is toString used for?
   a. A global variable
   b. A global variable which must be final
   c. A build-in Java method that allows us to do an object's string representation
   d. Does not exist

REFERENCES

- Java API Specifications
  http://www.oracle.com/technetwork/java/api-141528.html

- My Java programs that I use in my Java classes located at robinson.cs.fiu.edu

//END CHAPTER 10://EXTERNAL CLASSES, METHODS, THIS, CONSTRUCTORS

GUI
Simple
Applications

chapter
11

What is GUI (Graphical User Interface)?

In computer science the term GUI, usually pronounced gooey, is how users communicate with electronic machines such as monitors, cell phones, tablets, etc. using graphical images instead of text commands. For the user, the GUI usually makes the communication with the computer easier, simply point and click. The disadvantages are that the communication presented to the user is limited by the GUI's options.

Using non-GUI text commands to communicate with electronic machines allows the user total control of the machine.

What are Dialog Boxes?

In Graphical User Interface (GUI) programming we use dialog boxes to enable communication between the user and the program. In this chapter we are going to use two types of dialog boxes, message and input dialog boxes. In general, dialog boxes communicate information to the users, requesting a response from the users.

< 283 >

Message Dialog Boxes

These boxes usually contain a system icon, one or more buttons, and a short specific message.

Input Dialog Boxes

Input dialog boxes are used to interact with the user and retrieve information entered by the user. These boxes usually contain a system icon, multiple buttons, a short specific message, and a section where the user can input information.

These boxes stop the users from accessing other sections of the program before replying to the current dialog box.

All the information entered in the input dialog boxes is of string data type, regardless of what data was written in the input section.

Java provides the following methods to convert the data entered from string data type to the intended data type.

If the data entered is assigned to a variable called temp, it can be casted/converted as follows:

```
Integer  response = Integer.parseInt( temp );   //converts to Integer
Double   response = Double.parseDouble( temp );//converts to Double
Float    response = Float.parseFloat( temp );   //converts to Float
```

```
Long    response = Long.parseLong( temp );    //converts to Long
Short   response = Short.parseShort( temp );   //converts to Short
```

The following program will show us how to create dialog boxes.

```
/*
   Author   : Michael Robinson
   Program  : gui_1_dialogBoxes.java
   Purpose  : To present GUI dialog boxes
                - Message Dialog Boxes
                - Input Dialog Boxes

   Notes    : JOptionPane ALWAYS returns the input as STRING
              regardless of what was inputed

   Updated  : July 5th, 2099
*/


import javax.swing.JOptionPane;


public class gui_1_dialogBoxes
{

    //accepts input from user and returns it to caller
    public static String doInputBox( String question )
    {
        return( JOptionPane.showInputDialog( question ) );
    }


    //display message to users
    public static void doMessageBox( String message )
    {
        JOptionPane.showMessageDialog( null, message );
    }


    //accepts multiple variables of Object type, sort them
    //in descending order and return them as String data types
    public static String swap( Object ... numbers )
    {
```

```java
String array[] = new String[ 100 ];

int counter = 0;

String temp = "";


//processing all the Objects passed received
//using the enhanced for loop
for( Object x : numbers )
{
    array[ counter ] = x.toString();
    counter++;
}



//swap/sort array into descending order
if( array[ 0 ].compareTo(array[ 1 ]) > 0 )
{
    temp      = array[ 0 ];
    array[ 0 ] = array[ 1 ];
    array[ 1 ] = temp;
}

if( array[ 1 ].compareTo(array[ 2 ]) > 0 )
{
    temp      = array[ 1 ];
    array[ 1 ] = array[ 2 ];
    array[ 2 ] = temp;
}

if( array[ 0 ].compareTo(array[ 1 ]) > 0 )
{
    temp      = array[ 0 ];
    array[ 0 ] = array[ 1 ];
    array[ 1 ] = temp;
}


//JOptionPane ALWAYS returns the input as STRING regardless
//of what was inputed
return ( "Sorted :  " + array[ 0 ] + "  " + array[ 1 ] +
        "  " + array[ 2 ] );
```

```
}//end public static String swap( int ... numbers )


public static void main( String arg[] )
{
    doMessageBox( "Welcome, this is a Message Dialog Box..." );

    //assign the input from the method doInputBox
    //to the String fName
    String fName = doInputBox( "Enter your First Name" );


    //assign the input from the method doInputBox
    //to the String mName
    String mName = doInputBox( "Enter your Middle Name" );

    //assign the input from the method doInputBox
    //to the String lName
    String lName = doInputBox( "Enter your Last Name" );

    //call doMessageBox passing fName, mName and lName
    doMessageBox( "Nice to meet you\n" + fName + " " + mName +
                    " " + lName + "\nNow let's do some Sorting" );

    //assign the input from the method doInputBox
    //to the String fNum
    String fNum = ( doInputBox( "Enter First Object" ) );

    //assign the input from the method doInputBox
    //to the String sNum
    String sNum = ( doInputBox( "Enter Second Object" ) );

    //assign the input from the method doInputBox
    //to the String tNum
    String tNum = ( doInputBox( "Enter Third Object" ) );

    //call doMessageBox passing fName, fNum sNum tNum and
    //the result of calling swap method after also passing
    //the same fName, fNum sNum tNum and variables
    doMessageBox( "Objects Swap " + fName + "\n" + "Before :  " +
                    fNum + "  " + sNum + "  " + tNum +
                    "\n" + swap( fNum, sNum, tNum ) );
```

```
        System.exit(0);   //must use when using JOptionPane b/c it
                           //causes an additional task to run in the VM

   }//end public static void main( String arg[] )

}//end public static void main( String arg[] )
```

Your output (results) will look like this:

Notice that the line:

```
        public static void doMessageBox( String message )
```

Receives a string in the variable message.

The following line produces the message dialog box below

```
        JOptionPane.showMessageDialog( null, message );
```

The line

```
        String fName = doInputBox( "Enter your First Name" );
```

calls the following method passing a String that will appear in an input dialog box.

```
        public static String doInputBox( String question )
```

This method creates the input dialog box, requesting data from the user, accepts it, and returns it to the calling command above, as follows:

```
        return( JOptionPane.showInputDialog( question ) );
```

The following input dialog boxes used in this program are implemented as follows:

```
String fName = doInputBox( "Enter your First Name" );
```

```
String mName = doInputBox( "Enter your Middle Name" );
```

```
String lName = doInputBox( "Enter your Last Name" );
```

The data inputed by the user is then passed as follows:

```
doMessageBox( "Nice to meet you\n" + fName + " " + mName + " " +
              lName + "\nNow let's do some Sorting" );
```

to the following method:

```
public static void doMessageBox( String message )
{
    JOptionPane.showMessageDialog( null, message );
}
```

creates a message dialog box displaying the following results:

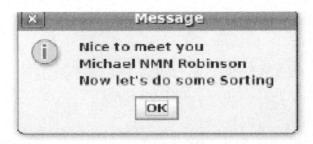

The following input dialog boxes will accept data of Object type using the following command:

```
String fNum = ( doInputBox( "Enter First Object" ) );
```

```
String sNum = ( doInputBox( "Enter Second Object" ) );
```

```
String tNum = ( doInputBox( "Enter Third Object" ) );
```

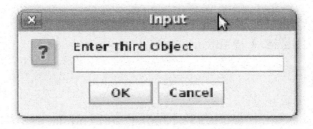

The data acquired by these input dialog boxes will be send to the following method:

```
public static String swap( Object ... numbers )
```

using the following command:

```
doMessageBox( "Objects Swap " + fName + "\n" + "Before :   " + fNum +
              "  " + sNum + "   " + tNum + "\n" +
           swap( fNum, sNum, tNum ) );
```

The swap method will sort its input in ascending order and return it to the calling command.

The original data and the sorted data will be displayed in a message dialog box.

Let's examine this code:

This program was highly documented, basically every line of code is documented in great detail. Please review program line by line.

What is a Frame?

In GUI programming, a frame is a window with a title and a border. GUI applications have at least one frame with button components that close, minimize or maximizes the window.

Creating a Frame

Creating a frame that is not full size is easier than a full size frame. When we execute a GUI program we expect a full screen. The following program will show how to create both.

Creating a Small Frame

```java
/*
  Author  : Michael Robinson
  Program : guiSmallFrame.java
  Purpose : To create a small GUI Frame

  Updated : July 5th, 2099
*/


import javax.swing.JFrame;


public class guiSmallFrame
{
    public static void createSmallFrame()
    {
        //create a frame also known as a window
        JFrame frame = new JFrame( "Small Frame" );
        frame.setVisible( true );
        frame.setSize( 400, 200 );
        frame.setDefaultCloseOperation( JFrame.EXIT_ON_CLOSE );

    }//end public static void createSmallFrame()


    public static void main( String arg[] )
    {
        createSmallFrame();

    }//end public static void main( String arg[] )

}//end public class guiSmallFrame
```

Your output (results) will look like this:

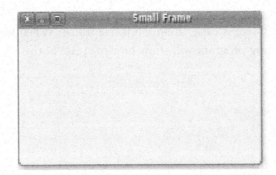

Let's examine this code:

We first need to import javax.swing.JFrame; to be able to access all the JFrame classes.

Using the JFrame class we create an object as follows:

```
JFrame frame = new JFrame( "Small Frame" );
```

The string inside the JFrame in this example "Small Frame" will appear on the top bar section of the frame.

```
frame.setVisible( true );
```

The previous line makes the Frame visible frame.setSize(400, 200);

creates a frame of size 400 by 200, you can set it to any size.

```
frame.setDefaultCloseOperation(JFrame.EXIT_ON_CLOSE);
```

when we press the X box on the bar the frame will close.

Creating a Full Size Frame

When we execute a GUI program we expect a full screen. The following program will show how to create one.

```
/*
  Author  : Michael Robinson
  Program : guiFullScreen.java
  Purpose : To create a full size GUI Frame

  Updated : July 5th, 2099
*/


import javax.swing.*;
import java.awt.Toolkit;
```

```java
public class guiFullScreen
{
    //private JFrame used on by this program
    private static JFrame frame;

    public static void createGuiFullScreen()
    {
        //create a new JFrame called frame
        frame = new JFrame( "Full Screen" );

        //create Toolkit tk class which allows
        //the construction of a Full Screen GUI
        Toolkit tk = Toolkit.getDefaultToolkit();

        //create a variable with the Width of the frame
        int xSize = ( (int) tk.getScreenSize().getWidth() );

        //create a variable with the Height of the frame
        int ySize = ( (int) tk.getScreenSize().getHeight() );

        //set the size of the full frame
        frame.setSize( xSize, ySize );

        //make the frame visible
        frame.setVisible( true );

    }//end public static void createGuiFullScreen()


    public static void main( String args[] )
    {
        //creates and displays full screen GUI
        createGuiFullScreen();

    }//end public static void main(String[] args)

}//end public class GuiFullScreen
```

Your output (results) will look like this:

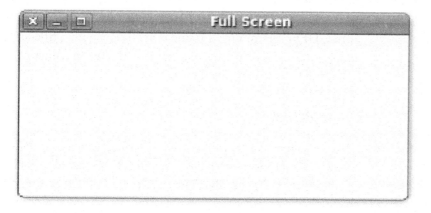

Let's examine this code:

This program was highly documented, basically every line of code is documented in great detail. Please review program line by line.

Summary

This chapter covers an introductory section on how to create GUI (Graphical User Interfaces) using Java. At this time there are other languages that concentrate in GUI programming in a larger extend. JavaApplets, part of the Java language, as well as Flash from Acrobat, stopped being processed by browsers such as Chrome beginning on September 1st, 2015.

Key Terms

Frame. What is a Frame?	In GUI programming, a frame is a window with a title and a border. GUI applications have at least one frame with button components that close, minimize or maximizes the window.
	Please see the following two programs: guiSmallFrame.java guiFullScreen.java
GUI (Graphical User Interface)	In computer science the term GUI, usually pronounced gooey, is how users communicate with electronic machines such as monitors, cell phones, tablets, etc. using graphical images instead of text commands.
	For the user, the GUI usually makes the communication with the computer easier, simply point and click. The disadvantages are that the communication presented to the user is limited by the GUI's options.
	Using non-GUI text commands to communicate with electronic machines allows the user total control of the machine.
GUI. Dialog Boxes	In Graphical User Interface (GUI) programming we use dialog boxes to enable communication between the user and the program.
	In this chapter we use two types of GUI dialog boxes, the message and the input dialog boxes.
	In general, dialog boxes communicate information to the users, requesting a response from the users.

GUI. Input Dialog Boxes	Input dialog boxes are used to interact with the user and retrieve information entered by the user. These boxes usually contain a system icon, multiple buttons, a short specific message, and a section where the user can input information.
	These boxes stop the users from accessing other sections of the program before replying to the current dialog box.
	All the information entered in the input dialog boxes is of string data type, regardless of what data was written in the input section.
	Java provides the following methods to convert the data entered from string data type to the intended data type. If the data entered is assigned to a variable called temp, it can be casted/converted as follows:
	//converts to Integer
	Integer response = Integer.parseInt(temp);
	//converts to Double
	Double response = Double.parseDouble(temp);
	//converts to Float Float response = Float.parseFloat(temp);
	//converts to Long Long response = Long.parseLong(temp);
	//converts to Short Short response = Short.parseShort(temp);
Message Dialog Boxes	These boxes usually contain a system icon, one or more buttons, and a short specific message.

Exercises

1. Create a program that will display a message dialog box.

2. Create a program that will display an input dialog box.

3. Create a program that will display a small frame.

4. Create a program that will display a full frame.

5. Create a program that will display an input frame and then a message frame.

6. What is GUI (Graphical User Interface)?
   a. The only way for users to access computers
   b. A usually beautiful graphical display that allows us to easily work with most types of computers, including cellular phones
   c. Use only in cellular phones
   d. Use only in laptop computers and tablets

7. What are dialog boxes?
   a. Java graphical tools that allows us to communicate with the users
   b. Java graphical tools used in websites only
   c. Java programs that allows us to speak to computers
   d. Programs used in Apple computers only

8. What are message dialog boxes?
   a. Java graphical tools that allow us to display messages
   b. Java graphical tools used in reply to messages
   c. Java programs that allows to input messages
   d. Java icons to change messages fonts

9. What are input dialog boxes?
   a. Java graphical tools that allow us to communicate with the users
   b. Java graphical tools that allow us to input data
   c. Java programs used in websites only
   d. Programs used in Orange computers only

10. What are frames?
    a. Java graphical tools used for icons only
    b. Java graphical tools used in websites only
    c. GUI applications that have a window with sections such as a borders, title name, and buttons to close the window
    d. Programs used in terminal mode operating systems only

REFERENCES

- Java API Specifications
  http://www.oracle.com/technetwork/java/api-141528.html

- My Java programs that I use in my Java classes located at robinson.cs.fiu.edu

//END CHAPTER 11: GUI SIMPLE APPLICATIONS

Sorting and Recursion

12

What is Sorting?

The fastest way of finding any information is when it is in order, usually when it is in ascending alphabetical order. When you look at the index in a book we know that the items beginning with m are after the a's and before the z's. Sorting is exactly that, a way of placing data in an orderly manner, either in ascending (a-z) or descending (z-a) order.

There are many specialized algorithms for sorting. The simplest and slowest is called bubble sort, one of the fastest is called quick sort. In this chapter we will learn the bubble sort. All sorts require that the items being examined be swapped/moved when necessary. The following program will teach us how to swap records.

Swap—Placing Data in Order

Swapping is the central process used in all sorting algorithms. Since all sorting algorithms require implement swap routines, I think we should learn how to implement them using small amounts of data. Here we will use three items.

In this example we sort three items using our swap method. We need three variables and an additional variable usually called temp which is used to temporarily move the data items that need to be swapped. Please examine the following program carefully, we must understand this process before going into the sorting algorithms.

< 301 >

```
/*
  Author  : Michael Robinson
  Program : swap.java
  Purpose : To place three items in ascending order

  Updated : December 22, 2099
*/


public class swap
{
    public static void swapThem( int fn, int sn, int tn )
    {
        int temp = 0;

        if( fn > sn)            // temp = 0  fn = 80   sn = 48     tn = 7
        {
            temp = fn;          // temp = 80 fn = 80   sn = 48     tn = 7
            fn   = sn;          // temp = 80 fn = 48   sn = 48     tn = 7
            sn   = temp;        // temp = 80 fn = 48   sn = 80     tn = 7

            System.out.printf( "After first swap  : %d %d %d\n",
                            fn, sn, tn);
        }

        if( sn > tn)            // temp = 80 fn = 48   sn = 80     tn = 7
        {
            temp = sn;          // temp = 80 fn = 48   sn = 80     tn = 7
            sn   = tn;          // temp = 80 fn = 48   sn = 7 tn = 7
            tn   = temp;        // temp = 80 fn = 48   sn = 7 tn = 80

            System.out.printf( "After second swap : %d %d %d\n",
                            fn, sn, tn);
        }

        if( fn > sn)            // temp = 80 fn = 48   sn = 7 tn = 80
        {
            temp = fn;          // temp = 48 fn = 48   sn = 7 tn = 80
            fn   = sn;          // temp = 48 fn = 7    sn = 7 tn = 80
            sn   = temp;        // temp = 48 fn = 7    sn = 48     tn = 80

            System.out.printf( "After third swap  : %d %d %d\n",
                            fn, sn, tn);
        }
```

```
    }//end public static void swapThem( int fn, int sn, int tn )


    public static void main( String arg[] )
    {
        int fn = 80;  //fn is first number
        int sn = 48;  //sn is second number
        int tn = 7;   //tn is third number

        System.out.printf( "Original items    : %d %d %d\n",
                            fn, sn, tn );

        swapThem( fn, sn, tn );

    }//end public static void main( String arg[] )

}//end public class swap
```

Your output (results) will look like this:

```
Original items     : 80 48 7

After first swap   : 48 80 7

After second swap  : 48 7 80

After third swap   : 7 48 80
```

Let's examine this code:

This program was highly documented, basically every line of code is documented in great detail. Please review program line by line.

Bubble Sort

Now that we know what sorting is, how to write a swap function and how to do constructors, we are going to implement this knowledge into the making of a sophisticated bubble sort.

This section contains four programs, bubbleSorter.java which is a regular calling program, and the following three classes: BubbleSort, IntBubbleSort, and StringBubbleSort.

Your will see the output produced by these programs at the end of this section.

```
/*
   Author  : Michael Robinson
   Program : bubleSorter.java
   Purpose : To present the bubble sort using constructors and classes
             I implemented two forms of sorting int and String arrays.

             The first implementation uses the BubbleSort.class
             which is a Constructor that accepts arrays of int and
             arrays of String.

             The second implementation uses the bubbleSort method in
             the IntBubbleSort class to sort and array of ints, and
             the bubbleSort method in the StringBubbleSort class,
             to sort and array of Strings.

             So it uses three programs, this program,
             the intBubbleSorter.class that sorts ints, and
             the stringBubbleSorter.class that sorts Strings.

             This section can be expanded to accept arrays of
             floats, doubles, and all other primitive types.

   Updated : July 22, 2099
*/


public class bubbleSorter
{
    // Create global arrays with test intValues.
    public static int intValues1[] =
                { 89, -9, 3, 0, -1, 5, 7, 6, 0, 34, 23, -3, 4, 36 };

    public static String stringValues1[] =
                { "zzz", "aaa", "cdet", "abcsd", "gatr" };

    public static int intValues2[] =
        { 5, 1, 4, 2, 12, 90, -9, -1, 5, 7, 6, 0, 34, 23, -3, 4, 36 };

    public static String stringValues2[] =
                { "one", "two", "five", "six", "ten" };

    public static int intValues3[] =
        { 90, 6, 4, 2, 12, 7, 01, 13, -1, 5, 7, 6, 0, 34 };
```

```java
public static String stringValues3[] =
        { "James", "Mariana", "999", "Sebastian", "Dan" };


public static void displayIntArray( int array[] )
{
    for ( int element : array )  //ENHANCED LOOP
    {
        System.out.print( element + " " );
    }

}//end public static void displayIntArray( int array[] )


public static void displayStringArray( String array[] )
{
    for( String element : array )  //ENHANCED LOOP
    {
        System.out.print( element + " " );
    }

}//end public static void displayStringArray( String array[] )


public static void useOneConstructor()
{
    System.out.println( "\n\nBubble sort using a constructor" );
    System.out.println( "-------------------------------" );

    //create an object no data passed
    BubbleSort one = new BubbleSort();

    //*********************************************************
    System.out.print( "\nOriginal: " );
    displayIntArray( intValues2 );

    //create an object passing an int array
    BubbleSort two = new BubbleSort( intValues2 );

    //get back the array sorted
    int arrayInt2[] = two.getIntBubbleSort();

    System.out.print( "\nSorted  : " );
    displayIntArray( arrayInt2 );

    //*******************************
```

```java
System.out.print( "\n\nOriginal: " );
displayStringArray( stringValues2 );

//create an object passing a String array
BubbleSort three = new BubbleSort( stringValues2 );

//get back the array sorted
String arrayString2[] = three.getStringBubbleSort();

System.out.print( "\nSorted   : " );
displayStringArray( arrayString2 );

//**********************************************************
System.out.println( "\n\nModify data in arrays" );
System.out.println( "---------------------" );

System.out.print( "Original: " );
displayIntArray( intValues3 );

//modified array values for object one
one.setIntBubbleSort( intValues3 );

//get back the array sorted
int arrayInt3[] = one.getIntBubbleSort();

System.out.print( "\nSorted   : " );
displayIntArray( arrayInt3 );

//**********************************
System.out.print( "\n\nOriginal: " );
displayStringArray( stringValues3 );

//modified array values for object one
one.setStringBubbleSort( stringValues3 );

//get back the array sorted
String arrayString3[] = three.getStringBubbleSort();

System.out.print( "\nSorted   : " );
displayStringArray( arrayString3 );

}//end public static void useOneConstructor()


public static void useMultipleClasses()
```

```
    {
        System.out.println(
                        "\n\n\nBubble sort using multiple classes" );
        System.out.println( "--------------------------------" );

        //************************************************
        System.out.print( "Original:     " );
        displayIntArray( intValues1 );

        //Sort the numeric array.
        IntBubbleSort.bubbleSort( intValues1 );

        System.out.print( "\nSorted   :    " );
        displayIntArray( intValues1 );

        //************************************************
        System.out.print( "\n\nOriginal: " );
        displayStringArray( stringValues1 );

        //Sort the string array.
        StringBubbleSort.bubbleSort( stringValues1 );

        System.out.print( "\nSorted   : " );
        displayStringArray( stringValues1 );

    }//end public static void useMultipleClasses()


    public static void main( String args[] )
    {
        useOneConstructor();

        useMultipleClasses();

        System.out.println( "\n--------------------------" );
        System.out.println( "End of BubleSorter Program" );

    }//end public static void main(String[] args)

}//end public class bubbleSorter
```

As we can see this program creates multiple arrays, then creates multiple objects using the following constructors which will sort the data in the arrays. Using the bubble sort, arrays can only hold one type of data, notice that we are using arrays of different data types and the constructors will handle them.

This constructor was used by the previous program. The following program is a constructor named: BubbleSort

```
/*
   Author  : Michael Robinson
   Program : BubbleSort.java  CONSTRUCTOR NO MAIN METHOD
   Purpose : To present the bubble sort algorithm using constructors.
             The intBubbleSort method performs the bubble sort on an
             int array.
             The stringBubbleSort method performing the bubble sort on
             a String array.

   Updated : July 22, 2099
*/


public class BubbleSort
{
    private static int    theIntArray[];
    private static String theStringArray[];



    //Constructors
    //***********************************************************
    public BubbleSort()
    {
        System.out.println( "\nDefault constructor no data send.\n" +
                            "Please send a Single Dimension array " +
                            "of ints or Strings" );
    }


    public BubbleSort( int arrayInt[] )
    {
        theIntArray = arrayInt;
    }


    public BubbleSort( String arrayString[] )
    {
        theStringArray = arrayString;
    }
```

```
//Setters
//************************************************************
public void setIntBubbleSort( int arrayInt[] )
{
    theIntArray = arrayInt;
}



public void setStringBubbleSort( String arrayString[] )
{
    theStringArray = arrayString;
}



//Getters
//************************************************************
public int[] getIntBubbleSort()
{
    return( intBubbleSort( theIntArray ) );
}



public String[] getStringBubbleSort()
{
    return( stringBubbleSort( theStringArray ) );
}



//a regular type of method that does the actual Bubble Sort
public static int[] intBubbleSort( int array[] )
{
    int maxElement;    // Marks the last element to compare
    int index;         // Index of an element to compare
    int temp;          // Used to swap to elements

    // The outer loop positions maxElement at the last element
    // to compare during each pass through the array. Initially
    // maxElement is the index of the last element in the array.
    // During each iteration, it is decreased by one.
    for( maxElement = array.length - 1; maxElement >= 0;
         maxElement-- )
    {
        // The inner loop steps through the array, comparing
        // each element with its neighbor. All of the elements
```

```
            // from index 0 through maxElement are involved in the

            // comparison. If two elements are out of order, they
            // are swapped.
            for( index = 0; index <= maxElement - 1; index++ )
            {
                // Compare an element with its neighbor.
                if ( array[index] > array[index + 1] )
                {
                    // Swap the two elements.
                    temp = array[index];
                    array[index] = array[index + 1];
                    array[index + 1] = temp;
                }//end if (array[index] > array[index + 1])

            }//end inner loop: for(index =0; index < =maxElement-1;
             //index++ )

        }//end outer loop: for(maxElement=array.length-1;
          //maxElement>= 0; maxElement--)

        return( array );

    }//end public static int[] intBubbleSort( int array[] )


    public static String[] stringBubbleSort( String array[] )
    {
        int maxElement;   // Marks the last element to compare
        int index;        // Index of an element to compare
        String temp;      // Used to swap to elements

        // The outer loop positions maxElement at the last element
        // to compare during each pass through the array. Initially
        // maxElement is the index of the last element in the array.
        // During each iteration, it is decreased by one.



        for( maxElement = array.length - 1; maxElement >= 0;
            maxElement-- )
        {
            // The inner loop steps through the array, comparing
            // each element with its neighbor. All of the elements
```

```
            // from index 0 through maxElement are involved in the
            // comparison. If two elements are out of order, they
            // are swapped.
            for( index = 0; index <= maxElement - 1; index++ )
            {
                // Compare an element with its neighbor.
                if( array[index].compareTo(array[index + 1]) > 0 )
                {
                    // Swap the two elements.
                    temp = array[index];
                    array[index] = array[index + 1];
                    array[index + 1] = temp;
                }//end if (array[index] > array[index + 1])

            }//end inner loop: for(index =0; index <= maxElement - 1;
            //index++ )

        }//end outer loop: for (maxElement = array.length - 1;
        //maxElement >= 0; maxElement--)

        return( array );

    }//end public static String[] stringBubbleSort( String array[] )

}//end public class BubbleSort
```

The above BubbleSort program is the first of the three constructors in this section.

The following program IntBubbleSorter.java is the second constructor.

This constructor performs the bubble sort algorithm for int arrays, it is a class and does not contain the main() method. Please read all the remarks in each method, I think they are self-explanatory. This program shows step by step how the bubble sort performs each move.

```
/*
  Author   : Michael Robinson
  Program  : IntBubbleSort.java   CLASS NO MAIN METHOD
  Purpose  : This CLASS performs the bubble sort algorithm for int
             arrays.
             Note: There is no main in this CLASS
                   It can be accessed from any program

  Updated  : July 22, 2099
*/
```

```java
public class IntBubbleSort
{
    public static void bubbleSort( int array[] )
    {
        int maxElement;    // Marks the last element to compare
        int index;         // Index of an element to compare
        int temp;          // Used to swap to elements

        // The outer loop positions maxElement at the last element
        // to compare during each pass through the array. Initially
        // maxElement is the index of the last element in the array.
        // During each iteration, it is decreased by one.
        for( maxElement = array.length - 1; maxElement >= 0;
             maxElement-- )
        {
            // The inner loop steps through the array, comparing
            // each element with its neighbor. All of the elements
            // from index 0 through maxElement are involved in the
            // comparison. If two elements are out of order, they
            // are swapped.
            System.out.print(
            "\n=============================================" );

            for( index = 0; index <= maxElement - 1; index++ )
            {
                // Compare each element with its neighbor.
                if( array[index] > array[index + 1] )
                {
                    // Swap the two elements.
                    temp = array[index];
                    array[index] = array[index + 1];
                    array[index + 1] = temp;
                }//end if (array[index] > array[index + 1])

                System.out.print( "\nmax,c=" + maxElement + "," +
                                  index + " " );
                if( index < 10 )
                {
                    System.out.print( " " );
                }

                showStep( array );
```

```
        }//end inner loop: for (index = 0; index <= maxElement -
        //1; index++ )


    }//end outer loop: for (maxElement = array.length - 1;
    // maxElement >= 0; maxElement--)


}//end public static void bubbleSort(int array[])



public static void showStep( int array[])
{
    System.out.print( " " );
    for( int element : array )   //ENHANCED LOOP
    {
        System.out.print( element + " " );
    }
}//end public static void showStep( int array[])
```

}//end public class IntBubbleSort

The following program StringBubbleSort.java is the third constructor.

This constructor performs the bubble sort algorithm for string arrays, it is a class and does not contain the main() method. Please read all the remarks in each method, I think they are self-explanatory. This program shows step by step how the bubble sort performs each move.

```
/*
  Author   : Michael Robinson
  Program  : StringBubleSort.java   CLASS NO MAIN METHOD.
  Purpose  : This CLASS performs the bubble sort algorithm for String
             arrays.
             Note: There is no main in this CLASS.
                   It can be accessed from any program.

  Updated  : July 22, 2099
*/



public class StringBubbleSort
{
    public static void bubbleSort( String array[] )
    {
        int maxElement;  // Marks the last element to compare
        int index;       // Index of an element to compare
        String temp;     // Used to swap to elements
```

```java
    // The outer loop positions maxElement at the last element
    // to compare during each pass through the array. Initially
    // maxElement is the index of the last element in the array.
    // During each iteration, it is decreased by one.
    System.out.print(
        "\n===============================================" );

    for( maxElement = array.length - 1; maxElement >= 0;
                maxElement-- )
    {
        // The inner loop steps through the array, comparing
        // each element with its neighbor. All of the elements
        // from index 0 through maxElement are involved in the
        // comparison. If two elements are out of order, they
        // are swapped.
        for( index = 0; index <= maxElement - 1; index++ )
        {
            // Compare each element with its neighbor.
            if( array[index].compareTo(array[index + 1]) > 0 )
            {
                // Swap the two elements.
                temp = array[index];
                array[index] = array[index + 1];
                array[index + 1] = temp;
            }//end if (array[index] > array[index + 1])

            System.out.print( "\nmax,c=" + maxElement + "," +
                            index + " " );
            if( index < 10 )
            {
                System.out.print( " " );
            }

            showStep( array );

        }//end inner loop: for( index =0; index <= maxElement- 1;
        //index++ )

    }//end outer loop: for (maxElement = array.length - 1;
    //maxElement >= 0; maxElement--)

}//end public static void bubbleSort(int array[])
```

```
public static void showStep( String array[] )
{
    System.out.print( " " );
    for( String element : array )  //ENHANCED LOOP
    {
        System.out.print( element + " " );
    }
}

}//end public class StringBubbleSort
```

Your output (results) will look like this:

Following you will see the output that the program bubbleSorter produces with the help of the three constructors BubbleSort, IntBubbleSort, and StringBubbleSort, all listed above.

```
Bubble sort using a constructor
-------------------------------

Default constructor no data send.

Please send a Single Dimension array of ints or Strings

Original: 5 1 4 2 12 90 -9 -1 5 7 6 0 34 23 -3 4 36
Sorted  : -9 -3 -1 0 1 2 4 4 5 5 6 7 12 23 34 36 90


Original: one two five six ten
Sorted  : five one six ten two


Modify data in arrays
---------------------
Original: 90 6 4 2 12 7 1 13 -1 5 7 6 0 34
Sorted  : -1 0 1 2 4 5 6 6 7 7 12 13 34 90


Original: James Mariana 999 Sebastian Dan
Sorted  : 999 Dan James Mariana Sebastian
```

```
Bubble sort using multiple classes
------------------------------------
Original:     89 -9 3 0 -1 5 7 6 0 34 23 -3 4 36
==================================================
max,c=13,0    -9 89 3 0 -1 5 7 6 0 34 23 -3 4 36
max,c=13,1    -9 3 89 0 -1 5 7 6 0 34 23 -3 4 36
max,c=13,2    -9 3 0 89 -1 5 7 6 0 34 23 -3 4 36
max,c=13,3    -9 3 0 -1 89 5 7 6 0 34 23 -3 4 36
max,c=13,4    -9 3 0 -1 5 89 7 6 0 34 23 -3 4 36
max,c=13,5    -9 3 0 -1 5 7 89 6 0 34 23 -3 4 36
max,c=13,6    -9 3 0 -1 5 7 6 89 0 34 23 -3 4 36
max,c=13,7    -9 3 0 -1 5 7 6 0 89 34 23 -3 4 36
max,c=13,8    -9 3 0 -1 5 7 6 0 34 89 23 -3 4 36
max,c=13,9    -9 3 0 -1 5 7 6 0 34 23 89 -3 4 36
max,c=13,10   -9 3 0 -1 5 7 6 0 34 23 -3 89 4 36
max,c=13,11   -9 3 0 -1 5 7 6 0 34 23 -3 4 89 36
max,c=13,12   -9 3 0 -1 5 7 6 0 34 23 -3 4 36 89
==================================================
max,c=12,0    -9 3 0 -1 5 7 6 0 34 23 -3 4 36 89
max,c=12,1    -9 0 3 -1 5 7 6 0 34 23 -3 4 36 89
max,c=12,2    -9 0 -1 3 5 7 6 0 34 23 -3 4 36 89
max,c=12,3    -9 0 -1 3 5 7 6 0 34 23 -3 4 36 89
max,c=12,4    -9 0 -1 3 5 7 6 0 34 23 -3 4 36 89
max,c=12,5    -9 0 -1 3 5 6 7 0 34 23 -3 4 36 89
max,c=12,6    -9 0 -1 3 5 6 0 7 34 23 -3 4 36 89
max,c=12,7    -9 0 -1 3 5 6 0 7 34 23 -3 4 36 89
max,c=12,8    -9 0 -1 3 5 6 0 7 23 34 -3 4 36 89
max,c=12,9    -9 0 -1 3 5 6 0 7 23 -3 34 4 36 89
max,c=12,10   -9 0 -1 3 5 6 0 7 23 -3 4 34 36 89
max,c=12,11   -9 0 -1 3 5 6 0 7 23 -3 4 34 36 89
==================================================
max,c=11,0    -9 0 -1 3 5 6 0 7 23 -3 4 34 36 89
max,c=11,1    -9 -1 0 3 5 6 0 7 23 -3 4 34 36 89
max,c=11,2    -9 -1 0 3 5 6 0 7 23 -3 4 34 36 89
max,c=11,3    -9 -1 0 3 5 6 0 7 23 -3 4 34 36 89
max,c=11,4    -9 -1 0 3 5 6 0 7 23 -3 4 34 36 89
max,c=11,5    -9 -1 0 3 5 0 6 7 23 -3 4 34 36 89
max,c=11,6    -9 -1 0 3 5 0 6 7 23 -3 4 34 36 89
max,c=11,7    -9 -1 0 3 5 0 6 7 23 -3 4 34 36 89
max,c=11,8    -9 -1 0 3 5 0 6 7 -3 23 4 34 36 89
max,c=11,9    -9 -1 0 3 5 0 6 7 -3 4 23 34 36 89
max,c=11,10   -9 -1 0 3 5 0 6 7 -3 4 23 34 36 89
==================================================
```

```
max,c=10,0    -9 -1 0 3 5 0  6  7 -3  4 23 34 36 89
max,c=10,1    -9 -1 0 3 5 0  6  7 -3  4 23 34 36 89
max,c=10,2    -9 -1 0 3 5 0  6  7 -3  4 23 34 36 89
max,c=10,3    -9 -1 0 3 5 0  6  7 -3  4 23 34 36 89
max,c=10,4    -9 -1 0 3 0 5  6  7 -3  4 23 34 36 89
max,c=10,5    -9 -1 0 3 0 5  6  7 -3  4 23 34 36 89
max,c=10,6    -9 -1 0 3 0 5  6  7 -3  4 23 34 36 89
max,c=10,7    -9 -1 0 3 0 5  6 -3  7  4 23 34 36 89
max,c=10,8    -9 -1 0 3 0 5  6 -3  4  7 23 34 36 89
max,c=10,9    -9 -1 0 3 0 5  6 -3  4  7 23 34 36 89
=================================================
max,c=9,0     -9 -1 0 3 0 5  6 -3  4  7 23 34 36 89
max,c=9,1     -9 -1 0 3 0 5  6 -3  4  7 23 34 36 89
max,c=9,2     -9 -1 0 3 0 5  6 -3  4  7 23 34 36 89
max,c=9,3     -9 -1 0 0 3 5  6 -3  4  7 23 34 36 89
max,c=9,4     -9 -1 0 0 3 5  6 -3  4  7 23 34 36 89
max,c=9,5     -9 -1 0 0 3 5  6 -3  4  7 23 34 36 89
max,c=9,6     -9 -1 0 0 3 5 -3  6  4  7 23 34 36 89
max,c=9,7     -9 -1 0 0 3 5 -3  4  6  7 23 34 36 89
max,c=9,8     -9 -1 0 0 3 5 -3  4  6  7 23 34 36 89
=================================================
max,c=8,0     -9 -1 0 0 3 5 -3  4  6  7 23 34 36 89
max,c=8,1     -9 -1 0 0 3 5 -3  4  6  7 23 34 36 89
max,c=8,2     -9 -1 0 0 3 5 -3  4  6  7 23 34 36 89
max,c=8,3     -9 -1 0 0 3 5 -3  4  6  7 23 34 36 89
max,c=8,4     -9 -1 0 0 3 5 -3  4  6  7 23 34 36 89
max,c=8,5     -9 -1 0 0 3 -3 5  4  6  7 23 34 36 89
max,c=8,6     -9 -1 0 0 3 -3 4  5  6  7 23 34 36 89
max,c=8,7     -9 -1 0 0 3 -3 4  5  6  7 23 34 36 89
=================================================
max,c=7,0     -9 -1 0 0 3 -3 4  5  6  7 23 34 36 89
max,c=7,1     -9 -1 0 0 3 -3 4  5  6  7 23 34 36 89
max,c=7,2     -9 -1 0 0 3 -3 4  5  6  7 23 34 36 89
max,c=7,3     -9 -1 0 0 3 -3 4  5  6  7 23 34 36 89
max,c=7,4     -9 -1 0 0 -3 3 4  5  6  7 23 34 36 89
max,c=7,5     -9 -1 0 0 -3 3 4  5  6  7 23 34 36 89
max,c=7,6     -9 -1 0 0 -3 3 4  5  6  7 23 34 36 89
=================================================
max,c=6,0     -9 -1 0 0 -3 3 4  5  6  7 23 34 36 89
max,c=6,1     -9 -1 0 0 -3 3 4  5  6  7 23 34 36 89
max,c=6,2     -9 -1 0 0 -3 3 4  5  6  7 23 34 36 89
max,c=6,3     -9 -1 0 -3 0 3 4  5  6  7 23 34 36 89
max,c=6,4     -9 -1 0 -3 0 3 4  5  6  7 23 34 36 89
max,c=6,5     -9 -1 0 -3 0 3 4  5  6  7 23 34 36 89
=================================================
```

```
max,c=5,0    -9 -1 0 -3 0 3 4 5 6 7 23 34 36 89
max,c=5,1    -9 -1 0 -3 0 3 4 5 6 7 23 34 36 89
max,c=5,2    -9 -1 -3 0 0 3 4 5 6 7 23 34 36 89
max,c=5,3    -9 -1 -3 0 0 3 4 5 6 7 23 34 36 89
max,c=5,4    -9 -1 -3 0 0 3 4 5 6 7 23 34 36 89
================================================
max,c=4,0    -9 -1 -3 0 0 3 4 5 6 7 23 34 36 89
max,c=4,1    -9 -3 -1 0 0 3 4 5 6 7 23 34 36 89
max,c=4,2    -9 -3 -1 0 0 3 4 5 6 7 23 34 36 89
max,c=4,3    -9 -3 -1 0 0 3 4 5 6 7 23 34 36 89
================================================
max,c=3,0    -9 -3 -1 0 0 3 4 5 6 7 23 34 36 89
max,c=3,1    -9 -3 -1 0 0 3 4 5 6 7 23 34 36 89
max,c=3,2    -9 -3 -1 0 0 3 4 5 6 7 23 34 36 89
================================================
max,c=2,0    -9 -3 -1 0 0 3 4 5 6 7 23 34 36 89
max,c=2,1    -9 -3 -1 0 0 3 4 5 6 7 23 34 36 89
================================================
max,c=1,0    -9 -3 -1 0 0 3 4 5 6 7 23 34 36 89
================================================
Sorted  :    -9 -3 -1 0 0 3 4 5 6 7 23 34 36 89


Original: zzz aaa cdet abcsd gatr
================================================
max,c=4,0    aaa zzz cdet abcsd gatr
max,c=4,1    aaa cdet zzz abcsd gatr
max,c=4,2    aaa cdet abcsd zzz gatr
max,c=4,3    aaa cdet abcsd gatr zzz
max,c=3,0    aaa cdet abcsd gatr zzz
max,c=3,1    aaa abcsd cdet gatr zzz
max,c=3,2    aaa abcsd cdet gatr zzz
max,c=2,0    aaa abcsd cdet gatr zzz
max,c=2,1    aaa abcsd cdet gatr zzz
max,c=1,0    aaa abcsd cdet gatr zzz


Sorted  : aaa abcsd cdet gatr zzz


--------------------------


End of BubbleSorter Program
```

Let's examine this code:

This program was highly documented, basically every line of code is documented in great detail. Please review program line by line.

Recursion

The term recursion has different meanings depending on the area being used ranging from logic to linguistics. The most common disciplines where it is used are mathematics and computer science. In computer science recursion is the process of creating functions where the function being created is applied/executed/called within its own definition. In other words a recursive method/function is a method/function that calls itself. Any recursive function needs to have a place where it terminates, otherwise it will be in a endless/infinity loop and will never end. This place is called the base case, when the function reaches its base case, it terminates.

Recursion is used to solve many algorithms, QuickSort the current fastest sorting algorithm uses recursion.

The following is the implementation of calculating the factorial of any integer using Recursion.

```
/*
  Author   : Michael Robinson
  Program  : recursion.java
  Purpose  : To implement recursion functions
             In this example we want to find the factorial of 7
             The mathematical representation is 7! = 5040
             which means  7 * 6 * 5 * 4 * 3 * 2 * 1

             We can find the factorial of any number by passing its
             value to the method factorial( int n )

             7! = 7*6! = 7*720 = 5040
             6! = 6*5! = 6*120 =  720
             5! = 5*4! = 5*24  =  120
             4! = 4*3! = 4*6   =   24
             3! = 3*2! = 3*2   =    6
             2! = 2*1! = 2*1   =    2
             1! = 1    = 1     =    1   //base case

             note 0! = 1 always

  Updated : January 13, 2099
*/
```

```java
class recursion
{
    public static long factorial( int n )
    {
        System.out.printf( "Processing factorial( %d )\n\n",  n );

        if( n <= 1 ) //base case
        {
            System.out.printf(
                    "Reached base case, returning %d\n\n", n);

            System.out.printf( "Now returning the accumulated " +
                    "values from RAM\n" );
            return 1;
        }
        else
        {
            System.out.printf( "Doing recursion by calling" +
                    "factorial( %d-1 )\n",  n );

            //doing recursion by calling factorial(n - 1)
            long counter = n * factorial(n - 1);

            System.out.printf( "Receiving results of " +
                    "factorial( %d ) =  %d * %d! =" +
                    " %d\n,  n, n, (n-1), counter );

            return counter;
        }

    }//end public static long fact(long n)


    public static void main(String args[])
    {
        System.out.println( "\nRecursion Program" );
        System.out.println( "=================" );

        System.out.println( "\nThe factorial of 7 = " +
                    factorial( 7 ) );
    }//end public static void main(String args[])

}//end class recursion
```

Your output (results) will look like this:

```
Recursion Program
=================

Processing factorial( 7 )
Doing recursion by callingfactorial( 7-1 )

Processing factorial( 6 )
Doing recursion by callingfactorial( 6-1 )

Processing factorial( 5 )
Doing recursion by callingfactorial( 5-1 )

Processing factorial( 4 )
Doing recursion by callingfactorial( 4-1 )

Processing factorial( 3 )
Doing recursion by callingfactorial( 3-1 )

Processing factorial( 2 )
Doing recursion by callingfactorial( 2-1 )

Processing factorial( 1 )

Reached base case, returning 1

Now returning the accumulated values from RAM

Receiving results of factorial( 2 )  =  2 * 1! = 2
Receiving results of factorial( 3 )  =  3 * 2! = 6
Receiving results of factorial( 4 )  =  4 * 3! = 24
Receiving results of factorial( 5 )  =  5 * 4! = 120
Receiving results of factorial( 6 )  =  6 * 5! = 720
Receiving results of factorial( 7 )  =  7 * 6! = 5040

The factorial of 7 = 5040
```

Let's examine this code:

This program is very short and very well documented, every line of code is documented, if not with remarks, then each chosen variable name reflects its purpose in the program for instance: Factorial, counter. Also the print commands describe what is being printed.

One of the main problems of recursion is that it is limited by the amount of RAM (Random Access Memory) in the computer in which it is being executed.

Summary

In this chapter we discuss two very important topics in computer science, sorting and recursion. We explained the meaning of sorting and how we use sorted data. Although it is not necessary, we extensibly used constructors in the bubble sort program example.

Recursion is a topic encountered in every programming language and usually it is a topic that most students like to avoid. It is said that recursion has a beginning point, an ending point called the "base case," and most important we must "believe that it works." When we try to trace what recursion does, it is very easy to get lost very fast. The recursion case that we showed in this chapter is very well documented and I think very easy to follow.

Key Terms

Bubble Sort	Now that we know what sorting is, how to write a swap function and how to do constructors, we are going to implement this knowledge into the making of a sophisticated bubble sort.

This section contains four programs:

bubbleSorter.java which is a regular calling program, and the following three classes:

BubbleSort.java

IntBubbleSort.java

StringBubbleSort.java |
| **Recursion** | The term recursion has different meanings depending on the area being used ranging from logic to linguistics. The most common disciplines where it is used are mathematics and computer science.

In computer science recursion is the process of creating functions where the function being created is applied/executed/called within its own definition. In other words a recursive method/function is a method/function that calls itself.

Any recursive function needs to have a place where it terminates, otherwise it will be in a endless/infinity loop and will never end. This place is called the base case, when the function reaches its base case, it terminates.

Recursion is used to solve many algorithms, QuickSort, the current fastest sorting algorithm uses recursion.

Our recursion.java program is the implementation of calculating the factorial of any integer using recursion. |
| **Sorting. What is Sorting?** | The fastest way of finding any information is when it is in order, usually when it is in ascending alphabetical order.

When you look at the index in a book we know that the items beginning with m are after the a's and before the z's. Sorting is exactly that, a way of placing data in an orderly manner, either in ascending (a-z) or descending (z-a) order.

There are many specialized algorithms for sorting, the simplest and slowest is called bubble sort, one of the fastest is called quick sort. In this chapter we will learn the bubble sort. All sorts require that the items being examined be swapped/moved when necessary.

Our swap.java program will teach us how to swap records. |

Swap - Placing Data in Order	Swapping is the central process used in all sorting algorithms. Since all sorting algorithms require implement swap routines, I think we should learn how to implement them using small amounts of data. Here we will use three items.
	In the swap.java example we sort three items using our swap method, we need three variables and an additional variable usually called temp which is used to temporarily move the data items that need to be swapped.
	Please examine our swap.java program carefully, we must understand this process before going into the sorting algorithms.

Exercises

1. Using the bubble sort, create a program that will sort, in ascending order, all numbers from 100 to 1.

2. Create a program that will swap 456, 32, 67 in ascending order.

3. Create a program that will swap maria, Maria, 456 in ascending order.

4. Create a program that will find the Factorial of 30.

5. Create a program that will verify if the answer in question 4 is correct.

6. In recursion what is the base case used for ?
   a. To start the process
   b. To stop the process and execute the return
   c. To divide by the two the processes being done
   d. None of the above

7. What happens when in recursion we encounter the return command?
   a. It stops the processing
   b. Prints the return values of each loop beginning with the loop in the middle
   c. Prints the return values of each loop beginning with the first loop
   d. Prints the return values of each loop beginning with the last loop

8. What is swap?
   a. It is the central process used in all sorting algorithms
   b. It is a theory that has not been proved
   c. It allows us to implement the binary search
   d. Allows data to the sorted in ascending order only

9. What is bubble sort?
   a. It is the easiest and slowest sorting algorithm
   b. Is a sorting algorithm for int data types only
   c. It allows to sort data of Object data types
   d. It is used by arrays

10. What is sorting?
    a. An algorithm to write data into text files
    b. An algorithm to divide and conquer software problems
    c. An algorithm that allows us to order data in ascending or descending order
    d. An algorithm to read data from text files

REFERENCES

- Java API Specifications
    http://www.oracle.com/technetwork/java/api-141528.html

- My Java programs that I use in my Java classes located at robinson.cs.fiu.edu

//END CHAPTER 12: SORTING AND RECURSION

Inheritance and Polymorphism

chapter

13

What is Inheritance?

The basic concept of inheritance is that some classes inherit methods and variables from other classes.

The class providing the inheritance is called the "super-class." It is also known as the "base-class."

The class inheriting is called the sub-class. It is also referred to as the "derived-class."

Here we will call them "super-class" and "sub-class."

The only condition for inheritance is that all variables and methods need to be declared public to be inheritable, if they are declared private the sub-classes can not see them.

As promised in the external classes section we are going to see a lot of them in this section.

For this section I have created the following programs:

```
cssDefautls.java          which is the super-class
webPageHome.java          which is a sub-class
webPage2.java             which is a sub-class
webPage3.java             which is a sub-class
inheritanceWebPage.java   which is the main program
```

< 327 >

The first step is to create an external class called cssDefautls.java, this class will be the super-class.

Then we are going to create multiple external classes that will define different web-pages: webPageHome, webPage2, and webPage3. These external classes will be the sub-classes that will inherit from the cssDefautls.java super-class.

Now that we have the super-class and a group of external classes we will create a program/class named inheritanceWebPage.java which will make use of the variables and methods of the above super-class and sub-classes.

This is how they are implemented:

This is cssDefautls.java, the super-class:

```
/*
   Author  : Michael Robinson
   Program : cssDefautls.java
   Purpose : THIS IS THE SUPER-CLASS
             This is the default class simulating
             css (Cascading Style Sheets) used in Web Design.
             css contains default formating which can be
             inherited by all pages.
             Each section in the default css can be overwritten
             in any page. Overwriting means that we can change
             whatever is in the original method.
             This inheritance concept in Java programming applies to
             to CSS in Web design somewhat. CSS is not Object
             oriented.

   Updated : July 31, 2099
*/



import java.util.Scanner;



//THIS IS THE SUPER-CLASS
public class cssDefaults
{

    private static void superClass()
    {
        System.out.println( "\t***I am the Super Class***" );
    }
```

```java
public void fontCSS()
{
    //call the superClass() method
    superClass();
    String fontType = "Times Roman"; //create data fields
    String fontSize = "12";          //create data fields

    System.out.println( "\tFont Type = " + fontType );
    System.out.println( "\tFont Size = " + fontSize );

}//end public static void fontCSS()


public void colorCSS()
{
    //call the superClass() method
    superClass();
    String foreGoundColor = "black"; //create data fields
    String backGoundColor = "white"; //create data fields

    System.out.println( "\tForeground Color = " +
                        foreGoundColor );

    System.out.println( "\tBackground Color = " +
                        backGoundColor );

}//end public static void colorCSS()


//This method allows us to pause the program at any time
public static void pause()
{
    //creates object to read the keyboard
    Scanner kb = new Scanner( System.in );

    System.out.print( "\n\t\t\tNice to see you again, " +
                "        press any key to continue -> " );

    kb.nextLine(); //this command waits for keyboard input

}//end public static void pause()

}//end public class cssDefaults
```

Let's examine this code:

This cssDefaults super-class contains the following methods:

```
private static void superClass()
public void fontCSS()
public void colorCSS()
public static void pause()
```

This private static void superClass() method is private and can not be directly inherited by any other class.

```
public void fontCSS()
public void colorCSS()
public static void pause()
```

are public and then can be inherited by any other class.

The following three classes are sub-classes that will inherit from the cssDefautls.java super-class and in some cases will override some methods from the super-class with their own local methods:

```
webPageHome.java          this is a sub-class
webPage2.java             this is a sub-class
webPage3.java             this is a sub-class
```

```
/*
  Author  : Michael Robinson
  Program : webPageHome.java
  Purpose : This class is called a SUB-CLASS because it INHERITS from
            the SUPER-CLASS cssDefaults
            This class can contain methods with the same name as the
            methods in the SUPER-CLASS overriding the SUPER-CLASS
            methods.
            This class can also have their own additional methods.

  Updated : July 31, 2099
*/



//extends means that this class inherits all the public code from an
//external class called ccsDefaults
public class webPageHome extends cssDefaults
{

}
```

Well, this class looks funny because it does not have any methods. In this case this class will inherit all the public methods and variables from the super-class, and even though this sub-class is empty, it will execute the methods inherited from the super-class. We will see the output when we execute the main program inheritanceWebPage, after we present all the sub-classes.

The following class is the second sub-class called webPage2.

```
/*
  Author   : Michael Robinson
  Program  : webPage2.java
  Purpose  : This class is called a SUB-CLASS because it INHERITS from
             the SUPER-CLASS cssDefaults.
             This class can contain methods with the same name as the
             methods in the SUPER-CLASS overriding the SUPER-CLASS
             methods.
             This class can also have their own additional methods.

  Updated  : July 31, 2099
*/



//extends means that this class inherits all the public code from an
//external class called ccsDefaults

public class webPage2 extends cssDefaults
{

    //The super-class cssDefaults has a method with the same
    //name of this method.
    //This method overrides the method in the super-class
    public void fontCSS()
    {
        System.out.println( "\n\t\t\t^^^I am the Sub Class^^^" );

        String fontType = "Courier";
        String fontSize = "10";

        System.out.println( "\t\t\tFont Type = " + fontType );
        System.out.println( "\t\t\tFont Size = " + fontSize );

    }//end public static void fontCSS()

}//end public class webPage2 extends cssDefaults
```

As we can see, this sub-class has only one method public void fontCSS(). Notice that this method has the same name and signature as a method in the super-class: public void fontCSS(). This is called "overriding a method" which means that when we execute this sub-class, the method in the sub-class will be used, ignoring the method in the super-class. We can do the same to variables, we can override them.

Now this is the last sub-class.

```
/*
   Author  : Michael Robinson
   Program : webPage3.java
   Purpose : This class is called a SUB-CLASS because it INHERITS from
             the SUPER-CLASS cssDefaults.
             This class can contain methods with the same name as the
             methods in the SUPER-CLASS overriding the SUPER-CLASS
             methods.
             This class can also have their own additional methods,
             not found in the SUPER-CLASS.

   Updated : July 31, 2099
*/



//extends means that this class inherits all the public code from an
//external class called ccsDefaults

public class webPage3 extends cssDefaults
{
    //The super-class cssDefaults has a method with the same
    //name of this method.
    //This method overrides the method in the super-class
    public void fontCSS()
    {
        System.out.println( "\n\t\t\t^^^I am the Sub Class^^^" );
        String fontType = "Loma";
        String fontSize = "15";

        System.out.println( "\t\t\tFont Type = " + fontType );
        System.out.println( "\t\t\tFont Size = " + fontSize );

    }//end public static void fontCSS()


    //The super-class cssDefaults has a method with the same
    //name of this method.
    //This method overrides the method in the super-class
```

```
    public void colorCSS()
    {
        System.out.println( "\n\t\t\t^^^I am the Sub Class^^^" );
        String foreGoundColor = "Blue";
        String backGoundColor = "Yellow";

        System.out.println( "\t\t\tForeground Color = " +
                            foreGoundColor );

        System.out.println( "\t\t\tBackground Color = " +
                            backGoundColor );

    }//end public static void colorCSS()

}//end public class webPage3 extends cssDefaults
```

As we can see, this sub-class overrides two classes found in the super-class.

```
    public void fontCSS() and public void colorCSS()
```

When we call/execute this sub-class it will override the two methods in the super-class that have the same name and signature.

Now we present the calling program that uses the super-class and the sub-classes.

```
/*
  Author  : Michael Robinson
  Program : inheritanceWebPage.java
  Purpose : This program uses multiple classes to make use of
            INHERITANCE.

            The class cssDefault.java is called the SUPER-CLASS and
            contains some methods that are inherited by other
            classes, by using the extends command in their signature.

            The classes WebPageHome, WebPage2, and WebPage3 are
            called SUB-CLASSES because they inherit/extends from the
            cssDefault SUPER-CLASS.

            These SUB-CLASSES can use all the methods of the SUPER-
            CLASS. At the same time these classes can have methods
            with the same names used in the SUPER-CLASS with
            different content. If a SUB-CLASS does this, it is said
```

that it is OVERIDING such method(s). SUB-CLASSES can have their own additional methods, not found in the SUPER-CLASS.

The calling program that uses a SUB-CLASS, first checks to see if there are methods with the same name in the SUPER-CLASS, if there are, it will use the methods inside the SUB-CLASS overriding the methods in the SUPER-CLASS.

```java
   Updated : July 31, 2099
*/



import java.util.Scanner;
import java.awt.*;



//This is the calling program that uses the super-class and the
//sub-classes.
public class inheritanceWebPage
{
    //this variable is private therefore it can not be inherited
    private static int end = -1;

    //this variable is public therefore it can be inherited
    public final double interestRate = .25;


    public static void page3()
    {
        System.out.println( "  Welcome to WebPage3, these are your" +
                            " settings:" );

        //this is an external class which also is a sub-class
        webPage3 wp3 = new webPage3();
        wp3.fontCSS();
        wp3.colorCSS();

    }//end public static void page3()


    public static void page2()
    {
        System.out.println( "  Welcome to WebPage2, these are your" +
                            " settings:" );
```

```
        //this is an external class which also is a sub-class
        webPage2 wp2 = new webPage2();
        wp2.fontCSS();
        wp2.colorCSS();

}//end public static void page2()


public static void home() //user enters 1
{
        System.out.println( "  Welcome Home, these are your" +
                        " settings:" );

        //this is an external class which also is a sub-class
        webPageHome wpHome = new webPageHome();
        wpHome.fontCSS();
        wpHome.colorCSS();

}//end public static void home() //user enters 1


public static void menu()
{
        System.out.println( "\n\n\t\t\t************************" );
        System.out.println( "\t\t\t*    Enter :              *" +
                        "\n\t\t\t*    0 to end program    *" +
                        "\n\t\t\t*    1 for HOME page    *" +
                        "\n\t\t\t*    2 for Page 1        *" +
                        "\n\t\t\t*    3 for Page 2        *"
                    );

        System.out.println( "\t\t\t************************" );

}//end public static void menu()


public static void controlMethod()
{
    //creates and object to access the keyboard
    Scanner kb = new Scanner( System.in );

    while( true )
    {
        //this method accepts user manual input
```

```java
        menu();

        end = kb.nextInt(); //reads the keyboard

        if( end == 0 )
        {
            break;
        }
        else if( end == 1 )
        {
            home();
        }
        else if( end == 2 )
        {
            page2();
        }
        else if( end == 3 )
        {
            page3();
        }

    }//end while(true)

}//end public static void controlMethod()


public static void welcome( int time, int recursion )
                        throws InterruptedException
{

    int x = 0;

    String heading = "Welcome back --->";

    System.out.print( "\t\t\t" );


    for( x = 0; x < heading.length(); x++ )
    {
        //prints one character at the time
        //from beginning to end
        System.out.print( heading.charAt(x) );

        //program goes to sleep for time value
        //1000 = 1 second
```

```
            Thread.sleep( time );
        }


    System.out.print( "    " );


    for( x = heading.length()-1; x > -1; x--)
    {
        //prints one character at the time
        //from end to beginning
        System.out.print( heading.charAt(x) );

        //program goes to sleep for time value
        //1000 = 1 second
        Thread.sleep( time );
    }


    System.out.println();

    //calls the pause method in the SUPER-CLASS
    cssDefaults.pause();

    if( recursion == 0 )
    {
        //change font type, appearance and size
        Font font = new Font( "Verdana", Font.BOLD, 12 );
        font = font.deriveFont( 20.0f );
        welcome( 0, 1 );
    }

}//end public static void welcome(int time, int recursion)throws
 //InterruptedException


public static void screenSize()
{
    //creates an object called toolkit of the ToolKit class
    Toolkit toolkit =  Toolkit.getDefaultToolkit();

    //The Dimension Class encapsulates the height and width
    //values of a component. In this case is the screen's
```

```
        //height and width
        Dimension dim = toolkit.getScreenSize();

        System.out.println( "\n\t\t\tYour Screen Dimensions Are:" );

        System.out.println( "\t\t\tWidth  : " + dim.width +
                            " pixels" );

        System.out.println( "\t\t\tHeight : " + dim.height +
                            " pixels" );
    }//end public static void screenSize()


    public static void main( String arg[] )
                            throws InterruptedException
    {
        welcome( 100, 0 );

        screenSize();

        controlMethod();

        System.out.println( "Thank you!!" );

        System.exit(0);

    }//end public static void main( String arg[] )
      //throws InterruptedException

}//end public class inheritanceWebPage
```

Let's examine this code:

See details in the following section.

Your output (results) will look like this:

```
        Welcome back --->    >--- kcab emocleW

        Nice to see you again,      press any key to continue

        Welcome back --->    >--- kcab emocleW

        Nice to see you again,      press any key to continue
```

```
Your Screen Dimensions Are:
Width  : 1366 pixels
Height : 768 pixels


* * * * * * * * * * * * * * * * * * * * *
*    Enter :                *
*    0 to end program       *
*    1 for HOME page        *
*    2 for Page 1           *
*    3 for Page 2           *
* * * * * * * * * * * * * * * * * * * * *
```

At this point we select choice "1 for HOME page" obtaining the following results:

```
Welcome Home, these are your settings:

    ***I am the Super Class***
    Font Type = Times Roman
    Font Size = 12

    ***I am the Super Class***
    Foreground Color = black
    Background Color = white


* * * * * * * * * * * * * * * * * * * * *
*    Enter :                *
*    0 to end program       *
*    1 for HOME page        *
*    2 for Page 1           *
*    3 for Page 2           *
* * * * * * * * * * * * * * * * * * * * *
```

Here we created an object from the sub-class webPageHome which does NOT have any methods,

```
webPageHome wpHome = new webPageHome();
```

but it inherits all the methods from the super class cssDefaults and we used the following methods:

```
wpHome.fontCSS();
wpHome.colorCSS();
```

When we select option "2 for Page 1" we obtain:

```
Welcome to WebPage2, these are your settings:

              ^^^I am the Sub Class^^^
              Font Type = Courier
              Font Size = 10

     ***I am the Super Class***
     Foreground Color = black
     Background Color = white


         ***********************
         *    Enter :          *
         *    0 to end program *
         *    1 for HOME page   *
         *    2 for Page 1      *
         *    3 for Page 2      *
         ***********************
```

This time we created an object from the webPage2 class which does NOT have any methods,

```
          webPage2 wp2 = new webPage2();
```

but it inherits all the methods from the super class cssDefaults and we used the following methods:

```
               wp2.fontCSS();
               wp2.colorCSS();
```

We then selected option "3 for Page 2" and obtained:

```
Welcome to WebPage3, these are your settings:

              ^^^I am the Sub Class^^^
              Font Type = Loma
              Font Size = 15

              ^^^I am the Sub Class^^^
              Foreground Color = Blue
              Background Color = Yellow
```

```
* * * * * * * * * * * * * * * * * * * *
*    Enter :                *
*    0 to end program       *
*    1 for HOME page        *
*    2 for Page 1           *
*    3 for Page 2           *
* * * * * * * * * * * * * * * * * * * *
```

Here we created an object from the webPage3 sub-class

```
webPage3 wp3 = new webPage3();
```

which has its own classes fontCSS and colorCSS overriding the classes with the same names in the super-class cssDefaults

```
wp3.fontCSS();
wp3.colorCSS();
```

Finally when we select "0 to end program" the program terminates with this message:

```
Thank you!!
```

In this section of inheritance, we implemented three concepts in the class inheritanceWebPage and shortly, we will see in detail.

a - recursion and threads in the method:

```
public static void welcome( int time, int recursion )
                       throws InterruptedException
```

b - The "Toolkit" to find the screen size, in the method:

```
public static void screenSize()
```

Make sure to understand this topic of inheritance because some of the future sections depend on understanding this section.

Polymorphism

Polymorphism is an extension of inheritance, it allows us to use multiple super-classes and multiple sub-classes from calling programs, which I refer to as main or calling programs. Remember that super-classes and sub-classes do not have the main method.

This is the diagram of all classes that I am using in this polymorphism section:

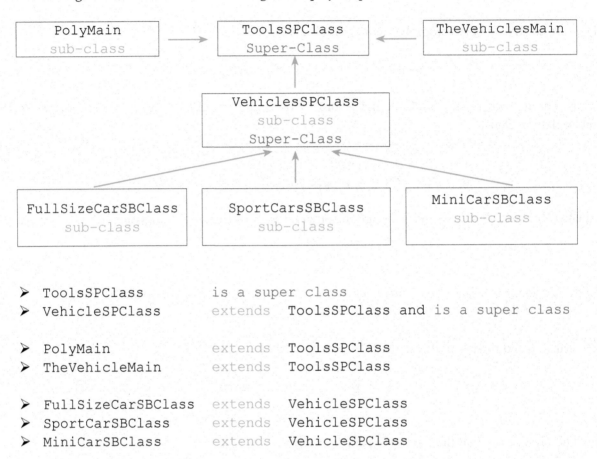

> ToolsSPClass   is a super class
> VehicleSPClass   extends   ToolsSPClass and is a super class

> PolyMain   extends   ToolsSPClass
> TheVehicleMain   extends   ToolsSPClass

> FullSizeCarSBClass   extends   VehicleSPClass
> SportCarSBClass   extends   VehicleSPClass
> MiniCarSBClass   extends   VehicleSPClass

The following is the super-class ToolsSPClass. It contains multiple methods that we call tools, which will be inherited by all the sub-classes and in some cases they will be overridden.

```
/*
   Author  : Michael Robinson
   Program : ToolsSPClass.java
   Purpose : This is a super-class that contains multiple methods
             which perform specific jobs and can be inherited by any
             other class.
```

The methods in this class are tools which can be used
(inherited) by other classes:

```
setMyName( String )        //modifies a string
getMyName();               //returns a String

//accept variable amount of ints
addInts( int ... items )

//accept variable amount of floats
addFloats( float ... items )

//accept variable amount of doubles
addDoubles( double ... items )

p( Object anyKey )         //System.out.print( any Object )
pl()                       //System.out.println()
pl( Object anyKey )        //any Object
pl( Object anyKey[] )      //any array of Objects

//pauses displaying any String send by user
pause( String display )

//prints backwards any array of Objects
printBackwards( Object data[] )

//returns the maximum number in the ints received
max( int ... data )

//returns the minimum number in the ints received
min( int ... data )

//returns the average of multiple doubles
average( double ... numbers )

  Updated : September 12, 2099
*/


import java.util.Scanner;
```

```java
public class ToolsSPClass //this is a super class
{
    //create a global private variable
    private static String myName = "";


    //set a value using the setMyName method
    public static void setMyName( String name )
    {
        myName = name;

    }//end public static void setMyName( String name )


    //returns the value in my getMyName method
    public static String getMyName( )
    {
        return myName;

    }//end public static String getMyName( )


    //adds any amount of ints, returning the total
    public static int addInts( int ... items )
    {

        int total = 0;

        for( int unit : items )
        {
            total = total + unit;
        }

        return total;

    }//end public static int addInts( int ... items )


    //adds any amount of floats, returning the total
    public static float addFloats( float ... items )
    {
        float total = 0;

        for( float unit : items )
        {
```

```java
            total = total + unit;
        }

        return total;

    }//end public static float addFloats( int ... items )


    //adds any amount of doubles, returning the total
    public static double addDoubles( double ... items )
    {
        double total = 0;

        for( double unit : items )
        {
            total = total + unit;
        }

        return total;

    }//end public static double addDoubles( double ... items )


    //Executes System.out.print
    public static void p( Object anyKey )
    {
        System.out.print( anyKey );

    }//end public static void p( Object anyKey )


    //executes System.out.println
    public static void pl()
    {
        System.out.println();

    }//end public static void pl()


    //System.out.println any Object
    public static void pl( Object anyKey )
    {
        System.out.println( anyKey );
```

```java
    }//end public static void pl( Object anyKey )


    //System.out.println any array of Objects
    public static void pl( Object anyKey[] )
    {
        for( Object x : anyKey )
        {
            System.out.print( x + " " );
        }

    }//end public static void pl( Object anyKey[] )


    //pauses displaying any String send by user
    public static void pause( String display )
    {
        pl( display );
        Scanner kb = new Scanner( System.in );
        String temp = kb.nextLine();
        temp = null;
        kb   = null;

    }//end public static void pause( String display )


    //prints backwards any array of Objects
    public static void printBackwards( Object data[] )
    {
        for( int x = data.length-1 ; x > -1; x-- )
        {
            System.out.print( data[x] + " " );
        }

    }//end public static void printBackwards( Object data[] )


    //returns the maximum number in the ints received
    public static int max( int ... data )
    {
        int max = data[0];

        for( int temp : data )
        {
            if ( max < temp  )  //compareTo
```

```
            {
                max = temp;
            }
        }

        return max;

    }//end public static int max( int ...data )


    //returns the minimum number in the ints received
    public static int min( int ... data )
    {
        int min= data[0];

        for( int temp : data )
        {
            if ( min >  temp  )
            {
                min = temp;
            }
        }

        return min;

    }//end public static  int min( int ... data )


    //returns the average of multiple doubles
    public static double average( double ... numbers )
    {
        double average = 0;
        int counter = 0;

        for( double items : numbers )
        {
            average = average + items;
            counter++;
        }

        return average/counter;

    }//end public static double average( double ... numbers )

}//end public class toolsSPClass
```

As we can see in the previous class, every method has a specific job, so they are tools that can be used by the other classes.

Now we are going to see how another super-class "VehicleSPClass" becomes a sub-class of the previous super-class "ToolsSPClass," and at the same time it contains methods that will be inherited by lower sub-classes.

```
/*
   Author  : Michael Robinson
   Program : VehicleSPClass.java
   Purpose : This is a super-class that contains  multiple methods
             which perform specific jobs and can be inherited by any
             other class.

             At the same time this class is inheriting from the
             ToolsSPClass super-class, making this class a sub-class.

             The methods in this class can be accessed from a main
             program and they can also be overridden by other sub-
             classes that can inherit this class.

   Updated : September 23, 2099
*/


//This is also a super class to other subclasses
public class VehicleSPClass extends ToolsSPClass
{
    public static void myInfo()
    {
        System.out.println( "I am the VehicleSPClass" );

    }//end public static void myInfo()


    public static void brandName()
    {
        System.out.println( "I am the brandName in the" +
                            " VehicleSPClass" );

    }//end public static void brandName()
```

```java
public static void exteriorColor()
{
    System.out.println( "I am the exteriorColor in the" +
                        " VehicleSPClass" );

}//end public static void exteriorColor()


public static void interiorColor()
{
    System.out.println( "I am the interiorColor in the" +
                        " VehicleSPClass" );

}//end public static void interiorColor()


public static void tires()
{
    System.out.println( "My car has tires in the" +
                        " VehicleSPClass" );

}//end public static void tires()


public static void doors()
{
    System.out.println( "My car has 4 doors in the" +
                        " VehicleSPClass" );

}//end public static void doors()


public static void capacity()
{
    System.out.println( "My car seats 5 people in the" +
                        " VehicleSPClass" );

}//end public static void capacity()


public static void mpg()
{
```

```
        System.out.println( "My car's mpg is 200 in the" +
                        " VehicleSPClass" );

    }//end public static void mpg()

}//end public class VehicleSPClass extends toolsSPClass
```

As we can see this class now contains, by inheritance, all the methods and variables of the super-class ToolsSPClass. This class will be inherited by the following sub-classes.

```
/*
  Author  : Michael Robinson
  Program : FullSizeCarSBClass.java
  Purpose : This is a sub-class inheriting from the VehicleSPClass
            super-class.

            This class overrides the method myInfo().

  Updated : September 23, 2099
*/


public class FullSizeCarSBClass extends VehicleSPClass
{
    //this method overrides myInfo in VehicleSPClass super-class
    public static void myInfo()
    {
        System.out.println( "I am the FullSizeCar myInfo" );

        //calls setName method at ToolsSPClass super-class
        setMyName( "from FullSizeCar to ToolsSPClass" );

    }//end public static void myInfo()

}//end public class FullSizeCar extends VehicleClass
```

The above class overrides the method myInfo in VehicleSPClass super-class. It also calls the setName method at ToolsSPClass super-class.

This is the SportCarSBClass class which inherites from VehicleSPClass.

```java
/*
  Author  : Michael Robinson
  Program : SportCarSBClass.java
  Purpose : This is a sub-class inheriting from the VehicleSPClass
            super-class.

            This class overrides several methods and has its own
            variable private static String myName = ""; which
            overrides an exact variable in the super-class
            ToolsSPClass.

  Updated : September 23, 2099
*/



public class SportCarSBClass extends VehicleSPClass
{
    private static String myName = "";

    //overrides setMyName at ToolsSPClass super-class
    public static void setMyName( String name )
    {
        myName = name;

    }//end public static void setMyName( String name )



    //overrides getMyName at ToolsSPClass super-class
    public static String getMyName( )
    {
        return myName;

    }//end public static String getMyName( )



    //this method overrides myInfo in VehicleSPClass super-class
    public static void myInfo()
    {
        setMyName( "from SportsCarSBClaSS at " +
                   "VehicleSPClass.setMyName" );

        System.out.println( "I am myInfo() at SportCarSBClass" );
```

```
    }//end public static void myInfo()


    //calls mpg and myInfo methods from super-class VehicleSPClass
    void superSample()
    {
        super.mpg();
        super.myInfo();

    }//end void superSample()

}//end public class SportCar extends VehicleClass
```

As we can see this class overrides three methods and what is new is that it makes direct calls to two methods from its super-class in the superSample() method:

```
        super.mpg();
        super.myInfo();
```

Now we implement the last sub-class called MiniCarSBClass which also inherits from the VehicleSPClass.

```
/*
  Author  : Michael Robinson
  Program : MiniCarSBClass.java
  Purpose : This is a sub-class inheriting from the VehicleSPClass
            super-class.

            This class overrides the method myInfo().

  Updated : September 23, 2099
*/


public class MiniCarSBClass extends VehicleSPClass
{
    //this method overrides myInfo in VehicleSPClass super-class
    public static void myInfo()
    {
        System.out.println( "I am the MiniCar" );

    }//end public static void myInfo()

}//end public class MiniCar extends VehicleClass
```

At this point we are going to make use of all the previous super- and sub-classes. From the main() method we call the following methods:

```
showSportCars();
polyCar();
SportCarSBClass.myInfo();
SportCarSBClass.doors();
```

We have included a lot of documentation inside this program and after it we explain in more detail the polyCar() method.

```
/*
  Author   : Michael Robinson
  Program  : TheVehiclesMain.java
  Purpose  : This is a super-class which also is
             a sub-class of another super-class.

             This class contains one variable and
             multiple methods which will be inherited by
             other sub-classes:

             double gpa = 4.00;
             public static void showSportCars()
             public static void polyCar()

  Updated : September 12, 2099
*/


public class TheVehiclesMain
{
    double gpa = 4.00;

    public static void showSportCars()
    {
        //calls tires method which is inside SportCarSBClass
        SportCarSBClass.tires();

        //calls mpg method which is inside MiniCarSBClass
        MiniCarSBClass.mpg();

    }//end public static void showSportCars()
```

```
    public static void polyCar()
    {
        //calls method capacity() inside object clone1 but
        //since class MiniCarSBClass() inherits from
        //VehicleSPClass super-class, the method capacity()
        //can be in the super-class and/or the sub-class
        VehicleSPClass clone1 = new MiniCarSBClass();

        clone1.capacity();

    }//end public static void polyCar()


    public static void main( String arg[] )
    {
        showSportCars();
        polyCar();
        SportCarSBClass.myInfo();
        SportCarSBClass.doors();

    }//end public static void main( String arg[] )

}//end public class TheVehiclesMain
```

Note on the above public static void polyCar() method we create the clone1 object of data type VehicleSPClass, but we assign new MiniCarSBClass() to it.

```
    VehicleSPClass clone1 = new MiniCarSBClass();
    clone1.capacity();
```

This previous TheVehiclesMain programs shows a very simple use of the super-classes and sub-classes above.

The following main program PolyMain inherits from the ToolsSPClass super-class making extensive use of all super-classes and sub-classes mentioned above.

```
/*
  Author  : Michael Robinson
  Program : polyMain.java
  Purpose : This class uses the SUPER-CLASS ToolsSPClass
            and some SUB-CLASSES to implement:
            polymorphism and inheritance

  Updated : July 31, 2099
*/
```

```java
public class PolyMain extends ToolsSPClass
{
    public static void showPolymorphism()
    {
        //inherits from ToolsSPClass super-class
        pause( "Using ToolsSPClass full = new " +
                " FullSizeCarSBClass(); .. enter" );

        pl( "---------------------------------------------------" );

        //creates object "full" of ToolsSPClass data type
        //controlling sub-class FullSizeCarSBClass()
        ToolsSPClass full = new FullSizeCarSBClass();

        full.setMyName( "I am testing the full size" );

        pl( full.getMyName().toUpperCase() + " as an object" );

        full.setMyName( "I am using substring method full size" );

        pl( full.getMyName().substring(2, 15).toUpperCase().concat(
            " about time" ).toUpperCase() + " as a static" );

        pl( "---------------------------------------------------\n");

        pause( "Using ToolsSPClass sport = new SportCarSBClass();" +
                " .. enter" );
        pl( "---------------------------------------------------" );

        //creates object "sport" of ToolsSPClass data type
        //controlling sub-class SportCarSBClass()
        ToolsSPClass sport = new SportCarSBClass();

        sport.setMyName( "I am testing the sports size as " +
                        "an object" );
        pl( sport.getMyName() );

        sport.setMyName( "I am testing the sports size" );

        pl( getMyName() + " as a static" );

        pl( "---------------------------------------------------\n" );

        pause( "Using ToolsSPClass mini = new MiniCarSBClass();" +
```

```java
                " .. enter" );
        pl( "---------------------------------------------" );

        //creates object "mini" of ToolsSPClass data type
        //controlling sub-class MiniCarSBClass()
        ToolsSPClass mini = new MiniCarSBClass();

        mini.setMyName( "I am testing the mini size as an object" );

        pl( mini.getMyName() );

        mini.setMyName( "I am testing the mini size " );

        pl( getMyName() + " as a static" );

        pl( "---------------------------------------------\n" );

        pause( "Calling  methods from different classes .. enter" );

        pl( "---------------------------------------------\n" );

        pl( "" + full.getMyName().toUpperCase() );

        pl( "" + sport.getMyName().toUpperCase() );

        pl( "\nThe Maximun number of 6,2,3,18,8,12,15 is : " +

        full.max( 6,2,3,18,8,12,15 ) );

        pl( "The Minimum number of 6,2,3,18,8,12,15 is : "   +
             full.min( 6,2,3,18,8,12,15 ) );

        pl( "---------------------------------------------\n" );

}//end public static void showPolymorphism()


public static void dataManipulation()
{
        //calling methods from the ToolsSPClass super-class
        Object data[] = { 49, 33, 'a', "michael"  };

        pl();
```

```java
        pl( "I want to print backwards the following array of " +
            "Objects: " );

        pl( data );

        pl();

        printBackwards( data ) ;

        pl();

        pause( "Let's continue.." );

}//end public static void dataManipulation()


public static void someMath() //tools from
{
        //calling methods from the ToolsSPClass super-class
        System.out.println( "Adding ints    3, 5, 6 = " +
                        addInts( 3, 5, 6 ) );

        System.out.println( "Adding doubles 3, 5, 6 = " +
                        addDoubles( 3, 5, 6 ) );

        System.out.println( "Adding floats  3, 5, 6 = " +
                        addFloats( 3, 5, 6 ) );

        System.out.printf( "The average of 3, 5, 6 = %.02f",
                        average( 3, 5, 6 ) );

        pl();

        pl( "The Maximum number of 6,2,3,18,8,12,15 is:" +
            max(6,2,3,18,8,12,15) );

        pl( "The Minimum number of 6,2,3,18,8,12,15 is:" +
            min(6,2,3,18,8,12,15) );

        pl();

        pause( "Lets manipulate some data, press ..." +
               " well you know you know what to do ..." );
```

```
    }//end public static void someMath()


    public static void whoAmI()
    {
        //calling methods from the ToolsSPClass super-class
        setMyName( "Michael" );

        p( "Howdy my name is " );

        pl( getMyName() );

        pause( "Let's do some math, press any key to continue .." );

    }//end public static void whoAmI()


    public static void main( String arg[] )
    {
        whoAmI();;

        someMath();

        dataManipulation();

        showPolymorphism();

        pl( "Thank you for using PolyMain, hope to see you " +
            "again soon" );

        pl( "=================================================" +
            "======" );

    }//end public static void main( String arg[] )

}//end public class PolyMain extends toolsSPClass
```

Let's examine this code:

At this point what we do is compile the PolyMain program that extends/inherits from ToolsSPClass, which in turn compiles all the super- and sub-class being used by this program. The details of each program will be displayed in the following section.

Your output (results) will look like this:

```
Howdy my name is Michael

Let's do some math, press any key to continue ..


Adding ints    3, 5, 6 = 14

Adding doubles 3, 5, 6 = 14.0

Adding floats  3, 5, 6 = 14.0

The average of 3, 5, 6 = 4.67

The Maximum number of 6,2,3,18,8,12,15 is:18

The Minimum number of 6,2,3,18,8,12,15 is:2


Lets manipulate some data, press ... well you know you know what to do
...


I want to print backwards the following array of Objects:

49 33 a michael

michael a 33 49

Let's continue..


Using ToolsSPClass full = new  FullSizeCarSBClass(); .. enter

---------------------------------------------------

I AM TESTING THE FULL SIZE as an object

AM USING SUBS ABOUT TIME as a static

---------------------------------------------------
```

```
Using ToolsSPClass sport = new SportCarSBClass(); .. enter

---------------------------------------------------

I am testing the sports size as an object

I am testing the sports size as a static

---------------------------------------------------

Using ToolsSPClass mini = new MiniCarSBClass(); .. enter

---------------------------------------------------

I am testing the mini size as an object

I am testing the mini size  as a static

---------------------------------------------------


Calling  methods from different classes .. enter

---------------------------------------------------

I AM TESTING THE MINI SIZE

I AM TESTING THE MINI SIZE

The Maximum number of 6,2,3,18,8,12,15 is : 18

The Minimum number of 6,2,3,18,8,12,15 is : 2
---------------------------------------------------

Thank you for using PolyMain, hope to see you again soon
===================================================
```

This is the diagram of all classes that I am using in following section:

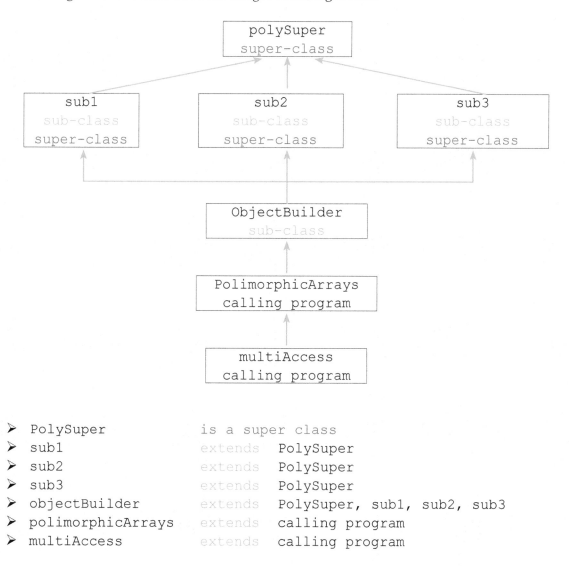

> PolySuper   is a super class
> sub1   extends   PolySuper
> sub2   extends   PolySuper
> sub3   extends   PolySuper
> objectBuilder   extends   PolySuper, sub1, sub2, sub3
> polimorphicArrays   extends   calling program
> multiAccess   extends   calling program

The above program has a more detailed implementation of polymorphism, and it contains inheritance and also creates objects of a sub-class with super-class data type.

This is the heart of polymorphism. We can create an object of a sub-class of data type super-class.

Polymorphism also allows us to create arrays of data type super-class and have in each index of the array a different object of a different sub-class.

If we have a method that accepts objects of type super-class, this method can also accept objects of the such super-class's sub-classes, without having to create new methods for each sub-class.

The following class objectBuilder.java contains the method processing(String who, polySuper temp) which accepts data of type polySuper which is a super-class.

```
/*
   Author  : Michael Robinson
   Program : objectBuilder.java
   Purpose : This is a class that accepts objects of a super-class
             and its sub-classes

   Updated : September 23rd, 2099
*/


public class objectBuilder
{
    //the type polySuper is a super-class
    public void processing( String who, polySuper temp )
    {
        System.out.print( who + " " );

        temp.myName();

    }//end public static void processing( polySuper temp )

}//end public class objectBuilder
```

This is the polySuper.java super-class which implements polymorphic arrays:

```
/*
   Author  : Michael Robinson
   Program : polySuper.java
   Purpose : This is a super-class.
             Implementing polymorphic arrays.

   Updated : September 23rd, 2099
*/


public class polySuper
{
    public void myName()
    {
        System.out.println( "Hi, I am the super-class polySuper" );
```

```
        }//end public static void myName()

}//end public class polySuper
```

The following is the sub1.java sub-class:

```
/*
   Author   : Michael Robinson
   Program  : sub1.java
   Purpose  : This class inherits from polySuper
              Implementing polymorphic arrays

   Updated : September 23rd, 2099
*/


public class sub1 extends polySuper
{
     public void myName()
     {
            System.out.println( "Hi, I am sub1" );

     }//end public static void myName()

}//end public class sub1
```

This is the sub2 sub-class:

```
/*
   Author   : Michael Robinson
   Program  : sub2.java
   Purpose  : This class inherits from polySuper
              I are implementing polymorphic arrays

   Updated : September 23rd, 2099
*/


public class sub2 extends polySuper
{
    public void myName()
    {
```

```
            System.out.println( "Hi, I am sub2" );

        }//end public static void myName()

}//end public class sub2
```

This is the sub3 sub-class:

```
/*
   Author  : Michael Robinson
   Program : sub3.java
   Purpose : This class inherits from polySuper
             I are implementing polymorphic arrays

   Updated : September 23rd, 2099
*/


public class sub3 extends polySuper
{
      public void myName()
      {
            System.out.println( "Hi, I am sub3" );

      }//end public static void myName()

}//end public class sub3
```

This is the calling program called multiAccess.java which passes objects of super-class and sub-classes to the objectBuilder class.

```
/*
   Author  : Michael Robinson
   Program : multiAccess.java
   Purpose : This program passes objects of a super-class and its sub-
             classes to a class that accepts objects of a super-class
             data type.

   Updated : September 23rd, 2099
*/
```

```
public class multiAccess
{
    public static void main( String arg[] )
    {
        //this object takes an argument type polySuper
        objectBuilder test = new objectBuilder();

        //to be used as a parameter in the test object.
        //notice polyObject is of type and class polySuper
        polySuper polyObject = new polySuper();

        //passing the super-class
        test.processing( "super", polyObject );


        //*********************************************
        //to be used as a parameter in the test object.
        //notice sub1Object is of type polySuper
        //and class sub1, a sub-class
        polySuper sub1Object = new sub1();
        polySuper sub2Object = new sub2();
        polySuper sub3Object = new sub3();

        //passing the sub-classes
        test.processing( "sub1", sub1Object );
        test.processing( "sub2", sub2Object );
        test.processing( "sub3", sub3Object );

    }//end public static void main( String arg[] )

}//end public class multiAccess
```

Your output (results) will look like this:

When we run java multiAccess, this is the output:

```
super Hi, I am the super-class polySuper
sub1 Hi, I am sub1
sub2 Hi, I am sub2
sub3 Hi, I am sub3
```

Let's examine this code:

Notice that the signature for all the methods in these classes, except for the calling programs, does not contain the statement "static," so they look as follows:

```
public void myName()
public void processing( String who, polySuper temp )
```

Notice that polimorphicArrays and multiAccess are the only two programs that have a main method. Both programs are calling programs that are calling multiple sub-classes and super-classes.

Now we will have some examples of polymorphic arrays.

```
/*
  Author  : Michael Robinson
  Program : polimorphicArrays.java
  Purpose : This program creates an array of objectBuilder data type
            then it loads sub-classes into array
            prints backwards array contents
            prints forwards array contents


  Updated : September 23rd, 2099
*/


public class polimorphicArrays
{
    public static void main( String arg[] )
    {

        //create an array of objectBuilder data type
        polySuper array[] = new polySuper[3];

        //load sub-classes into array
        array[0] = new sub1();
        array[1] = new sub2();
        array[2] = new sub3();

        //print array contents backwards
        for( int temp = array.length -1; temp > -1; temp-- )
        {
            array[temp].myName();
        }
```

```
        System.out.println();

        //print forwards array contents
        for( polySuper temp : array )
        {
            temp.myName();
        }

    }//end public static void main( String arg[] )

}//end public class polimorphicArrays
```

Let's examine this code:

Here we have created an array of polySuper data type that accepts three sub-classes objects with the data type being polySuper.

Your output (results) will look like this:

When we run polimorphicArrays.java the output is this:

```
Hi, I am sub3
Hi, I am sub2
Hi, I am sub1


Hi, I am sub1
Hi, I am sub2
Hi, I am sub3
```

Final Methods

Now that we have learned about inheritance, we know what super-classes and sub-classes are.

Final methods can NOT be overridden by sub-classes. This is just like in the case of the final variables, final methods are used to prevent any changes to be made to a method in a super-class.

The following is a simple example of a final method.

```
/*
   Author  : Michael Robinson
   Program : theFinalMethodClass.java
   Purpose : Simple example of a final method
             which can not be modified by any sub-class.

   Updated : August 18, 2099
*/


public class theFinalMethodClass
{

    public static final void theFinalMethod()
    {
        System.out.println( "I am theFinalMethod() and you can" +
                            " NOT override me." );

    }//end public static final void theFinalMethod()

}//end public class theFinalMethodClass
```

If we try to override the theFinalMethod() method in the above class using the following program:

```
/*
   Author  : Michael Robinson
   Program : finalMethodClass.java
   Purpose : This class extends theFinalMethodClass
             and tries to override the final method
             theFinalMethod() of the super-class

   Updated : August 18, 2099
*/


public class finalMethodClass extends theFinalMethodClass
{
    public static final void theFinalMethod()
    {

    }//end public static final void theFinalMethod()
```

```
public static void main( String arg[] )
{

    theFinalMethod();

}//end public static void main( String arg[] )

}//end public class finalMethodClass extends theFinalMethodClass
```

we will get the following error:

```
finalMethodClass.java:14:  error:  theFinalMethod()  in  finalMethodClass
cannot override theFinalMethod() in theFinalMethodClass

    public static final void theFinalMethod()
                            ^
  overridden method is static,final

1 error
```

Final Classes

We make a class FINAL when we want to prevent any other class from inheriting from it. Final classes can not have sub-classes. We usually do this for security reasons. Classes from the Java API standard library such as Java.lang.System, java.util.Collections, java.util.Arrays, and Java.lang.String are final. All the methods in a final class are automatically treated as final methods.

The following is a simple example of a final class:
```
/*
  Author   : Michael Robinson
  Program  : aFinalClass.java
  Purpose  : We make a class FINAL when we want to prevent any other
             class from inheriting from it. Final classes can not
             have sub-classes. We usually do this for security
             reasons.

  Updated  : August 18, 2099
*/


public final class aFinalClass
{
    public static void main( String arg[] )
```

```
    {
        System.out.println( "Hi I am a FINAL class" );

    }//end public static void main( String arg[] )

}//end public final class aFinalClass
```

Your output (results) will look like this:

When we run aFinalClass the output is this:

```
Hi I am a FINAL class
```

Protected Classes Methods and Variables

There are three types of access for classes, methods, and variables: public, protected and private.

Protected is the access mode that is between public and private. These are the scopes of the three access modes:

```
Modifier        Class   Package    Subclass    Everybody
public            Y        Y           Y           Y
protected         Y        Y           Y           N
no modifier       Y        Y           N           N
private           Y        N           N           N
```

The following are examples of how to implement a protective method.

```
/*
  Author   : Michael Robinson
  Program  : protectedWay.java
  Purpose  : How protected methods can be used

            Protected Methods Access Levels
            Modifier      Class    Package     Subclass  Everybody
            public          Y        Y            Y         Y
            protected       Y        Y            Y         N
            no modifier     Y        Y            N         N
            private         Y        N            N         N


  Updated  : October 24, 2099
*/
```

```
public class protectedWay
{
    protected static void protectedName()
    {
        System.out.println( "\nMy name is THE PROTECTED METHOD" );

    }//end protected static void protectedName()


    public static void publicName()
    {

        System.out.println( "\nMy name is THE PUBLIC METHOD" );

    }//end public static void publicName()

}//end public class protectedWay
```

The following program calls the protected methods of the above program:

```
/*
  Author  : Michael Robinson
  Program : protectedTesting.java
  Purpose : How to use protected methods
            Protected Methods Access Levels
            Modifier        Class    Package    Subclass  Everybody
            public          Y        Y          Y         Y
            protected       Y        Y          Y         N
            no modifier     Y        Y          N         N
            private         Y        N          N         N

  Updated : October 24, 2099
*/


public class protectedTesting
{

    public static void main( String arg[] )
    {
        protectedWay.publicName();

        protectedWay.protectedName();
```

```
    }//end public static void main( String arg[] )

}//end public class protectedTesting
```

Your output (results) will look like this:

```
My name is THE PUBLIC METHOD

My name is THE PROTECTED METHOD
```

Let's examine this code:

In the protectedWay.java program the publicName() method is declared as a public method:

```
           public static void publicName()
```

and it is then called in the protectedTesting class as follows:

```
            protectedWay.publicName();
```

In the protectedWay.java program the protectedName() method is declared as a protected method:

```
          protected static void protectedName()
```

and it is then called in the protectedTesting class as follows:

```
          protectedWay.protectedName();
```

Summary

In this chapter we covered two of the most important topics in the Java programming language, inheritance and polymorphism.

The basic concept of inheritance is that some classes inherit methods and variables from other classes. The class providing the inheritance is called the "super-class." It is also known as the "base-class." The class inheriting is called the sub-class. It is also referred to as the "derived-class."

The only condition for inheritance is that all variables and methods need to be declared public to be inheritable, if they are declared private the sub-classes can not see them.

Polymorphism is an extension of inheritance, it allows us to use multiple super-classes and multiple sub-classes from calling programs, which we refer to as main/calling programs. Remember that super-classes and sub-classes do not have the main method.

Final Methods. Final methods can NOT be overridden by sub-classes. This is just like in the case of the final variables, final methods are used to prevent any changes to be made to a method in a super-class.

Final Classes. We make a class FINAL when we want to prevent any other class from inheriting from it. Final classes can not have sub-classes. We usually do this for security reasons. Classes from the Java API standard library such as Java.lang.System, java.util.Collections, java.util.Arrays, and Java.lang.String are final. All the methods in a final class are automatically treated as final methods.

Protected Classes Methods and Variables. There are three types of access for classes, methods, and variables: public, protected, and private. Protected is the access mode that is between public and private. These are the scopes of the three access modes:

Modifier	Class	Package	Subclass	Everybody
public	Y	Y	Y	Y
protected	Y	Y	Y	N
no modifier	Y	Y	N	N
private	Y	N	N	N

Key Terms

Final Classes	We make a class FINAL when we want to prevent any other class from inheriting from it. Final classes can not have sub-classes. We usually do this for security reasons. Classes from the Java API standard library such as Java.lang.System, java.util.Arrays, Java.lang.String and java.util.Collections are final. All the methods in a final class are automatically treated as final methods. Our aFinalClass.java program is a simple example of a final class.
Final Methods	Now that we have learned about inheritance, we know what super-classes and sub-classes are final methods that can NOT be overridden by sub-classes. This is just like in the case of the final variables, final methods are used to prevent any changes to be made to a method in a super-class. Our theFinalMethodClass.java is a simple example of a final method.
Inheritance	The basic concept of inheritance is that some classes inherit methods and variables from other classes. The class providing the inheritance is called the "super-class," It is also known as the "base-class." The class inheriting is called the sub-class. It is also referred to as the "derived-class." Here we will call them "super-class" and "sub-class." The only condition for inheritance is that all variables and methods are declared public to be inheritable, if they are declared private sub-classes we can not see them. For this section we have created the following programs: cssDefautls.java is the super-class webPageHome.java is a sub-class webPage2.java is a sub-class webPage3.java is a sub-class inheritanceWebPage.java is the main program The first step is to create an external class called cssDefautls.java, this class will be the super-class. Then we create multiple external classes that will define different web-pages: webPageHome, webPage2, and webPage3. These external classes will be the sub-classes that will inherit from the cssDefautls.java super-class. Now that we have the super-class and a group of external classes we will create a class named inheritanceWebPage.java which will make use of the variables and methods of the above super-class and sub-classes.

Polymorphism	Polymorphism is an extension of inheritance. It allows us to use multiple super-classes and multiple sub-classes from calling programs, which I refer to as main or calling programs. Remember that super-classes and sub-classes do not have the main method.
	Please review the following .java programs:
	ToolsSPClass is a super class VehicleSPClass extends ToolsSPClass and is a super class PolyMain extends ToolsSPClass TheVehicleMain extends ToolsSPClass FullSizeCarSBClass extends VehicleSPClass SportCarSBClass extends VehicleSPClass MiniCarSBClass extends VehicleSPClass
Variables. Protected Classes Methods and Variables	There are three types of access for classes, methods, and variables: public, protected, and private.
	Protected is the access mode that is between public and private, these are the scopes of the three access modes:

Modifier	Class	Package	Subclass	Everybody
public	Y	Y	Y	Y
protected	Y	Y	Y	N
no modifier	Y	Y	N	N
private	Y	N	N	N

Exercises

1. Write a program that inherits from another program called homes, and have it override a method called roomOne which accepts two variables.

2. Create a super-class with methods that can not be inherited.

3. Create a program with final variables and methods only.

4. Create a program with one final method, one protected method, and one public method.

5. Create a program with one final variable, one protected variable, and one public variable.

Multiple choice questions. Choose all that apply:

6. What is inheritance?

   a. Classes can inherit public methods and variables from other classes
   b. Most classes inherit methods and variables from other classes
   c. All classes can inherit all methods from other classes
   d. All classes can inherit all variables from other classes

7. What is polymorphism?

   a. An extension of inheritance, it allows us to use multiple super-classes and multiple sub-classes using calling programs
   b. Programs that must have super-classes, sub-classes and the main method
   c. A way of inheriting final methods from public classes
   d. How we allow inheritance to extend final classes

8. What are final methods?

   a. The last method in a program
   b. Methods found in public classes only
   c. Methods found in final classes only
   d. Methods that can not be inherited and modified

9. What are final classes?

   a. Final Classes are the last classes in a program
   b. They do not exist
   c. Classes that can not be inherited
   d. Classes that can not be modified

10. What are protected classes methods and variables?

    a. Classes with Class, Package, Subclass and Everybody scope
    b. Classes with Class, Package, and Subclass scope
    c. Classes that protect Inheritance
    d. The do not exist

REFERENCES

- Java API Specifications
  http://www.oracle.com/technetwork/java/api-141528.html

- My Java programs that I use in my Java classes located at robinson.cs.fiu.edu

//END CHAPTER 13: INHERITANCE AND POLYMORPHISM

Interfaces and Abstraction

What is an Interface?

An interface is a class that contains methods that only have headings. It is also referred as "an interface is a group of related methods with empty bodies." These methods are considered to be "templates" without bodies. Interfaces can be implemented in any other class and all the methods in the interface must be used in the class that is implementing the interface. One of the main purposes of using interfaces is to establish uniformity in the software development, so that every class that uses a specific interface will implement all its methods. Another advantage is that each method in the interface can have its own implementation defined by the need of the class that is using it. Everything in an interface is "abstract."

There are two types of contents that we can have in an interface:

- Methods can be of type public and abstract ONLY.
- Variables can be of type public, static and final ONLY.

If we do not give a type to the methods or the variables, by default interfaces automatically treat the methods as "public abstract" and the variables as "public static final."

Since variables are "public static final" we must assign a value to them when we declare them. Since we can not have definitions in an interface, we can not have constructors in an interface.

Interfaces can inherit multiple interfaces since they are abstract.

Classes can only inherit one class.

< 379 >

A class can inherit an interface by using:

```java
public static class demo implements interfaceDemo
{

}
```

An interface to maintain a student record can be as follows:

```java
/*
  Author  : Michael Robinson
  Program : studentIDinterface.java
  Purpose : This is an Interface example

  Updated : September 1, 2099
*/


public interface studentIDinterface
{
    public String SchoolID = "UNI_87945";

    void studentID( int studentID );
    void studentLastName( String studentLastName );
    void studentFirstName( String studentFirstName );
    void studentMiddleName( String studentMiddleName );
    void studentAddress1( String studentAddress1 );
    void studentAddress2( String studentAddress2 );
    void studentCity( String studentCity );
    void studentState( String studentState );
    void studentCountry( String studentCountryName );
    void studentZipCode( String studentZipCode );
    void studentTelNumber( String studentTelNumber );

}//end public interface studentIDinterface
```

We can directly access the variables inside the interfaces as follows:

```java
System.out.println( studentIDinterface.SchoolID );
```

however, to implement the interface in any other class we must use all the methods in the interface and create the bodies for each method:

```java
/*
  Author   : Michael Robinson
  Program  : setStudentID.java
  Purpose  : This is a class that implements
             the studentIDinterface  interface

  Updated : September 1, 2099
*/



class setStudentID implements studentIDinterface
{
    //creating global public variables
    public int    studentID;
    public String studentLastName;
    public String studentFirstName;
    public String studentMiddleName;
    public String studentAddress1;
    public String studentAddress2;
    public String studentCity;
    public String studentState;
    public String studentCountry;
    public String studentZipCode;
    public String studentTelNumber;



    public void studentSchool( )
    {
        //the SchoolID variable used here is the
        //public global variable from the interface
        System.out.println( SchoolID );

    }//end public void studentSchool( String SchoolID )


    public void studentID( int studentID )
    {
        //assigns received studentID value to
        //global studentID variable
        this.studentID = studentID;

        System.out.println( this.studentID );
```

```java
    }//end public void studentID( int studentID )


    public void studentLastName( String studentLastName )
    {
        //assigns received studentLastName value to
        //global studentLastName variable
        this.studentLastName = studentLastName;

        System.out.println( this.studentLastName );

    }//end public void studentLastName( String studentLastName )


    public void studentFirstName( String studentFirstName )
    {
        //assigns received studentFirstName value to
        //global studentFirstName variable
        this.studentFirstName = studentFirstName;

        System.out.println( this.studentFirstName );

    }//end public void studentFirstName( String studentFirstName )


    public void studentMiddleName( String studentMiddleName )
    {
        //assigns received studentMiddleName value to
        //global studentMiddleName variable
        this.studentMiddleName = studentMiddleName;

        System.out.println( this.studentMiddleName );

    }//end public void studentMiddleName( String studentMiddleName )


    public void studentAddress1( String studentAddress1 )
    {
        //assigns received studentAddress1 value to
        //global studentAddress1 variable
        this.studentAddress1 = studentAddress1;

        System.out.println( this.studentAddress1 );

    }//end public void studentAddress1( String studentAddress1 )


    public void studentAddress2( String studentAddress2 )
    {
        //assigns received studentAddress2 value to
        //global studentAddress2 variable
        this.studentAddress2 = studentAddress2;
```

```java
        System.out.println( this.studentAddress2 );

}//end public void studentAddress2( String studentAddress2 )


public void studentCity( String studentCity )
{
    //assigns received studentCity value to
    //global studentCity variable
    this.studentCity = studentCity;

    System.out.println( this.studentCity );

}//end public void studentCity( String studentCity )


public void studentState( String studentState )
{
    //assigns received studentState value to
    //global studentState variable
    this.studentState = studentState;

    System.out.println( this.studentState );

}//end public void studentState( String studentState )


public void studentCountry( String studentCountry )
{
    //assigns received studentCountry value to
    //global studentCountry variable
    this.studentCountry = studentCountry;

    System.out.println( this.studentCountry );

}//end public void studentCountry( String studentCountry )


public void studentZipCode( String studentZipCode )
{
    //assigns received studentZipCode value to
    //global studentZipCode variable
    this.studentZipCode = studentZipCode;

    System.out.println( this.studentZipCode );

}//end public void studentZipCode( String studentZipCode )


public void studentTelNumber( String studentTelNumber )
{
```

```
            //assigns received studentTelNumber value to
            //global studentTelNumber variable
            this.studentTelNumber = studentTelNumber;

            System.out.println( this.studentTelNumber );

    }//end public void studentTelNumber( String studentTelNumber )


    public static void main( String arg[] )
    {
            //create and object of the interface type
            //from our own class that is implementing the interface
            studentIDinterface MySetStudentID = new setStudentID();

            //call the implemented methods from the interface
            //passing our own data, except for the schoolID that
            //we will get from the interface, see studentSchool()
            //method
            MySetStudentID.studentSchool();

            MySetStudentID.studentID( 1234567 );

            MySetStudentID.studentLastName( "Hamilton" );

            MySetStudentID.studentFirstName( "Joseph" );

            MySetStudentID.studentMiddleName( "Michael" );

            MySetStudentID.studentAddress1( "123 main st" );

            MySetStudentID.studentAddress2( "apt #456" );

            MySetStudentID.studentCity( "Miami" );

            MySetStudentID.studentState( "Florida" );

            MySetStudentID.studentCountry( "USA" );

            MySetStudentID.studentZipCode( "76512" );

            MySetStudentID.studentTelNumber( "555-555-5555" );

    }//end public void main( String arg[] )

}//end class setStudentID implements studentIDinterface}
```

Your output (results) will look like this:

```
1234567
Hamilton
Joseph
Michael
123 main st
apt #456
Miami
Florida
USA
76512
555-555-5555
```

Let's examine this code:

When we implement an interface we are required to create all the methods that appear in the interface. Any data variables in the interface can be used by the program, but it is not required to use the them. This is our interface signature:

```
interface studentIDinterface
```

and this is how we implement it:

```
class setStudentID implements studentIDinterface
```

The above implementation is very well documented. Please read each line.

Data Abstraction

Java has abstract classes and methods. Abstracts are not defined. An abstract classes exists to be extended. It can only be used for inheritance or polymorphism, we can not create objects from an abstract class:

```
abstract public class abstractClass //this is an  abstract class
{

}//end abstract public class abstractClass
```

Abstract classes contain abstract methods, abstract methods do NOT contain a body, just the heading:

```
abstract void hello(); //this is an abstract method NO BODY NEEDED
```

Abstract classes can also contain regular methods:

```
public static void methodOne()
{
    System.out.println( "I am methodOne, a regular method " +
                        "inside an the abstractClass" );


}//end public static void methodOne()
```

This is an example of an abstract class:

```
/*
  Author  : Michael Robinson
  Program : abstractClass.java
  Purpose : this is an abstract class,
            it can contain as many abstract methods as needed.
            Abstract classes can also contain as many
            regular methods as needed.

  Updated : September 9th, 2099
*/


abstract public class abstractClass //this is an  abstract class
{
    //this is an abstract method NO BODY NEEDED
    //but this method MUST be overridden if this
    //abstract class is  extended
    abstract void hello();


    //this is a regular method inside an abstract class
    public static void methodOne()
    {
        System.out.println( "I am methodOne, a regular method " +
                            "inside an the abstractClass" );

    }//end public static void methodOne()


    //does not need to be implemented
    public static void methodTwo()
    {
        //not all regular methods need to be implemented in an
        //abstract class
```

```
    }

}//end abstract public class abstractClass
```

All classes that extend an abstract class MUST override all the abstract methods in the abstract class.

The following is a class that inherits the previous "abstractClass:"

```
/*
  Author   : Michael Robinson
  Program  : extendsAbstractClass.java
  Purpose  : This class  extends the abstract class named
             abstractClass, It overrides the abstract hello method in
             the abstract class.

  Updated  : September 9th, 2099
*/


public class extendsAbstractClass extends abstractClass
{
    //this method is an abstract method implementation
    public void hello()
    {
        System.out.println( "I am the implementation of the hello" +
          " abstract method\n inside the extendsAbstractClass.java" );

    }//end public void hello()


    public static void methodOne()
    {
        System.out.println( "I am methodOne inside the " +
                            "extendsAbstractClass.java." );

    }//end public static void methodOne()

}//end public class extendsAbstractClass extends abstractClass
```

As we can see, here we override the hello abstract method and the regular method methodOne() from the abstract class.

Now we will use the extendsAbstractClass class to inherit all methods from it and the abstract class as well:

```
/*
   Author  : Michael Robinson
   Program : usingAbstract.java
   Purpose : This class uses a class called:
             extendsAbstractClass.java which inherits from an
             ABSTRACT CLASS called abstractClass.java

   Updated : September 9th, 2099
*/


public class usingAbstract
{
    public static void main( String arg[] )
    {
        System.out.println( "I am at: usingAbstract.java's main" +
                            " method\n" );

        //create an object of a class that inherits an abstract class
        extendsAbstractClass one = new extendsAbstractClass();

        //use a method from this new object called one
        one.hello();
        System.out.println();

        //use overridden regular method in the extendsAbstractClass
        extendsAbstractClass.methodOne();

        System.out.println();

        //use a regular method in the abstract class
        abstractClass.methodOne();

    }//end public static void main( String arg[] )

}//end public class usingAbstract
```

Your output (results) will look like this:

```
I am at: usingAbstract.java's main method

I am the implementation of the hello abstract method inside the
extendsAbstractClass.java

I am methodOne inside the extendsAbstractClass.java.

I am methodOne, a regular method inside an the abstractClass
```

Let's examine this code:

```
The three above programs are very short and are very well documented.
Please read the comments inside the programs.
```

Data Abstraction vs Interfaces

Sometimes we ask why we need interfaces when we can use abstract classes. The answer is simple. Every method in an interface MUST be implemented, while in abstract classes only the abstract methods MUST be implemented.

Interfaces can only have methods that are abstract, while abstract classes can have both abstract and regular methods.

Summary

In this chapter we covered Interfaces, Data abstraction and Data Abstraction vs Interfaces.

An interface is a class that contains methods that only have headings. It is also referred as "an interface is a group of related methods with empty bodies." These methods are considered to be "templates" without bodies. Interfaces can be implemented in any other class and all the methods in the interface must be used in the class that is implementing the interface. One of the main purposes of using interfaces is to establish uniformity in the software development, so that every class that uses a specific interface will implement all its methods. Another advantage is that each method in the interface can have its own implementation defined by the need of the class that is using it. Everything in an interface is "abstract."

Data abstraction. An abstract class exists to be extended. It can only be used for inheritance or polymorphism, we can not create objects from an abstract class. Java has abstract classes and methods.

Data Abstraction vs Interfaces. Every method in an interface MUST be implemented while in abstract classes only the abstract methods MUST be implemented. Interfaces can only have methods that are abstract, while abstract classes can have both abstract and regular methods.

Key Terms

Data abstraction	Java has abstract classes and methods. Abstracts are not defined. An abstract classes exists to be extended. It can only be used for inheritance or polymorphism, we can not create objects from an abstract class:
	
	 //this is an abstract class
	 abstract public class abstractClass
	 {
	
	 }//end abstract public class abstractClass
	
	 Abstract classes contain abstract methods, abstract methods do NOT contain a body, just the heading:
	 abstract void hello(); //this is an abstract method NO BODY NEEDED

Data Abstraction vs Interfaces	Sometimes we ask why we need interfaces when we can use abstract classes. The answer is simple. Every method in an interface MUST be implemented while in abstract classes only the abstract methods MUST be implemented. Interfaces can only have methods that are abstract, while abstract classes can have both abstract and regular methods.
What is an Interface?	An interface is a class that contains methods that only have headings. It is also referred as "an interface is a group of related methods with empty bodies." These methods are considered to be "templates" without bodies. Interfaces can be implemented in any other class and all the methods in the interface must be used in the class that is implementing the interface. One of the main purposes of using interfaces is to establish uniformity in the software development, so that every class that uses a specific interface will implement all its methods. Another advantage is that each method in the interface can have its own implementation defined by the needs of the class that is using it. Everything in an interface is "abstract." There are two types of contents that we can have in an interface: methods can only be of type public and abstract, and variables are of type public, static and final. If we do not give a type to the methods or the variables, by default interfaces automatically treat the methods as "public abstract" and the variables as "public static final." Since variables are "public static final" we must assign a value to them when we declare them. Because we can not have definitions in an interface, we can not have constructors in an interface.

Exercises

1. Make a program to create an interface.

2. Implement the interface on question 1.

3. Create an abstract class with two abstract methods and one regular method.

4. Create a program to extend the previous abstract class.

5. Create a program to use the program # 4.

Multiple choice questions. Choose all that apply:

6. What is an interface?

    a. A class that contains abstract methods only
    b. A class that contains methods that only have headings
    c. A class that contains final methods only
    d. A class that contains global protected methods only

7. What is data abstraction?

    a. An abstract class exists to be extended—it can only be used for inheritance or polymorphism
    b. An abstract class with methods that only have headings
    c. An abstract class that can not be used in polymorphism
    d. An abstract class that can only be used in inheritance

8. What is the difference between data abstraction and interfaces?

    a. Interfaces are used for polymorphism only and abstraction for inheritance only
    b. Abstractions work on virtual box VMs, interfaces do not
    c. Every method in abstract classes need to be implemented while not in the interface
    d. Every method in an interface MUST be implemented while in abstract classes only the abstract methods MUST be implemented

9. What can we create from abstract classes?

    a. We can create objects from an abstract class
    b. Abstract classes allows us to implement inheritance or polymorphism
    c. Abstract classes allows interfaces
    d. Abstract classes are used to create constructors

10. Can interfaces inherit multiple interfaces since they are abstract?

    a. Yes, as many as necessary
    b. Only if they are not abstract
    c. No interfaces can not inherit interfaces
    d. They can only inherit one non-abstract interface

REFERENCES

- Java API Specifications
  http://www.oracle.com/technetwork/java/api-141528.html

- My Java programs that I use in my Java classes located at robinson.cs.fiu.edu

//END CHAPTER 14: INTERFACES AND ABSTRACTION

Data Structures Implementations

chapter 15

Linked List

Linked lists have many similarities to single dimensional arrays the major difference is:

- Linkedlist are data structures that do not have a set size as in arrays. What we know in arrays as indexes, in linked lists we call them nodes.

- In linked lists we can always extend or reduce the amount of nodes. In arrays we can not change their amount of indexes, once created.

Linked lists are better than arrays in some areas, and arrays are better than linked lists in other areas. In this chapter we will learn how to implement them. Full semester courses in data structures deal with the detailed study of linked lists and other data structures.

A linked list is referred to as a linear collection of nodes, they are also defined as a finite sequence of nodes. Except for the first node, each node contains one pointer field that points to the next node, and another pointer field that points to the previous node. The first node only points to the next node. The pointer in the last node points to null, which is always the end of the linked list.

The following program shows how to create linked lists, add data into new nodes, print all nodes forward and backwards, delete nodes and merge multiple linked lists.

< 395 >

```java
/*
  Author  : Michael Robinson
  Program : linkedListSample.java
  Purpose : Here we learn how to create link lists
            A data structure that is very efficient to
            add nodes in a list.
            The drawback of link lists is the search time
            to find a node is very expensive in time.

  Updated : October 15, 2099
*/


import java.util.*;


public class linkedListSample
{
    public static void createLinkedList()
    {
        System.out.println( "\nCreating food Linked List" );

        //this is a one dimensional array of String data type
        String foodsArray[] =
            { "Chicken_soup", "Wild_Rice", "Bread", "Lasagna" };



        //this is a linked list of String data type
        List<String> foodsList = new LinkedList<String>();



        //this for loop reads one item at the time
        for( String foods: foodsArray )
        {

            //adding the array item foods to the linked list
            foodsList.add(foods);

            System.out.printf( "adding %s\n", foods );

        }

        System.out.println( "\nCreating people Linked List" );
```

```java
            //creating another single dimensional array of String type
            String peopleArray[] = { "Joe", "Maria", "Bobby", "Tony" };


            //this is a linked list of String data type
            List<String> peopleList = new LinkedList<String>();


            //this for loop reads one item at the time
            for( String people: peopleArray )
            {
                //adding the array item people to the linked list
                peopleList.add(people);

                System.out.printf( "adding %s\n", people );
            }

            System.out.println( "\nMerging Linked Lists" );

            //merge Linked List peopleList into foodsList
            foodsList.addAll( peopleList );

            for( String temp : foodsList )
            {

                System.out.printf( "%s\n", temp );

            }

            printListFoward( foodsList );

            printListBackward( foodsList );


            //remove nodes from location 4 to 6
            removeItems( foodsList, 4, 6 );

            printListFoward( foodsList );

            printListBackward( foodsList );

    }//end public static void createLinkedList()
```

```java
public static void printListFoward( List<String> foodsList )
{

    System.out.print( "\nPrinting nodes Forward    : " );

    for( String temp : foodsList )
    {

        System.out.printf( "[%s] ", temp );

    }

}//end public static void printListFoward(List<String> foodsList)


public static void printListBackward( List<String> foodsList )
{

    System.out.print( "\nPrinting nodes Backwards : " );

    ListIterator<String> itr =
            foodsList.listIterator( foodsList.size() );

    while( itr.hasPrevious() )
    {

        System.out.printf( "[%s] ", itr.previous() );

    }

}//end public static void
 //printListBackward(List<String> foodsList)



public static void removeItems(
                List<String> foodsList, int from, int to )
{

    foodsList.subList( from, to ).clear();

    System.out.printf( "\n\nRemoving items %d to %d\n",
                    from, to );

}//end public static void
 //removeItems(List<String> foodsList,int from, int to)
```

```
    public static void main( String arg[] )
    {
        createLinkedList();

    }//end public static void main( String arg[] )

}//end public class linkList
```

output (results) will look like this:

```
Creating food Linked List
adding Chicken_soup
adding Wild_Rice
adding Bread
adding Lasagna

Creating people Linked List
adding Joe
adding Maria
adding Bobby
adding Tony

Merging Linked Lists
Chicken_soup
Wild_Rice
Bread
Lasagna
Joe
Maria
Bobby
Tony

Printing nodes Forward   : [Chicken_soup] [Wild_Rice] [Bread]
[Lasagna] [Joe] [Maria] [Bobby] [Tony]

Printing nodes Backwards : [Tony] [Bobby] [Maria] [Joe] [Lasagna]
[Bread] [Wild_Rice] [Chicken_soup]

Removing items 4 to 6

Printing nodes Forward   : [Chicken_soup] [Wild_Rice] [Bread]
[Lasagna] [Bobby] [Tony]

Printing nodes Backwards : [Tony] [Bobby] [Lasagna] [Bread] [Wild_
Rice] [Chicken_soup]
```

Let's examine this code:

The detailed comments in the above program and the topic introduction is abundantat and adding more detail is not necessary. Please read the comments in detail.

Overloading

Overloading is a great tool in Java that allows us to use a single method name, to accept different amounts of variables, of various data types, in different order. It behaves similarly to the System.out.print(? ?) Java command.

```
/*
   Author  : Michael Robinson
   Program : overloading.java
   Purpose : Using the same method name for multiple methods.

             By having different amount of variables being
             accepted, and/or different data types, we can
             use methods with the same name.

             This will allows us to use the same method name
             passing multiple variables of different data types,
             like when we using the print commands.

   Updated : October 19, 2099
*/

public class overloading
{

    //accepts unknown amount of ints
    public static int addNumbers( int ... numbers )
    {
        int total = 0;

        //add all int variables in numbers
        for( int temp : numbers )
        {
            total += temp;
        }

        return ( total );

    }//end public static int addNumbers( int ... numbers )
```

```
//accepts one int, one double and another int
public static double addNumbers( int fn, double sn, int tn )
{
    return ( fn + sn + tn );

}//end public static double addNumbers(int fn, double sn, int tn)


//accepts one int, one double and another double
public static double addNumbers( int fn, double sn, double tn )
{
    return ( fn + sn + tn );

}//end public static double addNumbers(
 //                      int fn, double sn, double tn )


//calls multiple methods to be overloaded. All methods have
//the same name addNumbers( ? ? ? ) accepting different types
//and amounts of variables
public static void process()
{

    int fn  = 5;
    int sn  = 3;
    int tn  = 2;
    int fon = 1;

    double done = 3.9;
    double dtwo = 4.1;

    System.out.printf( "\nAdding two ints %3d + %3d = %3d\n",
                    fn, sn, addNumbers( fn, fn ) );


    System.out.printf( "\nAdding four ints " +
                "%3d + %3d + %3d + %3d = %3d\n",
            fn, sn, tn, fon, addNumbers( fn, sn, tn, fon ) );


    System.out.printf( "\nAdding three numbers " +
                "%3d + %3.2f + %3.2f = %3.2f\n",
            fn, done, dtwo, addNumbers( fn, done, dtwo ) );
```

```
        System.out.printf( "\nAdding three numbers " +
                           "%3d + %3.2f + %3d = %3.2f\n",
                    fn, done, sn, addNumbers( fn, done, sn ) );

    }//end public static void process()


    public static void main( String arg[] )
    {
        //calls multiple methods to be overloaded
        process();

    }//end public static void main( String arg[] )

}//end public class overloading
```

Your output (results) will look like this:

```
Adding two ints    5 +   3 =  10

Adding four ints    5 +   3 +   2 +   1 =  11

Adding three numbers    5 + 3.90 + 4.10 = 13.00

Adding three numbers    5 + 3.90 +   3 = 11.90
```

Let's examine this code:

The previous program and this topic's introduction are very detailed and well documented. Please refer to them.

Stacks

Stack is a data structure that allows us to place data items on top of each other. It uses the LIFO (last in, first out) method of processing. The last item placed in the stack is the first item to be extracted.

To create an object of the stack class we use:

```
Stack stackName = new Stack();
```

To place items in the stack we use the command:

```
                    stackName.push( item );
```

To extract items in the stack we use the command:

```
                    stackName.pop();
```

To find the location of an item in the stack we use:

```
                    stackName.search( item );
```

To see the item that is on top of the stack we use:

```
                    stackName.peek();
```

The following program shows us the implementation of a simple stack.

```
/*
  Author   : Michael Robinson
  Program  : simpleStack.java
  Purpose  : Stack is a data structure that allows us to place
             data items on top of each other.

             It uses the LIFO (last in, first out) method of
             processing.
             The last item placed in the stack is the first
             item to be extracted.

             To create an object of the Stack class we use:
                Stack stackName = new Stack();

             To place items in the stack we use the command
                stackName.push( item );

             To extract items in the stack we use the command
                stackName.pop();

             To find the location of an item in the stack we use:
                stackName.search( item );

             To see the item that is on top of the stack we use:
                stackName.peek();

             The Stack class inherits from several classes, e.i:
```

```
            Iterator iter = stack.iterator();

            and many others. For more details see :

            http://docs.oracle.com/javase/6/docs/api/java/util/Stack.html

    Updated : October 26, 2099
*/


import java.util.*;


public class simpleStack
{

    public static void
                printTheStack( Stack<String> stack, String message )
    {
        if( !stack.empty() )
        {
            System.out.printf( "  %s size = %d : %s\n",
                            message, stack.size(), stack );
        }

    }//end public static void
     //printTheStack( Stack<String> stack, String message )


    public static void        stackPop( Stack<String> stack )
    {

        String message = "Poping stack item =";

        while ( !stack.empty() )
        {
            //lets see what is on top
            System.out.printf( "\n  Lets see what is on top : %s",
                            (String)stack.peek() );

            //find and remove the last element from the stack
            System.out.printf( "\n  %s %s\n",
                            message, (String)stack.pop() );
```

```java
        printTheStack( stack, "Items in the stack " );
    }

    System.out.printf( "\nNow we have an empty stack," +
                    " size = %d, items = %s",
                        stack.size(), stack );

}//end public static void stackPop( Stack<String> stack )


public static void fullStack( Stack<String> stack )
{
    System.out.printf( "\nNow that we are playing with a " +
                "full stack let's see what we can do\n\n" );

    System.out.printf( "  Full stack = %s of size %d\n\n",
                    stack, stack.size() );

    String item = "";

    Iterator iter = stack.iterator();

    while(iter.hasNext())
    {
        item = (String)iter.next();
        System.out.printf( "  while loop at location %d the" +
        " stack contains : %s.\n", stack.search( item ), item );
    }

    System.out.println();


    //enhanced for  loop
    for( String temp : stack)
    {
        System.out.printf( "  enhanced for at location %d the" +
                    "  stack contains : %s.\n, " +
                        stack.search( temp ), temp );
    }

    System.out.println();
```

```
        //inline iterator new for loop in Java NO STEP section
        for( Iterator<String> it = stack.iterator(); it.hasNext(); )
        {
            item = (String)it.next();
            System.out.printf( "  inline iterator at location %d " +
                            "the stack contains : %s.\n"," +
                            stack.search( item ), item );
        }

}//end public static void fullStack( Stack<String> stack )


public static void stackPush( Stack<String> stack )
{
        System.out.printf(
                "We start with an empty stack : %s\n\n", stack );

        String message = "Pushing items is the stack,";

        stack.add( "First" );
        printTheStack( stack, message );

        stack.add( "Second" );
        printTheStack( stack, message );

        stack.add( "Third" );
        printTheStack( stack, message );

        stack.add( "Four" );
        printTheStack( stack, message );

}//end public static void stackPush( Stack<String> stack )


public static void  main( String arg[] )
{
        Stack<String> stack = new Stack<String>();

        stackPush( stack );

        fullStack( stack );

        stackPop( stack );
```

```
    }//end public static void  main( String arg[] )

}//end public class simpleStack
```

Your output (results) will look like this:

```
We start with an empty stack : []

  Pushing items is the stack, size = 1 : [First]
  Pushing items is the stack, size = 2 : [First, Second]
  Pushing items is the stack, size = 3 : [First, Second, Third]
  Pushing items is the stack, size = 4 : [First, Second, Third, Four]

Now that we are playing with a full stack let's see what we can do:

  Full stack = [First, Second, Third, Four] of size 4
  while loop at location 4 the stack contains : First.
  while loop at location 3 the stack contains : Second.
  while loop at location 2 the stack contains : Third.
  while loop at location 1 the stack contains : Four.

  enhanced for at location 4 the  stack contains : First.
  enhanced for at location 3 the  stack contains : Second.
  enhanced for at location 2 the  stack contains : Third.
  enhanced for at location 1 the  stack contains : Four.

  inline iterator at location 4 the stack contains : First.
  inline iterator at location 3 the stack contains : Second.
  inline iterator at location 2 the stack contains : Third.
  inline iterator at location 1 the stack contains : Four.

  Lets see what is on top : Four
  Poping stack item = Four

  Items in the stack  size = 3 : [First, Second, Third]

  Lets see what is on top : Third
  Poping stack item = Third

  Items in the stack  size = 2 : [First, Second]
  Lets see what is on top : Second
  Poping stack item = Second
```

```
Items in the stack  size = 1 : [First]
Lets see what is on top : First
Poping stack item = First
```

```
Now we have an empty stack, size = 0, items = []
```

Let's examine this code:

The previous program and this topic's introduction are very detailed and well documented. Please refer to them.

Queue

Queue is a data structure that allows us to place data items one after another. It uses the FIFO (first in, first out) processing method. The first item placed in the queue is the first item to be extracted/processed.

To create an object of the queue class we use:

> Queue<String> queue = new LinkedList<String>();

To place items in the queue we use the command:

> queue.add("FirstQ");

To extract items in the queue we use the command:

> queue.poll();

if we are using an iterator such as:

> Iterator itq = queue.iterator();

we first need to check if the queue has more items:

> itq.hasNext();

then we remove the data using:

> itqProcess.remove();

we can see the first item in the queue using:

        queue.peek();

The following program queue.java is a data structure that allows us to place data items one after another.

```
/*
  Author  : Michael Robinson
  Program : queue.java
  Purpose : Queue is a data structure that allows us to place
            data items one after another.

            It uses the FIFO (First In, First Out) processing method.
            The first item placed in the queue is the first
            item to be extracted/processed.

            To create an object of the Queue class we use:
                Queue<String> queue = new LinkedList<String>();

            To place items in the queue we use the command
                queue.add( "FirstQ" );

            To extract items in the queue we use the command
                queue.poll();

                if we are using an iterator such as:
                    Iterator itq = queue.iterator();

                we first need to check if the queue has more items:
                    itq.hasNext()

                then we remove the data using:
                itqProcess.remove();

                we can see the first item in the queue using:
                queue.peek();

        For more details see :

        http://docs.oracle.com/javase/6/docs/api/java/util/Queue.html

        There is another type of queue called priority queue.

  Updated : October 26, 2099
*/
```

```java
import java.util.Iterator;
import java.util.LinkedList;
import java.util.Queue;


public class queue
{
    public static void printTheQueue(
                    Queue<String> queue, String message )
    {
        System.out.printf( "  Adding...  %d = Size of Queue : %s\n",
                        queue.size(), queue );
    }


    public static void reqularQueue()
    {
        String message = "Adding items is the queue,";

        Queue<String> queue = new LinkedList<String>();

        System.out.printf( "We now start with an empty queue :" +
                        " %s\n\n", queue );

        //add data into the queue
        queue.add( "FirstQ" );
        printTheQueue( queue, message );

        //add data into the queue
        queue.add( "SecondQ" );
        printTheQueue( queue, message );

        //add data into the queue
        queue.add( "ThirdQ" );
        printTheQueue( queue, message );

        //add data into the queue
        queue.add( "FourQ" );
        printTheQueue( queue, message );

        System.out.println("\nFIFO order means, First In First Out");

        System.out.println( "\nLet's see the top of the Queue in" +
                        " FIFO order : " + queue.peek() );
        Iterator itq = queue.iterator();
```

```java
        //print all the data inside the queue
        System.out.printf( "\nLet's see what is in the Queue in " +
                        "FIFO order: %s\n", queue );

        System.out.printf("\n  Let's see again \t .. left in queue");

        //starting at the top of the queue, display all data in queue
        while( itq.hasNext() )
        {
            System.out.printf( " %s ", ( String )itq.next() );
        }

        //display first data in queue
        System.out.printf( "\n  removing  %s", queue.peek() );
        queue.poll();

        System.out.printf( "\t .. data left in queue %s\n", queue );

        Iterator itqProcess = queue.iterator();

        //starting at the top of the queue
        while( itqProcess.hasNext() )
        {
            System.out.printf( "  removing  %s ", ( String )
                            itqProcess.next() );

            itqProcess.remove();

            System.out.printf("\t .. left in queue %s \n", queue );
        }

        System.out.println( "\nFinal Size of Queue : " +
                        queue.size() );

        System.out.printf( "We end with an empty queue : %s\n\n",
                        queue );

}//end  public static void reqularQueue()


public static void main(String[] args)
{
    reqularQueue();
```

```
    }//public static void main(String[] args)

}//end public class queue
```

Your output (results) will look like this:

```
We now start with an empty queue : []

    Adding...   1 = Size of Queue : [FirstQ]
    Adding...   2 = Size of Queue : [FirstQ, SecondQ]
    Adding...   3 = Size of Queue : [FirstQ, SecondQ, ThirdQ]
    Adding...   4 = Size of Queue : [FirstQ, SecondQ, ThirdQ, FourQ]

FIFO order means, First In First Out

Let's see the top of the Queue in FIFO order : FirstQ

Let's see what is in the Queue in FIFO order: [FirstQ, SecondQ,
ThirdQ, FourQ]

    Let's see again     .. left in queue FirstQ  SecondQ  ThirdQ  FourQ
    removing  FirstQ    .. data left in queue [SecondQ, ThirdQ, FourQ]
    removing  SecondQ   .. left in queue [ThirdQ, FourQ]
    removing  ThirdQ    .. left in queue [FourQ]
    removing  FourQ     .. left in queue []

Final Size of Queue : 0
We end with an empty queue : []
```

Let's examine this code:

The previous program documentation and each line as well as the desciption of this topic's introduction is very well documented. Please read the comments above.

Summary

In this chapter we covered four very important topics. We started with linked lists, we continue with overloading, then stacks and finished with queues.

A linked list is refered to as a linear collection of nodes, they are also defined as a finite sequence of nodes. Except for the first node, each node contains one pointer field that points to the next node, and another pointer node that points to the previous node. The first node only points to the next node. The pointer in the last node points to null, which is always the end of the linked list.

Overloading is a great tool in Java that allows us to use a single method name to accept different amounts of variables, of various data types, in different order. It behaves similarly to the System.out.print(? ?) Java command.

A stack is a data structure that allows us to place data items on top of each other. It uses the LIFO (last in, first out) method of processing. The last item placed in the stack is the first item to be extracted.

Queue is a data structure that allows us to place data items one after another. It uses the FIFO (first in, first out) processing method. The first item placed in the queue is the first item to be extracted/processed.

Key Terms

Linked List	A linked list is refered to as a linear collection of nodes, they are also defined as a finite sequence of nodes. Except for the first node, each node contains one pointer field that points to the next node, and another pointer node that points to the previous node. The first node only points to the next node. The pointer in the last node points to null, which is always the end of the linked list. Linked lists have many similarities to single dimensional arrays the major difference is: Linked lists are data structures that do not have a set size as in arrays. What we know in arrays as indexes, in linked lists we call them nodes. In linked lists we can always extend or reduce the amount of nodes. In arrays we can not change their amount of indexes, once created.
Overloading	Overloading is a great tool in Java that allows us to use a single method name to accept different amounts of variables, of various data types, in different order. It behaves similarly to the System.out.print(? ?) Java command.
Queue	Queue is a data structure that allows us to place data items one after another. It uses the FIFO (first in, first out) processing method. The first item placed in the queue is the first item to be extracted/processed.
Stack	A stack is a data structure that allows us to place data items on top of each other. It uses the LIFO (last in, first out) method of processing. The last item placed in the stack is the first item to be extracted.

Exercises

1. Create a program with three methods that will overload as follows: one int, two ints, one double, one float and one double.

2. Write a program that will create a linked list, add 3 nodes and then remove the middle node.

3. Create a queue with 4 nodes, print them.

4. Create a program that will pop the first 3 items in program 3.

5. Create a stack with 4 items. Print all items usign the FIFO processing method program that.

Multiple choice questions. Choose all that apply:

6. What is overloading?
   a. A difficult student
   b. A program with multiple methods with the same name and different parameters
   c. A program with multiple methods with the same name and identical parameters
   d. None of the above

7. What is a queue?
   a. A difficult student
   b. A program with multiple methods with the same name and different parameters
   c. A program with multiple methods with the same name and identical parameters
   d. None of the above

8. What is wtack?
   a. A data structure equivalent to an array
   b. A data structure that allows search data using the LIFO method
   c. A data structure that allows search data using the FIFO method
   d. A data structure that allows search data using the LILO method

9. What is linked list?
   a. A finite sequence of nodes
   b. A sequence of nodes with a minimun of 3 pointers
   c. A fixed sequence of nodes with one pointer
   d. A fixed sequence of nodes with no pointers

REFERENCES

- Java API Specifications
  http://www.oracle.com/technetwork/java/api-141528.html

- My Java programs that I use in my Java classes located at robinson.cs.fiu.edu

//END CHAPTER 15: DATA STRUCTURES IMPLEMENTATIONS

chapter 16

Complex Programming

In this chapter we present programs that are a little more challenging than the typical material we learned in the previous chapters. Here we are trying to implement the previous knowledge adquired, to present new solutions.

Caller Program

This first program multiClasses.java is the main caller program where all parts come together. It uses the following classes:

```
public class multiClasses
public interface customerInterface
public class superCustomer implements customerInterface
public class retailCustomer extends superCustomer
public class wholesaleCustomer extends superCustomer
```

The multiClasses.java program contains the following inner classes:

Abstract Classes

```
abstract public static class abstractClass
containing the methods:
  methodOne() and
  methodTwo()
```

< 417 >

```
   public static class extendsAbstractClass extends abstractClass
containing the methods:
   usingAbstractClass()
   methodOne()
   methodTwo()
   usingAbstractClass()
   polyMethod( superCustomer obj )
   usingInterface() and
   main( String arg[])
```

Classes Inside Classes

The first class is the outer class and the other two classes are inner classes with their corresponding methods.

These programs are fully documented and I hope that documentation will be sufficient.

```
/***************************************************
   Author  : Michael Robinson
   Program : multiClasses.java
   Purpose : This project will cover the following:
             Interfaces
             Classes inside classes.
             Polymorphism
             More Inheritance
             Abstract classes
             Abstract methods

             This project does the following:
             1 - Create an Interface named customerInterface
             2 - Create a class called superCustomer
                 to implement the customerInterface.
                 This class will also be a Super-class.
             3 - Create two subclasses named wholesaleCustomer and
                 retailCustomer both inheriting from superCustomer

   Updated : September 9th, 2099
***********************************************************/

public class multiClasses
{
   /***********************************************************
   Author  : Michael Robinson
   Program : abstractClass.java
```

```
Purpose : this is an abstract class,
          it can contain as many abstract methods as needed.
          Abstract classes can also contain as many
          regular methods as needed.

Updated : September 9th, 2099
************************************************************/


//this is an  abstract class
abstract public static class abstractClass
{
    //this is an abstract method NO BODY NEEDED
    abstract void hello();


    public static void methodOne()
    {
        System.out.println( "I am methodOne, a regular method " +
                            "inside the  abstractClass" );

    }//end public static void methodOne()


    public static void methodTwo()
    {
        System.out.println( "I am methodTwo, a regular method " +
                            "inside an the abstractClass" );

    }//end public static void methodTwo()

}//end abstract public class abstractClass



/************************************************************
Author  : Michael Robinson
Program : extendsAbstractClass.java
Purpose : This class  extends the abstract class named
          abstractClass,
          It overrides the abstract hello method in the abstract
          class.

Updated : September 9th, 2099
************************************************************/
```

```java
public static class extendsAbstractClass extends abstractClass
{
    //this method is an abstract method implementation
    public void hello()
    {
        System.out.println( "I am the implementation of the " +
        "hello abstract method,\n" +
        "                inside the extendsAbstractClass.java" );

    }//end public void hello()


    public static void methodOne()
    {
        System.out.println( "I am methodOne inside the " +
                        "extendsAbstractClass.java." );

    }//end public static void methodOne()\n


    public static void methodTwo()
    {
        System.out.println( "I am methodTwo inside the " +
                        "extendsAbstractClass.java." );

    }//end public static void methodOne()

}//end public class extendsAbstractClass extends abstractClass


public static void usingAbstractClass()
{
    System.out.println( "This section will use ABSTRACTION " +
        "and inheritance.\nThere is an abstract class called " +
        "abstractClass\nwith one abstract method called "       +
        "abstractClass\n hello and two\nlocal methods called " +
        "methodOne and methodTwo\nThe abstract hello method "   +
        "will be implemented\nand the other two methods will " +
        "be overridden\nby a class called extendsAbstract.\n" );

    //use a regular method in the abstract class
    abstractClass.methodOne();
    abstractClass.methodTwo();

    System.out.println( "\nNow I will create an " +
                    "extendsAbstractClass object\n" );
```

```java
        //create an object of a class that
        //inherits an abstract class
        extendsAbstractClass one = new extendsAbstractClass();

        //use a method from this new method
        one.hello();

        //use an overridden regular method
        //in the extendsAbstractClass
        extendsAbstractClass.methodOne();
        extendsAbstractClass.methodTwo();
        System.out.println();

}//end public static void main( String arg[] )


public static void polyMethod( superCustomer obj )
{
    System.out.print( "Hi I am the " + obj.getCustomerType() );
    System.out.print( ", my name is " + obj.getCustomerName() );
    System.out.println( ". These are my data fields:" );

}//end public static void polyMethod( superCustomer obj )


public static void usingInterface()
{
    //Polymorphism: Creating object rCust of retailCustomer()
    //sub-class with super-class superCustomer() data type
    superCustomer rCust = new retailCustomer();

    System.out.println( "Using an object of retailCustomer " +
                        "class and superCustomer data type" );

    //accessing methods in rCust sub-class
    polyMethod( rCust );


    //getting data from rCust sub-class object
    String theArray[] = rCust.getCustomerData();

    for( String temp : theArray )
    {
        System.out.print( temp + " " );
    }
```

```java
        System.out.println( "\n\nNow I will use arrays containing " +
                            "sub-classes" );

        //creating an array of superCustomer data type
        superCustomer array[] = new superCustomer[2];

        //loading array[0] with object of retailCustomer sub-class
        array[0] = new retailCustomer();

        //loading array[1] with object of wholesaleCustomer sub-class
        array[1] = new wholesaleCustomer();

        //processing the sub-classes
        for( superCustomer arrayIndex : array  )
        {
            polyMethod( arrayIndex );

            for( String inner :  arrayIndex.getCustomerData() )
            {
                System.out.print( inner + " " );
            }

            System.out.println( "\n" );

        }//for( superCustomer temp : array )

        System.out.println( "End of Polymorphism examples\n\n" );

    }//end public static void usingInterface()


    public static void main( String arg[] )
                            throws InterruptedException
    {
        usingInterface();

        usingAbstractClass();

    }//end public static void main( String arg[] )
     //                              throws InterruptedException

}//end public class multiClasses
```

Interfaces

This is the interface which will be implementing the super-class.

```
/*
  Author  : Michael Robinson
  Program : customerIDinterface.java
  Purpose : This is an Interface example

  Updated : September 1, 2099
*/


public interface customerInterface
{
    public String   customerType = "I am the interface";
    public String   customerID = "";
    public String   customerLastName = "";
    public String   customerFirstName = "";
    public String   customerMiddleName = "";
    public String   customerAddress1 = "";
    public String   customerAddress2 = "";
    public String   customerCity = "";
    public String   customerState = "";
    public String   customerCountry = "";
    public String   customerZipCode = "";
    public String   customerTelNumber = "";

    public void setCustomerType( String customerType );
    public void setCustomerID( String customerID );
    public void setCustomerLastName( String customerLastName );
    public void setCustomerFirstName( String customerFirstName );
    public void setCustomerMiddleName( String customerMiddleName );
    public void setCustomerAddress1( String customerAddress1 );
    public void setCustomerAddress2( String customerAddress2 );
    public void setCustomerCity( String customerCity );
    public void setCustomerState( String customerState );
    public void setCustomerCountry( String customerCountryName );
    public void setCustomerZipCode( String customerZipCode );
    public void setCustomerTelNumber( String customerTelNumber );

}//end public interface customerInterface
```

The following class implements the previous interface and in addition it contains three more methods.

```
/*
   Author   : Michael Robinson
   Program  : superCustomer.java
   Purpose  : This is a super-class that implements the
              customerInterface interface.
              From this super-class two sub-classes are inheriting,
              in addition it contains three methods:
              public String[] getCustomerData()
              public String getCustomerType(), and
              public String getCustomerName()

   Updated  : September 1, 2099
*/


public class superCustomer implements customerInterface
{
    //implement interface variables
    public String  name                = "superCustomer Guy";
    public String  customerType         = "superCustomer Type";
    public String  customerID           = "id";
    public String  customerLastName     = "Last Name";
    public String  customerFirstName    = "First Name";
    public String  customerMiddleName   = "Middle Name";
    public String  customerAddress1     = "Address 1";
    public String  customerAddress2     = "Address 2";
    public String  customerCity         = "City";
    public String  customerState        = "State";
    public String  customerCountry      = "Country";
    public String  customerZipCode      = "Zip";
    public String  customerTelNumber    = "Telephone";


    // set all variables implemented from customerInterface
    public void setCustomerType( String customerType )
    {
        this.customerType = customerType;

    }//end public void setCustomerType( String customerType )


    public void setCustomerID( String customerID )
```

```
    {

        this.customerID = customerID;


    }//end public void setCustomerID( String customerID )



    public void setCustomerLastName( String customerLastName )
    {

        this.customerLastName = customerLastName;


    }//end public void setCustomerLastName(
    //String customerLastName )



    public void setCustomerFirstName( String customerFirstName )
    {

        this.customerFirstName = customerFirstName;


    }//end public void setCustomerFirstName(
     //String customerFirstName )



    public void setCustomerMiddleName( String customerMiddleName )
    {

        this.customerMiddleName = customerMiddleName;


    }//end public void setCustomerMiddleName( String
      //customerMiddleName )



    public void setCustomerAddress1( String customerAddress1 )
    {

        this.customerAddress1 = customerAddress1;


    }//end public void setCustomerAddress1( String
     //customerAddress1



    public void setCustomerAddress2( String customerAddress2 )
    {

        this.customerAddress2 = customerAddress2;


    }//end public void setCustomerAddress2( String
     //customerAddress2 )
```

```java
public void setCustomerCity( String customerCity )
{
    this.customerCity = customerCity;

}//end public void setCustomerCity( String customerCity )


public void setCustomerState( String customerState )
{
    this.customerState = customerState;

}//end public void setCustomerState( String customerState )


public void setCustomerCountry( String customerCountry )
{
    this.customerCountry = customerCountry;

}//end public void setCustomerCountry( String customerCountry )


public void setCustomerZipCode( String customerZipCode )
{
    this.customerZipCode = customerZipCode;

}//end public void setCustomerZipCode( String customerZipCode )


public void setCustomerTelNumber( String customerTelNumber )
{
    this.customerTelNumber = customerTelNumber;

}//end public void setCustomerTelNumber( String
 //customerTelNumber )


//create an array with all variables and return it
public String[] getCustomerData()
{
    String customerData[] = new String[]
    {
        customerID,
        customerLastName,
        customerFirstName,
```

```
                customerMiddleName,
                customerAddress1,
                customerAddress2,
                customerCity,
                customerState,
                customerCountry,
                customerZipCode,
                customerTelNumber
        };

        return customerData;

    }//end public String[] getCustomerData()


    public String getCustomerType()
    {
        return ( customerType );

    }//end public String getCustomerType()


    public String getCustomerName()
    {
        return ( name );

    }//end public String getCustomerName()

}//end public class superCustomer implements customerInterface
```

Extends/Inhereting

The following is the sub-class retailCustomer which extends superCustomer.

```
/*
  Author  : Michael Robinson
  Program : retailCustomer.java
  Purpose : This is a sub-class that inherits from
            the superCustomer super-class

  Updated : September 1, 2099
*/
```

```
public class retailCustomer extends superCustomer
{
     public static String  name = "The Pizza Places";
     public static String  customerType = "retailCustomer";


     public String getCustomerName()
     {
          return ( name );

     }//end public String getCustomerName()


     public String getCustomerType()
     {
          return ( customerType );

     }//end public String getCustomerType()

}//end public class retailCustomer   extends superCustomer
```

Now this is the sub-class wholesaleCustomer which extends superCustomer.

```
/*
   Author   : Michael Robinson
   Program  : wholesaleCustomer.java
   Purpose  : This is a sub-class that inherits from
              the superCustomer super-class

   Updated  : September 1, 2099
*/


public class wholesaleCustomer extends superCustomer
{
     public String  name = "The Cheese Makersss";
     public String  customerType = "wholesaleCustomer";


     public String getCustomerName()
     {
          return ( name );

     }//end public String getCustomerName()
```

```
    public String getCustomerType()
    {
        return ( customerType );

    }//end public String getCustomerType()


}//end public class wholesaleCustomer  extends superCustomer
```

Your output (results) will look like this:

```
Using an object of retailCustomer class and superCustomer data type

Hi I am the retailCustomer, my name is The Pizza Places. These are my
data fields:

id Last Name First Name Middle Name Address 1 Address 2 City State
Country Zip Telephone


Now I will use arrays containing sub-classes

Hi I am the retailCustomer, my name is The Pizza Places. These are my
data fields:

id Last Name First Name Middle Name Address 1 Address 2 City State
Country Zip Telephone


Hi I am the wholesaleCustomer, my name is The Cheese Makersss. These
are my data fields:

id Last Name First Name Middle Name Address 1 Address 2 City State
Country Zip Telephone



End of Polymorphism examples


This section will use ABSTRACTION and inheritance.

There is an abstract class called abstractClass
```

with one abstract method called abstractClass

hello and two

local methods called methodOne and methodTwo

The abstract hello method will be implemented

and the other two methods will be overridden

by a class called extendsAbstract.

I am methodOne, a regular method inside the abstractClass

I am methodTwo, a regular method inside an the abstractClass

Now I will create an extendsAbstractClass object

I am the implementation of the hello abstract method,

                inside the extendsAbstractClass.java

I am methodOne inside the extendsAbstractClass.java.

I am methodTwo inside the extendsAbstractClass.java.

Let's examine this code:

The previous program documentation and each line as well as the desciption of this topic's introduction is very well documented. Please read the comments above.

Summary

In this chapter we present programs that are a little more challenging than the typical material we learned in the previous chapters. Here we are trying to implement the previous knowledge adquired to present new solutions.

This first program multiClasses.java is the main caller program where all parts come together. It uses the following classes:

```
public class multiClasses
public interface customerInterface
public class superCustomer implements customerInterface
public class retailCustomer extends superCustomer
public class wholesaleCustomer extends superCustomer
```

The multiClasses program contains the following inner classes:

```
abstract public static class abstractClass
containing the methods:
  methodOne() and
  methodTwo()
```

```
public static class extendsAbstractClass extends
abstractClass
  containing the methods:
  usingAbstractClass()
  methodOne()
  methodTwo()
  usingAbstractClass()
  polyMethod( superCustomer obj )
  usingInterface() and
  main( String arg[])
```

The first class is the outer class and the other two classes are inner classes with their corresponding methods.

These programs are fully documented and I hope that documentation will be sufficient.

Key Terms

Abstract Classes	Java has abstract classes and methods. Abstracts are not defined. An abstract classes exists to be extended. It can only be used for inheritance or polymorphism, we can not create objects from an abstract class:
	
	//this is an abstract class
	abstract public class abstractClass
	{
	
	}//end abstract public class abstractClass
	
	Abstract classes contain abstract methods, abstract methods do NOT contain a body, just the heading: abstract void hello(); //this is an abstract method NO BODY NEEDED
	
	Abstract classes contain as many abstract methods and regular methods as needed.

Caller Methods	Methods that call other methods. Usually is the main method in a program.

Classes Inside Classes	<pre>public class multiClasses
	{
	    //this is an abstract class
	    abstract public static class abstractClass
	    {
	        //this is an abstract method
	        //NO BODY NEEDED
	
	        abstract void hello();
	
	        public static void methodOne()
	        {
	            System.out.println("I am methodOne,
	                inside the abstractClass");
	
	        }//end public static void methodOne()
	
	    }//end abstract public class abstractClass
	
	    public static class extendsAbstractClass
	                    extends abstractClass</pre>

| Classes inside Classes (cont.) | ```
            {
                System.out.println( "Implementation
                   of the hello abstract method,\n";
               }//end public void hello()

           }//end public class extendsAbstractClass
            // extends abstractClass

           public static void main( String arg[] )
                         throws InterruptedException
           {
                usingAbstractClass();

           }//end public static void main(String arg[])

       }//end public class multiClasses
``` |
Extends/ Inhereting	Classes that use the content (methods, variables) of other programs usually called super-classes.
Interfaces	An interface is a class that contains methods that only have headings. It is also referred as "an interface is a group of related methods with empty bodies."
	These methods are considered to be "templates" without bodies. Interfaces can be implemented in any other class and all the methods in the Interface must be used in the class that is implementing the interface.
```

Exercises

1. Create an interface with 4 variables.

2. Create a super-class to implement previous interface.

3. Create a progam to extend previous super-class.

4. Create another program to extend previous super-class.

5. Create a caller program to implement all previous programs.

Select all answers that apply

6. What is an interface?
   a. A program that is inhereted by other programs
   b. A super-class program
   c. A group of related methods with empty bodies
   d. A class that contains methods that only have headings

7. What is a super-class program?
   a. A class that is more powerful than a regular class
   b. A program that is inhereted by other programs
   c. A group of related methods with empty bodies
   d. A program that is implemented by other programs

8. What is extending another program?
   a. Inhereting other program(s)
   b. Implementing methods with empty bodies
   c. Creating a calling program
   d. Inhereting private methods from other programs

9. What is an abstract class?
   a. A super-class program
   b. A group of related methods with empty bodies
   c. A program that is implemented by other programs
   d. A program that is inhereted by other programs

REFERENCES

- Java API Specifications
  http://www.oracle.com/technetwork/java/api-141528.html

- My Java programs that I use in my Java classes located at robinson.cs.fiu.edu

//END CHAPTER 16: COMPLEX PROGRAMMING

chapter 17

Miscellaneous

Generic Methods

The use of generic methods allows us to replace the use of methods overloading. We can use one method to pass different types of data. We can use the same method to received and process integers, characters, doubles, strings, objects, and other types of data, without having to write one method for each data type as is required when using overloading.

```
/*
  Author  : Michael Robinson
  Program : genericMethods.java
  Purpose : To present generic methods that
            accept any type of data

  Updated : July 28th, 2099
*/


public class genericMethods
{
    public static <T> void showMe( T[] multiDataType )
    {
        for( T elements : multiDataType )
```

< 437 >

```java
        {
            System.out.printf( "%s ", elements );
        }
        System.out.println();

}//end public static <T> void showMe( T[] multiDataType )


/*
   generic  return  method use only objects that:
   inherits from  returns  method name
     Comparable   generic  accepting genetic data
                  T data    a, c, and c     */
public static < T extends Comparable<T> > T maxMethod(
                T firstItem, T middleItem, T lastItem )
{
    System.out.printf( "The max value of %s %s %s is ",
                    firstItem, middleItem, lastItem );

    T maximum = firstItem;

    if( middleItem.compareTo( maximum ) > 0 )
    {
        maximum = middleItem;
    }

    if( lastItem.compareTo(maximum) > 0 )
    {
        maximum = lastItem;
    }

    return maximum;

}//end public static < T extends Comparable<T> > T maxMethod(
 // T firstItem,T middleItem,T lastItem )


public static void main( String arg[] )
{
    Object ob[] =  { "one", 2, 2.5, "last" };
    showMe( ob );

    Integer In[] = { 1, 2, 3, 4, 5 };
    showMe( In );
```

```
        Double Dou[] = { 1.1, 2.2, 3.3, 4.4 };
        showMe( Dou );

        String St[] = { "Joe", " goes", " to", " FIU" };
        showMe( St );

        Character Ch[] = { 'a', 'b', 'c', 'd', 'e' };
        showMe( Ch );

        System.out.println( maxMethod( "one", "four",  "three" ) );
        System.out.println( maxMethod( 188, 103, 44 ) );

    }//end public static void main( String arg[] )

}//end public class genericMethods
```

Your output (results) will look like this:

```
one 2 2.5 last
1 2 3 4 5
1.1 2.2 3.3 4.4
Joe  goes  to  FIU
a b c d e
The max value of one four three is three
The max value of 188 103 44 is 188
```

Let's examine this code:

The previous program documentation and each line as well as the desciption of this topic's introduction are very well documented. Please read the comments above.

Introduction to Java Collection Interface

A collection is an object that groups elements into a single unit. Collections are used to store, retrieve, manipulate, and communicate aggregate data. Usually they represent data items that form a group of similar data, such as a list of employees.

There are many data structures that are part of the collections interface such as lists, maps and hashTables. In this section we will use lists to demostrate collections. Collections are also known as containers.

```
/*
  Author    : Michael Robinson
  Program   : collectionsClass.java
  Purpose   : A lot like an Array that holds stuff
              "holds references to other objects
              unlike an array Collections are DYNAMIC"
              A list or a Set (types of Collections) do not
              require a size to initialize they adjust by themselves
              as you work with them.
              List<type> = CAN contain duplicates

  Updated   : October 28th, 2099
*/


import java.util.*;


public class collectionsClass
{
    public static void removeFrom(
            Collection<String> listOne, Collection<String> listTwo )
    {
        Iterator<String> removeIt = listOne.iterator();

        while( removeIt.hasNext() )
        {
            if( listTwo.contains( removeIt.next() ) )
            {
                removeIt.remove();
            }
        }

    }//end public static void removeFrom(Collection<String> listOne,
     //Collection<String> listTwo)


    public static void displayList(Collection<String> collectionObj)
    {
        //display data in namesListOne
        Iterator<String> iterCollection = collectionObj.iterator();

        while( iterCollection.hasNext() )
        {
            System.out.print( "  " + iterCollection.next() );
        }
```

```
        System.out.println();

  }//end public static void displayList( Collection<String>
  //collectionObj )


public static void createList(
                String namesArray1[], String namesArray2[] )
{
    //*************************
    //   listOne
    //*************************
    //add array namesArray1 to List namesListOne
    System.out.println( "\n Copying the names in the first " +
                        "array into a first list" );

    //create a List of Strings
    List<String> namesListOne = new ArrayList<String>();

    //copy array namesArray2 to List namesListTwo
    for( String w : namesArray1 )
    {
        namesListOne.add(w);
    }

    displayList( namesListOne );

    //add more items into List namesListOne
    System.out.println( "\n  Adding Napoleon" );
    namesListOne.add( "Napoleon" );

    System.out.println( "  Adding Nathalie" );
    namesListOne.add( "Nathalie" );

    System.out.print( "\n Printing items in first list :  " );
    displayList( namesListOne );

    //*************************
    //   listTwo
    //*************************
    //add array namesArray2 to List namesListTwo
    System.out.println( "\n Copying the names in the second " +
                        "array into a second list" );
```

```java
        //create a List of Strings
        List<String> namesListTwo = new ArrayList<String>();

        //copy array namesArray2 to List namesListTwo
        for( String w : namesArray2 )
        {
            namesListTwo.add(w);
        }

        System.out.print( "\n Printing items in second list : " );
        displayList( namesListTwo );

        System.out.println( "\n Removing items in second list " +
                        "from first list" );

        removeFrom( namesListOne, namesListTwo );

        System.out.print( "\n Printing items in first list :   " );
        displayList( namesListOne );

        System.out.print( "\n Printing items in second list : " );
        displayList( namesListTwo );

}//end public static void createList( String namesArray1[],
 //String namesArray2[] )


public static void createArrays()
{
        //employees in graphics group
        System.out.println( "\n Creating array with employees " +
                        "names" );

        //create an array of Strings
        String namesArray1[] =
                    { "Lisa", "Dan", "Mike", "Jane",  "Phil" };

        //create an array of Strings
        String namesArray2[] =
                    { "Dennis", "Lisa", "Juan", "Jane", "Manny" };

        createList( namesArray1, namesArray2 );

}//end public static void createArrays()
```

```
public static void main( String arg[] )
{
    createArrays();

}//end public static void main( String arg[] )

}//end public class collectionsClass
```

Your output (results) will look like this:

Creating array with employees names

Copying the names in the first array into a first list

      Lisa Dan Mike Jane Phil

Adding Napoleon

Adding Nathalie

Printing items in first list :   Lisa Dan Mike Jane Phil Napoleon Nathalie

Copying the names in the second array into a second list

Printing items in second list : Dennis Lisa Juan Jane Manny

Removing items in second list from first list

Printing items in first list :   Dan Mike Phil Napoleon Nathalie

Printing items in second list : Dennis Lisa Juan Jane Manny

Let's examine this code:

The previous program documentation and each line as well as the description of this topic's introduction are very well documented. Please read the comments above.

Overriding equals and toString Methods

The toString method returns a string representation of an object. It is a string that "textually represents" the object. It is recommended that all classes override the toString method. If you do not override the toString method and you call it, it will return a string consisting of the object's name, the @ sign, and the unsigned hexadecimal representation of the hash code of the object, similar to this noToStringMethodDemo@384f14b0.

In this section we will see several programs that show how the toString method can be overritten using your own toString method.

The following program is the main program the_toStringObjectMain which calls the other two following theToStringDemoClass and noToStringMethodDemo.java programs.

```
/*
   Author  : Michael Robinson
   Program : the_toStringObjectMain.java
   Purpose : Here we learn to use the Java toString method
             toString is very easy to implement and very useful
             This is the main program where we create objects and
             pass data so that those objects can process and
             return the formatted data using their toString method.
             We also show what happens when we use the objects'
             default toString method.

   Updated : August 18, 2099
*/


public class the_toStringObjectMain
{

    public static void main( String arg[] )
    {
        //We created a class called theToStringDemoClass
        //in it we have a method called toString() to be used by this
        //program in several ways:
        //first creating an object of class theToStringDemoClass
        //this object will process and return passed data using the
        //toString method

        theToStringDemoClass toStringObj = new
                        theToStringDemoClass( 8, 18, 2099 );


        //or


        System.out.println( "\ntheToStringDemoClass toString method"+
                        toStringObj );
```

```java
//or

System.out.println( "\ntheToStringDemoClass.toString() " +
                "method " + toStringObj.toString() );

System.out.println( "\n----------------------------------" +
                "------------------\n" );

//This is a different way of create an object and pass data
System.out.println( "\nThis is a different way of create " +
                "an object and pass data" );

theToStringDemoClass myInfo = new
                theToStringDemoClass( 8, 18, 2099 );

System.out.println( "\nThis is myInfo class " + myInfo );

System.out.println( "\n----------------------------------" +
                "------------------\n" );

//*************************************************************
//Using a class that does NOT have a build in toString method
System.out.println( "\nClass that does NOT have a build " +
                "in toString method" );

noToStringMethodDemo noToStringObj = new
                noToStringMethodDemo( 8, 18, 2099 );

//or

//this object calls its toString method automatically
System.out.println( "\nObject's toString method " +
                "automatically " + noToStringObj );

//or

//this object call its toString method manually
System.out.println( "\nObject's toString method calling" +
                " it " + noToStringObj.toString() );

//this object calls it NoToString method manually
System.out.println( "\nObject's NoToString toString method "
                + noToStringObj.NoToString() );
```

```
        System.out.println( "\n----------------------------------" +
                            "-------------------\n" );

    }//end public static void main(String arg[])

}//end public class the_toStringObjectMain
```

The next program theToStringDemoClass.java is called by the previous the_toStringObjectMain.java program to create objects, accept data and return values formated as strings.

```
/*
    Author  : Michael Robinson
    Program : theToStringDemoClass.java
    Purpose : Learning to use the toString java method
              This is a class that is called by the
              the_toStringObjectMain.java main program

    Updated : August 18, 2012
*/



public class theToStringDemoClass
{
    private int day;
    private int month;
    private int year;


    public theToStringDemoClass( int myDay, int myMonth, int myYear)
    {
        day   = myDay;
        month = myMonth;
        year  = myYear;

        //when using the 'this' command (references the current
        //object) it calls it's toSring method
        System.out.println( "\nData received by the " +
                        " theToStringDemoClass constructor is " +
                        this );

    }//end public theToStringDemoClass( int d, int m, int y )
```

```
/* If the toString method is not declared in the class that is
   using the 'this' command to print, java will NOT give an
   error but it will print the name of the class and its address
*/


public String toString()
{

    //the return can be any format you need
    return String.format( "%d/%d/%d",  day, month, year );


}//end public String toString()

}//end public class theToStringDemoClass
```

The following program noToStringMethodDemo.java called by the main program the_toStringObject-Main.java is a constructor that creates objects, accepts a day, month and year and returns their values formated as strings using its NoToString() method.

```
/*
  Author   : Michael Robinson
  Program  : noToStringMethodDemo.java
  Purpose  : Learning to use the toString java method
             using this noToStringMethodDemo constructor

  Updated : August 18, 2099
*/



public class noToStringMethodDemo
{
    private int day;
    private int month;
    private int year;


    public noToStringMethodDemo(int myDay, int myMonth, int myYear )
    {

        day   = myDay;
        month = myMonth;
        year  = myYear;
```

```java
        //when using the 'this' command (references the current
        //object) it calls the toSring method
        System.out.println( "\nData received by the " +
                        "noToStringMethodDemo constructor: " +
                    this );

    }//end public theToStringDemoClass( int d, int m, int y )


    /* If the toString method is not declared in the class that is
     * using the 'this' command to print, java will NOT give an error
     * but it will print the name of the class and its address
     */


    public String NoToString()
    {

        //the return can be any format you need
        return String.format( "%d/%d/%d", day, month, year );

    }//public String NoToString()

}//end public class noToStringMethodDemo
```

Your output (results) will look like this:

```
Data received by the theToStringDemoClass constructor is 8/18/2099

theToStringDemoClass toString method 8/18/2099

theToStringDemoClass.toString() method 8/18/2099

------------------------------------------------------

This is a different way of create an object and pass data

Data received by the theToStringDemoClass constructor is 8/18/2099

This is myInfo class 8/18/2099


------------------------------------------------------

Class that does NOT have a build in toString method
```

```
Data received by the noToStringMethodDemo constructor:
noToStringMethodDemo@39862621

Object's toString method automatically noToStringMethodDemo@39862621

Object's toString method callingt it noToStringMethodDemo@39862621

Object's NoToString toString method 8/18/2099


------------------------------------------------------
```

Let's examine this code:

The previous programs documentation, almost each line in the source code, as well as the description of this topic's introduction are very well documented. Please read the comments above.

How to Reduce Typing

Sometimes we wish we could type less to do the same work, in Java to implement a print routine, we need to write System.out.print();. When we do a lot of printing, this can be time consumming. The following method is an example of how we can reduce the amount of typing. I am placing the pl() method inside a class so that you can run it, or just copy the method and use it in any program.

```
/*
  Author  : Michael Robinson
  Program : plClass.java
  Purpose : This program creates a method called pl()
            which allows us to type less when we need
            one line feed in a program.

  Updated : April 26, 2099
*/


public class plClass
{

    //This method saves us time. Instead of exececuting the command
    //System.out.println(); we just excuted pl();
    public static void pl()
    {
        System.out.println();
```

```
        }


        public static void main( String arg[] )
        {
                //call pl() instead of executing System.out.println();
                pl();

        }//end public static void main( String arg[] )

}//end public class plClass
```

Let's examine this code:

The previous program documentation and each line as well as the description of this topic's introduction are very well documented. Please read the comments above.

You can modify this pl() method and make it more useful by passing parameters.

ASCII Codes Program

The following program shows us how to produce the ASCII codes. We need to learn to use them since many characters that we need in programming can not be printed using the keyboard, such as the sound of the bell.

```
/*
  Author   : Michael Robinson
  Program  : ascii.java
  Purpose  : To present the American English ASCII codes
             and how to find any ASCII character

  Updated  : May 4, 2099
*/


public class ascii
{
    public static void asciiTable()
    {
        int x = 0;
        int y = 0;
```

```java
System.out.println( "\n These are ASCII values for " +
                    "some special characters" );
y = 1;

for( x = 32; x < 48; x++ )
 {
    System.out.printf( "'%c' = %d  ", x, x );
    if( y == 5 )
    {
        System.out.println();
        y = 0;
    }


    y++;
 }

System.out.println( "\n\n These are ASCII values from " +
                    "0 to 9" );
y = 1;
for( x = 48; x < 58; x++ )
{
    System.out.printf( "'%c' = %d  ", x, x );

    if( y == 5)
    {
        System.out.println();
        y = 0;
    }
    y++;
}

System.out.println( "\n These are ASCII values for some " +
                    "special characters" );
y = 1;

for( x = 58; x < 65; x++ )
{
    System.out.printf( "'%c' = %d  ", x, x );

    if( y == 5 )
    {
        System.out.println();
        y = 0;
    }
```

```
        y++;
    }

    System.out.println( "\n\n These are ASCII values from " +
                        "A to Z" );
    y = 1;
    for( x = 65; x < 91; x++ )
    {
        System.out.printf( "'%c' = %d  ", x, x );
        if( y == 5 )
        {
            System.out.println();
            y = 0;
        }
        y++;
    }

    System.out.println( "\n These are ASCII values for some " +
                        "special characters" );
    y = 1;

    for( x = 91; x < 97; x++ )
    {
        System.out.printf( "'%c' = %d  ", x, x );
        if( y == 5)
        {
            System.out.println();
            y = 0;
        }

        y++;
    }

    System.out.println( "\n\n These are all the ASCII values " +
                        "from a to z" );

    y = 1;
    for( x = 97; x < 123; x++ )
    {
        System.out.printf( "'%c' = %d  ", x, x );
        if( x < 100 )
        {
            System.out.print( "  " );
        }
```

```
        if( y == 5)
        {
            System.out.println();
            y = 0;
        }
        y++;
    }

    System.out.println( "\n These are ASCII values for some " +
                        "special characters" );

    y = 1;
    for( x = 123; x < 127; x++ )
    {
        System.out.printf( "'%c' = %d  ", x, x );
        if( y == 5)
        {
            System.out.println();
            y = 0;
        }
        y++;
    }

}//end public static void class ascii


public static void main( String arg[] )
{
    asciiTable();

}//end public static void main( String arg[] )

}//end public class ascii
```

The key in this program is this line of code:

```
        System.out.printf( "'%c' = %d  ", x, x );
```

As we can see, when using printf, we can display a value as a number, and as a character, in this case when we display the numeric variable x as a character using %c, we get the actual value of the ASCII code, e.g.: A = 65.

Your output (results) will look like this:

```
These are ASCII values for some special characters
' ' = 32   '!' = 33   '"' = 34   '#' = 35   '$' = 36
'%' = 37   '&' = 38   ''' = 39   '(' = 40   ')' = 41
'*' = 42   '+' = 43   ',' = 44   '-' = 45   '.' = 46
'/' = 47


These are ASCII values from 0 to 9
'0' = 48   '1' = 49   '2' = 50   '3' = 51   '4' = 52
'5' = 53   '6' = 54   '7' = 55   '8' = 56   '9' = 57


These are ASCII values for some special characters
':' = 58   ';' = 59   '<' = 60   '=' = 61   '>' = 62
'?' = 63   '@' = 64


These are ASCII values from A to Z
'A' = 65   'B' = 66   'C' = 67   'D' = 68   'E' = 69
'F' = 70   'G' = 71   'H' = 72   'I' = 73   'J' = 74
'K' = 75   'L' = 76   'M' = 77   'N' = 78   'O' = 79
'P' = 80   'Q' = 81   'R' = 82   'S' = 83   'T' = 84
'U' = 85   'V' = 86   'W' = 87   'X' = 88   'Y' = 89
'Z' = 90


These are ASCII values for some special characters
'[' = 91   '\' = 92   ']' = 93   '^' = 94   '_' = 95
'`' = 96


These are all the ASCII values from a to z
'a' = 97    'b' = 98    'c' = 99    'd' = 100   'e' = 101
'f' = 102   'g' = 103   'h' = 104   'i' = 105   'j' = 106
'k' = 107   'l' = 108   'm' = 109   'n' = 110   'o' = 111
'p' = 112   'q' = 113   'r' = 114   's' = 115   't' = 116
'u' = 117   'v' = 118   'w' = 119   'x' = 120   'y' = 121
'z' = 122


These are ASCII values for some special characters
'{' = 123   '|' = 124   '}' = 125   '~' = 126
```

Let's examine this code:

The previous program documentation and each line as well as the description of this topic's introduction are very well documented. Please read the comments above.

Javadoc

The symbols /** .... */ are used by javadoc, by placing javadoc comments just before declaration statements, we can add descriptions to classes, methods, variables, and other tools such as constructors, and interfaces, e.g.:

Javadoc is a Java tool that creates html documentation from javadoc comments /** */ created inside the program source code. Javadoc allows you to attach program docummentation descriptions to classes, methods, variables, and other tools such as constructors, and interfaces in the generated html documentation by placing Javadoc comments directly before their declaration statements.

```java
/** Creating javadocExample class
 *
 * @author  Michael Robinson
 * @version 1.0 March 1th 2099
 *
 *
 */

public class javadocExample
{
    /** declaring the variable studentID */
    public int studentID;


    /** declaring THE main method */
    public static void main( String arg[] )
    {

        // call all the methods
        System.out.println( "HI, I am Javadoc Example" );

    }//end public static void main(String arg[])


}
//end public class javadocExample
```

Your output (results) will look like this:

- Methods inherited from class java.lang.Object

  clone, equals, finalize, getClass, hashCode, notify, notifyAll, toString, wait, wait, wait

- Field Detail

  - **studentID**

  public int studentID
  declaring the variable studentID

- Constructor Detail

  - javadocExample

  public javadocExample()

- Method Detail

  - main

  public static void main(java.lang.String[] arg)
  declaring THE main method

Let's examine this code:

The documentation that we see above in the Your output (results) will look like this section is produced by running the following command:

```
javadoc javadocExample.java
```

which will produce the following steps and files:

```
Loading source file javadocExample.java...
```

```
Constructing Javadoc information...
```

```
Standard Doclet version 1.6.0_38
```

```
Building tree for all the packages and classes...

Generating /javadocExample.html...

Generating /package-frame.html...

Generating /package-summary.html...

Generating /package-tree.html...

Generating /constant-values.html...

Building index for all the packages and classes...

Generating /overview-tree.html...

Generating /index-all.html...

Generating /deprecated-list.html...

Building index for all classes...

Generating /allclasses-frame.html...

Generating /allclasses-noframe.html...

Generating /index.html...

Generating /help-doc.html...
```

All above html files can be viewed using your local browser.

Summary

Generic Methods. In this chapter we learned the use of generic methods which allows us to replace the use of methods overloading. We can use one method to pass different types of data. We can use the same method to received and process integers, characters, doubles, strings, objects, and other types of data, without having to write one method for each data type as is required when using overloading. In our program example genericMethods.java we present generic methods that accept any type of data.

A Java collection interface is an object that groups elements into a single unit. Collections are used to store, retrieve, manipulate, and communicate aggregate data. Usually they represent data items that form a group of similar data, such as a list of employees. There many data structures that are part of the collections interface such as lists, maps and hashTables. In this section we will use lists to demostrate collections. Collections are also known as containers.

Overriding equals and toString methods. The toString method returns a string representation of an object. It is a string that "textually represents" the object. It is recommended that all classes override the toString method. If you do not override the toString method and you call it, it will return a string consisting of the object's name, the @ sign, and the unsigned hexadecimal representation of the hash code of the object, similar to this noToStringMethodDemo@384f14b0.

In this section we saw several programs that showed how the toString method can be overritten using your own toString method.

How to reduce typing. Sometimes we wish we could type less to do the same work, in Java to implement a print routine, we need to write System.out.println();. When we do a lot of printing, this can be time consumming, the following method is an example of how we can reduce the amount of typing. I am placing the pl() method inside a class so that you can run it, or just copy the method and use it in any program.

ASCII. The American Standard Code for Information Interchange codes, and how to find any ASCII character, is presented using our ascii.java program which shows us how to produce all ASCII codes. We need to learn to use them since many characters that we need in programming can not be printed using the keyboard, such as the sound of the bell.

Javadoc is a Java tool that creates html documentation from javadoc comments /** */ created inside the program source code. Javadoc allows you to attach program docummentation descriptions to classes, methods, variables, and other tools such as constructors, and interfaces in the generated html documentation by placing Javadoc comments directly before their declaration statements.

Key Terms

Generic Methods	Generic methods. In this chapter we learned the use of generic methods which allows us to replace the use of methods overloading. We can use one method to pass different types of data. We can use the same method to received and process integers, characters, doubles, strings, objects, and other types of data, without having to write one method for each data type as is required when using overloading. In Our program example genericMethods.java we present generic methods that accept any type of data.
Interface. **Java Collection** **Interface.**	A Java collection Interface is an object that groups elements into a single unit. Collections are used to store, retrieve, manipulate, and communicate aggregate data. Usually they represent data items that form a group of similar data, such as a list of employees. There are many data structures that are part of the collections interface such as lists, maps and hashTables. In this section we will use lists to demostrate collections. Collections are also known as containers.
toString. **Overriding** **Equals and** **toString Methods.**	Overriding equals and toString methods. The toString method returns a string representation of an object. It is a string that "textually represents" the object. It is recommended that all classes override the toString method. If you do not override the toString method and you call it, it will return a string consisting of the object's name, the @ sign, and the unsigned hexadecimal representation of the hash code of the object, similar to noToStringMethodDemo@384f14b0.
Reduce Typing. **How to Reduce** **Typing.**	Sometimes we wish we could type less to do the same work, in Java to implement a print routine, we need to write System.out.print();. When we do a lot of printing, this can be time consumming, the pl() method is an example of how we can reduce the amount of typing. I am placing the pl() method inside a class so that you can run it, or just copy the method and use it in any program.
ASCII. **The American** **Standard Code** **for Information** **Interchange.**	ASCII. The American Standard Code for Information Interchange codes, and how to find any ASCII character, is presented using our ascii.java program which shows us how to produce all ASCII codes. We need to learn to use them since many characters that we need in programming can not be printed using the keyboard, such as the sound of the bell.
Javadoc	Javadoc is a Java tool that creates html documentation from javadoc comments /** */ created inside the program source code. Javadoc allows you to attach program documentation descriptions to classes, methods, variables, and other tools such as constructors, and interfaces in the generated html documentation by placing Javadoc comments directly before their declaration statements.

Exercises

1. Create a program that will write your name, backwards in ASCII, leaving a space between each letter.

2. Following the idea of the pl() method in this chapter, create a method that will pause any java program while executing.

3. Create a program that will display all lowercase letters, backwards.

4. Create a program that will accept any type of data.

5. Create a program that uses generic methods.

Select all answers that apply

6. What value do we need to add to any ASCII uppercase letter to obtain its corresponding lowercase ASCII value?

   a. English has 26 uppercase letters so we add 26
   b. We subtract 26 from the uppercase letter
   c. We add 32 from the uppercase letter
   d. We subtract 32 from the uppercase letter

7. What is the purpose of Javadoc?

   a. To document classes, methods and variables in the source code
   b. To compile java programs that have abstract methods
   c. To display the warning produced when compiling
   d. To create HTML files with source code documentation

8. What is the purpose of the pl() method created in this chapter?

   a. To execute the break command
   b. To pause a running program
   c. To execute a line feed without having to type System.out.println;
   d. To execute a line feed

9. What are generic methods used for?

   a. Allows us to replace the use of methods overloading
   b. They can inherit Organic Methods
   c. We can use one method to pass different types of data
   d. To execute Java programs that contain other languages

10. What is a Java collection interface?

    a. Are used to store, retrieve, manipulate, and communicate aggregate data
    b. To replace inheritance
    c. Use to represent data items that form a group of similar data
    d. Is an object that groups elements into a single unit

REFERENCES

- Java API Specifications
  http://www.oracle.com/technetwork/java/api-141528.html

- My Java programs that I use in my Java classes located at robinson.cs.fiu.edu

//END CHAPTER 17: MISCELLANEOUS

Glossary

		CHAPTER

Abstract Classes	Java has abstract classes and methods. Abstracts are not defined. An abstract classes exists to be extended. It can only be used for inheritance or polymorphism, we can not create objects from an abstract class:
	
	//this is an abstract class
	abstract public class **abstractClass**
	{
	
	}//end abstract public class abstractClass
	
	Abstract classes contain abstract methods, abstract methods do NOT contain a body, just the heading:
	
	//this is an abstract method NO BODY NEEDED
	abstract void **hello()**;
	
	Abstract classes contain as many abstract methods and regular methods as needed.
		16

< 463 >

ArrayList	Array data structures have a size limitation, once an array declares its size it can not be modified. We can not add or delete rows or columns to/from it.	8
	ArrayLists are the solution. ArrayLists are another type of data structure; we can modify the ArrayList's size at any time, we can add or delete indexes from any location, ArrayLists are dynamic.	
	Let's create an ArrayList containing string type data as follows:	
	ArrayList<String> arrayList = new ArrayList<String>();	
	We create an ArrayList containing integer type data as follows:	
	ArrayList<Integer> arrayList = new ArrayList<Integer>();	
Arrays	Arrays are data structures that group data items of the same data type. Arrays can contain data of one data type at the same time such as int, char, float, double or any other primitive data type, but we can not mix data types in the same array.	7
	We can also declare arrays of wrapper data types such as Integer, Character, Float, Double, or String data type. Arrays of objects is a special case which will be addressed in Chapter 8.	
	Arrays can be of one or multiple dimensions.	
	Every location in an array is called an index. Arrays are very useful, but they have two short comings. First arrays can not have mixed data types, and once declared, their size can not be changed. Secondly, we can not add or delete indexes, however the data inside each index can be changed.	
Arrays. Allocating Space to Declared Arrays	When we declare an array as above, we create it, but we do not allocate space for it in RAM memory.	7
	The size of an array is specified when we allocate space for it, as follows:	
| | ```
//creates space for 3 ints
arrayOne[] = new int[ 3 ];

//creates space for 2 floats
arrayTwo[] = new float[ 2 ];

//creates space for 4 doubles
arrayThree[] = new double[ 4 ];

//creates space for 2 Strings
arrayFour[] = new String[ 2 ];
``` | |
```

Arrays.
Declare and
Allocate at the
Same Time
	We can also declare (create) an array and assign it space at the same time as follows:
	
	int arrayOne[] = new int[3];
	float arrayTwo[] = new float[2];
	double arrayThree[] = new double[4];
	String arrayFour[] = new String[2];
	
	When we have an array with 4 indexes:
	double arrayThree[] = new double[4];
	
	We say that this array is of length 4, and we know that is has indexes 0, 1, 2, and 3, therefore the indexes go from 0 to length-1.
	
	One of the most common mistakes when accessing an array is trying to access an index at location "length." This will give us the error "index out of range." We must remember that indexes begin at location 0 and end at location "length − 1," always!
		7

Arrays.
Load Data to a
Declared Array
	We can also load data directly into each index as follows:
	
	arrayOne[0] = 43;
	arrayOne[1] = 235;
	arrayOne[3] = 101;
	
	arrayTwo[0] = 12.54;
	arrayTwo[1] = 4.23;
	
	arrayThree[0] = 2.33;
	arrayThree[1] = 2.31;
	arrayThree[2] = 9.0;
	arrayThree[3] = 7.12;
	
	arrayFour[0] = { "Joe" };
	arrayFour[1] = { "Smith" };
		7

Arrays. One Dimension Array	A one dimension array contains one row and one or more columns. We refer to a location in an array as "the index" and we always name the row first then the column. If the data is in row 0 and column 3, we say that the data is at index location 0,3. "Red Cross" will help us remember R,C for Row,Column. We can also use "RC Cola," a soda found in parts of the United States or "RiCola" (RC), a famous medication of unique delicious taste for soothing of the mouth and throat. Always place the "row" before the "column," if we place the column before the row we will have unpredictable results.	7

Arrays. **Parallel Arrays**	Parallel arrays are used to combine multiple one dimensional arrays that might contain different data types, but each row in each array is related to each other: int studentID[] = { 50102, 23908, 12098 }; String studentName[] = { "Joe Ho", "Ann", "Mo" }; double studentBalance[] = { 10.00, 23.78, 1.07 }; Here we have three arrays, each containing three items, and each array holds a different type of data, int, string and double. Program arraysParallel.java creates a report showing the student's name, id and current balance owed. To create this report we use what is called parallel arrays. The only requirement is that all arrays must have the same amount of rows, in this case there are three rows in each array.	7

Arrays.
Printing All Values
Inside this Array
	```for(x = 0; x < 1,000,000; x++)```
	```{```
	``` System.out.printf("%d\n", array[x]);```
	```}```
		7

Arrays. **Three** **Multidimensional** **Arrays**	A three dimensional array is a group of two dimension arrays. I think that one of the best ways to explain what a three dimensional array is, is to use the representation of an apartment building, everybody knows what they look like. Please see program array3d.java	7
Arrays. **Copying Arrays** **into an ArrayList** **Modify and Back**	Remember that arrays have two shortcomings, an array contains only one type of data at the time: int, float, string, etc. and also once we declare an array we can not modify its size. Fortunately we can use ArrayList to modify any array's size, by moving the array's data into an ArrayList, then we can modify the size of the ArrayList by adding or removing elements in it. Once we get the new required size we copy the ArrayList data back into one or multiple new arrays. The program arrayToArrayListAndBack.java shows us how to do this by creating multiple arrays, an ArrayList, Iterators, and one enhanced for loop.	8

Arrays. Declaring/ Creating One Dimension Arrays	Creating one dimensional arrays:
	
	//creates the array arrayOne to hold ints
	int arrayOne[];
	
	//creates the array arrayTwo to hold floats
	float arrayTwo[];
	
	//creates the array arrayThree to hold doubles
	double arrayThree[];
	
	//creates the array arrayFour to hold Strings
	String arrayFour[];
		7

ASCII Codes Table	ASCII means American Standard Code for Information Interchange. Every character that a computer makes is assigned a numerical value, the ASCII code that represents the American English Language is limited to the first 128 characters/numbers, from 0 to 127. Codes from 128 to 255 represent other languages like French, Spanish and others. Codes after 255 are called Unicode. At the current time the Unicode has more than 107000 codes representing most of the languages used today. The first 255 Unicodes are the original ASCII codes. In the ASCII there are 33 non-printing control characters like esc, bell, etc. that affects how text and space is processed; 95 are printable characters such as a, b, c, 1, 2, H, Y, T, etc.	3
ASCII. The American Standard Code for Information Interchange.	ASCII. The American Standard Code for Information Interchange codes, and how to find any ASCII character, is presented using our ascii.java program which shows us how to produce all ASCII codes. We need to learn to use them since many characters that we need in programming can not be printed using the keyboard, such as the sound of the bell.	17
Binary Files	Binary files can only be seen with binary editors and usually they are compiled programs. To see how we handle binary files in Java, please see program FilesBinary.java	9

Binary Numerical System	Computers and all digital systems, such as cell phones, digital cameras, etc. use the binary systems or base-2 numeric system, which has 2 digits, 0 and 1.	3
	At first, it is hard to understand, but everything a digital system does, like video, sound, graphics, calculators, etc., is represented in binary.	
	When we use programming languages we write the programs in plain English commands, and the programming language, in this case Java, translates our work into binary, which is what digital systems understand, even the decimal system is translated into binary.	
Bubble Sort	Now that we know what sorting is, how to write a swap function and how to do constructors, we are going to implement this knowledge into the making of a sophisticated bubble sort.	12
	This section contains four programs: bubbleSorter.java which is a regular calling program, and the following three classes: BubbleSort. java, IntBubbleSort.java, StringBubbleSort.java	
Caller Methods	Methods that call other methods. Usually is the main method in a program.	4
Catching Errors Exceptions In Data Files	When we write Java programs we create at least three different types of errors:	9
	The most common is called "syntax error" which is a typographical error, for instance, instead of writing print we write frint.	
	We can also have "logical errors" in which we are telling the computer to do one thing, when we think we are telling it to do something else.	
	Lastly there are other errors called "runtime errors" that only happen when we run a program. For instance when we try to open a file that does not exist.	
	In Java, errors are called exceptions. As we will see in the following sections, every method that deals with files must have in their headings the command: throws IOException	
	This command will take care of any type of error that has to do with files.	
	If we try to open a file that does not exist we will get an error like this:	
	At 4 - addAllValuesInFile() : Exception in thread "main" java. io.FileNotFoundException: customer.txt (No such file or directory) at java.io.FileInputStream.open(Native Method) at java. io.FileInputStream.<init>(	
	FileInputStream.java:137)	

Classes Inside Classes	Please see our program multiClasses.java in Chapter 16.	16
Comments. Javadoc Comments	The symbols /** .... */ are used by Javadoc. By placing Javadoc comments just before declaration statements, we can add descriptions to classes, methods, variables, and other tools that we have not seen yet such as constructors, and interfaces, e.g.: /** creating JavadocExample class */ /** creating a class called JavadocExample */	2
Compiling in Java	Compiling a program is to transform your source/program into a language that the hardware can understand. When you compile a Java program its compiler (javac) translates your program (the source code) into instructions that the JVM (Java Virtual Machine) understands. In Java these instructions are known as byte codes and are created in a file that has the same name as your program name and replaces .java with .class at the end of the name. program name = myFirstProgram.java compiled name = myFirstProgram.class	1
Computer Programming Language	Just like English, Spanish and French are human languages used by humans to communicate with each other, Computer Programming Languages such as Java, C, Perl, PHP, etc. are used by humans to give instructions to computers. Computers do what we tell them to do through Programming Languages. There are two general types of Computer Languages, compiled and interpreted languages. A compiled language is a language that when compiled, gets translated into a type of code called binary that the computer can understand. Binary is the natural language of computers. C, Cobol and Assembly are some of the compiled languages. Interpreted languages get translated into binary code when the program runs. Java is an interpreted language. Since program written using compiled languages are already compiled, they are much faster than program written in interpreted languages.	1

Constructor. What is a Constructor?	A constructor is a class that contains methods with the same names as the class and accepts data with different signatures. Signatures are the data types and variables that are accepted by the methods. Up to now we have been using classes provided to us by Java, now we are going to learn how to create our own classes using constructors. Constructors create objects, also called an instance of a class. I also refer to them as clones because every object is an exact clone of its class. Java names all of its classes using a capital letter at the first character, see examples on page 250, I recommend to follow this custom, however, if you place a lower case letter at the first character of your homemade classes name, Java will NOT complain, but it will be very difficult to differentiate a class from a regular program by its name.	10
Contructors. Simple Constructors	Simple constructors have four sections: • The global variables • The constructors Methods with the same name as the class with unique signatures. • The mutators/setters methods Mutator methods are usually named "setSomething," and are used to receive variables from the calling program and assign them to the global variables. • The accessors/getters methods Accessors methods are usually named "getSomething," and are used to return the global values to the calling program. So before we can create objects/instance of aclass, we need to create the class, the Building.java program is a simple example.	10

Creating a Variable and Assigning a Value to it	In Java we can declare a variable without assigning a value to it, however, I recommend that you become used to assigning a value, if necessary zero, because in some languages like ANSI C, if you do not assign a value to a new variable, it assigns the value found at the memory location where the variable gets created, which can cause big problems.
	
	double speedOfLight = 186,282;
	float earthDiameter = 7,926.41;
	int myAge = 105;
	float myHeigth = 9.9;
		3

Creating Java Programs	Select an IDE (Integrated Development Environment) such as Eclipse or NetBeans or any editor of your choice. See detailed instructions in the corresponding section in Chapter 1.	1
	Once you are inside your code editor, start writing your program's source code file (your typed program). The program name requires three parts: the FirstName, one period/dot, and the word java. e.g., myFirstProgram.java.	
Data Abstraction	Java has abstract classes and methods. Abstracts are not defined. An abstract classes exists to be extended. It can only be used for inheritance or polymorphism, we can not create objects from an abstract class:	14

	//this is an abstract class
	abstract public class abstractClass
	{
	
	}//end abstract public class abstractClass	

	Abstract classes contain abstract methods, abstract methods do NOT contain a body, just the heading:	

	abstract void hello(); //this is an abstract method NO BODY NEEDED
	
	abstract void hello();	

Data Abstraction vs Interfaces	Sometimes we ask why we need interfaces when we can use abstract classes. The answer is simple. Every method in an interface MUST be implemented while in abstract classes only the abstract methods MUST be implemented.	14
	Interfaces can only have methods that are abstract, while abstract classes can have both abstract and regular methods.	
Data Type Boolean	The boolean type has only two values, true or false.	3
	When we declare a variable of type boolean we can only assign it to be either true or false.	
Data Type byte	An eight bit byte allows us to write data values from –128 to 128 or a maximum positive number of 255 by turning all 8 bits on, and then adding them. In this book we will only deal with positive numbers to describe bytes.	3
	Bit number 7 6 5 4 3 2 1 0 State on 1 1 1 1 1 1 1 1 Decimal value 128 64 32 16 8 4 2 1 = 255	

Data Type char	The char data type is used to place a single character, such as a letter, number, or symbol. Numbers of char data type are treated as characters not numbers.	3
Data Type double	A double holds whole numbers with decimals, with much greater values than the float, for ranges see table on page 39.	3
Data Type float	A float holds whole numbers with decimals, for ranges see table on page 39.	3
Data Type int	An int number will hold a whole number. If you placed a number with decimals into an int, the decimals will be dropped.	3
Data Type long	A long will also hold a whole number but of greater value than an int, see table on page 39.	3
Data Type short	A short number will also hold a whole number but of less value than an int, see table on page 39.	3
Data Types	In math we assign numbers to variables such as a, b, c, etc. e.g.: a = 5 where a becomes 5 b = 12.4 where b becomes 12.4 c = a + b where c becomes 17.4 In computer science a variable is a descriptive name given to a known amount of information so that we can use such a variable regardless of the value it represents. The value of variables can change during the life of the program. In Java we do the same, however before assigning a value to a variable, we assign what we call a data type to the variable.	3
Data Types String Class Data Types	To work with numbers we use the primitive data types, to work with characters such as "aec$ ^%FtaA01982.GA/}]" we use the string class. The string Java class has over 1,000 methods. This class is used for string variables containing a sequence of characters from 0 to 2gig in length, the characters in it can be the combination of any letters, numbers and/or symbols, e.g.: String myName = " Albert# &(723,.$ Einstein\? ";	3

Data Types. **Object Data Types**	We have been using primitive, wrappers and string data types from the beginning. In this chapter we used them to populate arrays and ArrayLists. Now that we are experts in using these data types, we are going to learn about another data type called Objects (notice here Objects are written with uppercase O). Remember that when we create an object of a class we refer to this using the lowercase o. Objects and objects are two different things. An object of a class is an identical copy of a class. I like to refer to objects of a class as clones, simply because they are exact clone copies of a class. In this section we learn about Object data types. An Object data type allows us to create data structures like arrays to accept data of multiple data types. Up to now, when we create an array or an ArrayList we make them to accept only one type of data. This new data type called Object data type allows us to accept the mixture of all previously learned data types into an array or ArrayList. Please see program ObjectsArraysArrayLists.java	8
Data Types. **Object Data Types**	The Object data type (notice Object with capital O), accepts data of all data types such as int, float, double, string, etc. We can use Object data types in data structures that accept data of only one type as int, float, double or string, such as arrays and arrayLists. The theObjectDataType.java program shows the implementation of the Object data type.	10
Decimal Format. **Printing Numbers.**	Now that we have learned how to work with files, we need to learn to print numeric data in with dollar signs, numbers separated with commas and periods, and multiple decimal numbers. For this, Java has a class called DecimalFormat. Please see program decimalFormatClass.java	9

Decimal Numerical System	We use this numerical system everyday. It contains 10 digits from 0 to 9 and it is known as base-10 numerical system because it has 10 numbers.
	
	Our common daily math computations are done with these 10 digits, e.g.:
	
	idNumber = 9876;
	x = 5 + 2;
	addNumbers(3, 7, 8, 123, 45);
		3

Documenting a Program	Java provides us with three ways to document our work, they are called REMARKS. Any documentation with REMARKS is ignored by the Java compiler, and is not part of the program instructions. The symbols /* begin a documentation area, and ends it with */ Such a section can be of any size, even thousands of pages, e.g.:
	
	`/*`
	  Author : Michael Robinson
	  Program : myFirstProgram.java
	  Purpose : To present, the Java class, the main
	                   method,
	                   one variable of data type int
	                   one variable of data type String
	                   and the three print command of Java
	
	  Updated : November 12th, 2099
	`*/`
	
	The symbols // can be placed in any line of code, anything written after them is a remark, therefore ignored by the compiler.
		2

Eclipse	A graphical user interface IDE to create Java programs. Download (FREE) from: http://www.eclipse.org/downloads/moreinfo/java.php	1
Editors	There are two types of editors. One is called IDE and the other Text Editor. Editors are programs that allows you to create your Java programs.	1

Exceptions Handling	In Java errors are called e-xceptions. There are a large amount of classes that handle errors, allowing us to maintain control of the program.
	
	To handle an exception, or control an error, Java requires the following import in the java.util.* package:
	
	import java.util.*;
	
	This is a typical code for exceptions handling:
	
	try
	{
	   String s = "";
	
	   BufferedWriter bw = new BufferedWriter(
	      new FileWriter("/home/mr/Bigtest"));
	
	(cont.)
		9

Exceptions Handling (cont.)	```
BufferedReader br = new BufferedReader(
    new FileReader("/home/mr/Bigtest"));

String sc = "12230381 Vallicos Inc";
int x = 0;

while(x < 99999999)
{
    sc = br.readLine();
    bw.write(sc + "\n");
    x++;
}
bw.close();
}
catch(Exception e)
{
    e.printStackTrace();
}
```

In the catch section we find ( Exception e ), this is the default exception handler which can handle any error. Java writes the error inside the variable e, which can then be printed. | 9 |
| Extends/ Inhereting | Classes that use the content (methods, variables) of other programs usually called super-classes. | 16 |
| External Classes | Up to this moment we have worked under the assumption that all Java programs must have one "public static void main( String args[] )" method.

If we go back to all the programs we have written so far, we can see that the word "class" is on the headings of all our programs, therefore all our programs are "classes."

We need to recognize that just like the Java classes that we used in our programs, such as string, scanner, etc., the programs we have written so far are also classes. They are classes that we wrote.

Now it is time to learn how to create "external classes" which do NOT have the "public static void main( String args[] )" method. These external classes only have variables and regular methods which can be used as additional classes, by any other program/class or external class. This means that we are extending the capabilities of the Java language by creating our own additional classes.

(cont.) | 10 |
```

External Classes (cont.)	External classes, just like methods, gives us three great benefits: • We can divide a large project into smaller pieces (divide and conquer). • When we have an error in a method, we can block that method allowing the rest of the project to continue working. • Re-use. This time any other class or method in our projects can re-use any method in any external class. We can also share our own external classes with other teams doing their own projects.	10
File. **What is a file?**	Files are data structures that are used to store data. Basically there are two types of data files, binary and text files. Text files are usually created using text editors. We can use operating systems commands to create text files. See details in the *Operating Systems for IT* book by Michael Robinson, published by Kendall-Hunt. Text files can be accessed with any text editor or any program that can access binary files. Binary files is the name given to any file that is not a text file and requires its corresponding program to access the data. Text editors can not access binary files. The Windows operating system uses a text editor named Notepad. There are other third party editors such as Notepad++ and EditPro that work in Windows. The Linux operating system has many text editors, among them Gedit, Nano, Pico, VM, VIM and many others. We also have IDEs (Integrated Development Environment) systems like NetBeans and Eclipse that allows us to write programs. IDEs have build in text editors. All the Java source code (programs) presented in this book were create using Gedit in Ubuntu Linux operating system. When we create a Java program with a text editor, we write lines of code and of course every line is made with characters. Any program can be viewed as a two dimensional array, it has rows and columns, every line of code is a row and every character is a column. Files are exactly the same. In files, every line/row is called a record. Every column is called a field.	9

Files. Large Files. Writing and Reading	I recommend to make sure that all students learn how to use all the classes in program filesLargeSize.java. These classes allow us to write, faster than the other above classes, files above the 2gig limit. In the filesLargeSize.java program, using the string class, we implement the substring, toUpperCase() and compareTo methods, as well as the Scanner(System.in) class to be able to read from the keyboard.	9

Files. Text Files	In this section we see several text and binary files program examples that demonstrate the following classes used in Java:
	
	FileWriter, PrintWriter
	FileReader, BufferedReader
	Formatter
	Scanner
	FileOutputStream, DataOutputStream
	BufferedWriter bw = new
	     BufferedWriter(new
	
	     FileWriter(filename))
		9

Files. Text Files using the File Class	Java uses the file class in java.io.File to obtain information about files and directories. The file class does not create files or allows us to make input or obtain output to/from files. Please see program filesFile.java	9
Files. Text Files using the Formatter Class	In Java there are several ways to create files, and using the formatter class is probably the easiest and fastest way to create a file. Formatter also allows us to write data into the file, however, make sure this file does NOT exist otherwise it will overwrite it (deletes it and re-creates it). Please see program filesFormatter.java	9

Files. **Text Files** **using the** **Scanner Class**	The scanner class is usually used to obtain data from the keyboard. Here we will see we can also use it to open text files and process them. For the program filesScanner.java, we use a text file called fileOne which contains the following data: Joe Smith CS Tom Richards IT Daniel Thomason Math Robert Lambert EE Miguel Gonzalez CS	9
Files. **Text Files** **using:** **FileWriter,** **PrintWriter,** **FileReader and** **BufferedReader**	Please see the appropiate programs in Chapter 9 for each type of the following text files: FileWriter PrintWriter FileReader BufferedReader	9
Final Classes	We make a class FINAL when we want to prevent any other class from inheriting from it. Final classes can not have sub-classes. We usually do this for security reasons. Classes from the Java API standard library such as Java.lang.System, java.util.Arrays, Java.lang.String and java.util.Collections are final. All the methods in a final class are automatically treated as final methods. Our aFinalClass.java program is a simple example of a final class.	13
Final Methods	Now that we have learned about inheritance, we know what super-classes and sub-classes are final methods that can NOT be overridden by sub-classes. This is just like in the case of the final variables, final methods are used to prevent any changes to be made to a method in a super-class. Our theFinalMethodClass.java is a simple example of a final method.	13

for Loops	There are two types of for loops in Java, the standard for loop which has three parts and the enhanced for loop (see Enhanced For Loops at the end of the arrays section in Chapter 7 - Data Structures - Arrays).
	
	The standard for loop looks as follows:
	for(start ; stop condition ; step)
	{
	   commands
	}
	
	The for loop requires a counter variable, in most cases the int x variable is selected.
	
	The start section determines the beginning of the loop, the loop can start at any location, 0, the end value, or any value in between.
	
	int x = 0;
	for(x = 0;
	for(x = lastValue;
	for(x = lastValue/2;
	
	The stop condition section tells the loop that when such condition is met to terminate the loop:
	
	     start stop
	for(x = 0; x <= 5
	
	The step section tells the for loop that every time it does a loop, execute whatever command is in the step:
	
	     start stop step
	for(x = 0; x <= 5; x++)
	
	x++ means add one to the current value of x.
		6

For. Enhanced for Loops	Now that we know how arrays work, lets see what "enhanced for loops" are. Enhanced for loops are a variation of the "for loop" that is used with arrays and other data structure called ArrayList which we will see in Chapter 8. enhancedForLoops.java	7
Frame. What is a Frame?	In GUI programming, a frame is a window with a title and a border. GUI applications have at least one frame with button components that close, minimize or maximizes the window. Please see the following two programs: guiSmallFrame.java guiFullScreen.java	11

Generic Methods	Generic methods. In this chapter we learned the use of generic methods which allows us to replace the use of methods overloading. We can use one method to pass different types of data. We can use the same method to received and process integers, characters, doubles, strings, objects, and other types of data, without having to write one method for each data type as is required when using overloading. In Our program example genericMethods.java we present generic methods that accept any type of data.	17
Graphical User Interface (GUI)	Graphical User Interface (GUI) are used by most people to access their computers. Computers using Windows, Linux, or Apple have beautiful graphical interfaces allowing the users easy management of their computer systems.	1
GUI (Graphical User Interface)	In computer science the term GUI, usually pronounced gooey, is how users communicate with electronic machines such as monitors, cell phones, tablets, etc. using graphical images instead of text commands. For the user, the GUI usually makes the communication with the computer easier, simply point and click. The disadvantages are that the communication presented to the user is limited by the GUI's options. Using non-GUI text commands to communicate with electronic machines allows the user total control of the machine.	11
GUI. Dialog Boxes	In Graphical User Interface (GUI) programming we use dialog boxes to enable communication between the user and the program. In this chapter we use two types of GUI dialog boxes, the message and the input dialog boxes. In general, dialog boxes communicate information to the users, requesting a response from the users.	11

GUI. Input Dialog Boxes	Input dialog boxes are used to interact with the user and retrieve information entered by the user. These boxes usually contain a system icon, multiple buttons, a short specific message, and a section where the user can input information.
	
	These boxes stop the users from accessing other sections of the program before replying to the current dialog box.
	
	All the information entered in the input dialog boxes is of string data type, regardless of what data was written in the input section.
	
	Java provides the following methods to convert the data entered from string data type to the intended data type. If the data entered is assigned to a variable called temp, it can be casted/converted as follows:
	
	`//converts to Integer`
	`Integer response = Integer.parseInt( temp );`
	
	`//converts to Double`
	`Double response = Double.parseDouble(temp);`
	
	`//converts to Float`
	`Float response = Float.parseFloat( temp );`
	
	`//converts to Long`
	`Long response = Long.parseLong( temp );`
	
	`//converts to Short`
	`Short response = Short.parseShort( temp );`
		11

Hexadecimal Numerical System	This numerical system is base-16 it goes for 0 – F, that is from 0–9 then ABCDEF
	
	`A = 10`
	`B = 11`
	`C = 12`
	`D = 13`
	`E = 14`
	`F = 15`
	
	At one time or another we have experienced computer problems where error messages show up on the screen such as:
	
	memory dump at: DA9F011231CCABDEDACF765
	
	What this means is that a RAM memory error occurred at memory location DA9F011231CCABDEDACF765.
		3

IDE Programming Editors	An IDE (Integrated Development Environment) is a programming tool that contains a code editor, a compiler, a debugger, and a GUI (Graphical User Interface) which allows the student to write programs easier. There are some disadvantages in using an IDE, such as all warnings are hidden therefore the student does not know that they exist. The best way to avoid this and other problems is to write the programs using text editors, which we will discuss in this book.	1

if Command	In my opinion the most used command in programming is the "if" command. In programming we are always making decisions, always asking what if?
	
	The great thing about the implementation of the "if" command is that it is almost identical in every programming language.
	A plain if is very useful and very easy to implement. The plain if statement has the following structure:
	
	if(condition)
	{
	   commands
	}
	
	If the condition is TRUE then the commands between the curly brackets will be executed:
	
	//create and load a float variable
	float temperature = 92.7;
	
	if(temperature > 90)
	{
	   System.out.println(" Oh man it is hot!!");
	}
		5

if else if	There are times that the if and else combination is not enough, then we use the "if else if" combination: Please see program if_else_if.java	5

if_else	The if statement has a sidekick called else, they work very well together, their structure is:
	
	if(condition)
	{
	   commands
	}
	else
	{
	   commands
	}
	
	If the "if" condition is NOT true then else takes charge and its commands are executed.
		5

if. nested if	The nested if is very powerful and sometimes complex. Please see program nestedIf.java	5
if. ternary If	The ternary (three way) "if" replaces some implementations of if else if statements expression1 ? expression2 : expression3 if expression1 is true then expression2 is selected else expression3 is selected other way to look at it is: condition ? value_if_true : value_if_false Please see program ternaryIf.java	5
Imports	Java is a very large programming language, when loaded it contains basic utilities that allows us to create a lot of programs, however to create some programs we need to import utilities into Java at the beginning of the program prior to the class header (see next section), e.g. If we want to obtain data from the keyboard we need to "import" a Java utility called Scanner as follows: import java.util.Scanner	2

Indentation. Java Indentation	Just like a book, programming must follow a structure that allows all persons working in any program to visually understand the sections in it.	2
	If every line in a book was left justified, and there were no headings it will be very difficult to read, the same happens in programming.	
	The class header and its two braces are left justified.	
	All methods inside the class MUST be indented the same amount of spaces, 3, 4, 5 or whatever is best for you.	
	All methods MUST be equally separated by 2 or 3 spaces.	
Inheritance	The basic concept of inheritance is that some classes inherit methods and variables from other classes. The class providing the inheritance is called the "super-class," It is also known as the "base-class."	13
	The class inheriting is called the sub-class. It is also referred to as the "derived-class."	
	Here we will call them "super-class" and "sub-class."	
	The only condition for inheritance is that all variables and methods are declared public to be inheritable, if they are declared private sub-classes we can not see them.	
	For this section we have created the following programs:	
	cssDefautls.java is the super-class webPageHome.java is a sub-class webPage2.java is a sub-class webPage3.java is a sub-class inheritanceWebPage.java is the main program	
	The first step is to create an external class called cssDefautls.java, this class will be the super-class.	
	Then we create multiple external classes that will define different web-pages: webPageHome, webPage2, and webPage3. These external classes will be the sub-classes that will inherit from the cssDefautls.java super-class.	
	Now that we have the super-class and a group of external classes we will create a class named inheritanceWebPage.java which will make use of the variables and methods of the above super-class and sub-classes.	

Interface. Java Collection Interface.	A Java collection Interface is an object that groups elements into a single unit. Collections are used to store, retrieve, manipulate, and communicate aggregate data. Usually they represent data items that form a group of similar data, such as a list of employees. There are many data structures that are part of the collections interface such as lists, maps and hashTables. In this section we will use lists to demostrate collections. Collections are also known as containers.	17
Interfaces	An interface is a class that contains methods that only have headings. It is also referred as "an interface is a group of related methods with empty bodies." These methods are considered to be "templates" without bodies. Interfaces can be implemented in any other class and all the methods in the Interface must be used in the class that is implementing the interface.	16
Iterator	The iterator class is very powerful, in a way it is similar to the for loop. It allows us to see if we have data/elements in a data structure, it moves forwards element by element, and remove any element in the data structure. Iterator exists in several data structures, among them the ArrayList and the List. We use an iterator to go through a data structure. The items inside the structure are called elements. This is how an iterator is created and used: First we need to create an instance of the iterator, in this case we will call it itr: //create an Iterator object using Iterator. Iterator<Integer> itr = arrayList.iterator(); Here we created the "itr" iterator for the ArrayList called arrayList that we created in the previous ArrayList section. Java iterators have three methods: hasNext, next and remove	8
Java	The programming language Java is known as "write once run every-where." This means that we can write our programs on any device, convert it into a standard code and run it in any device that contains a JVM (Java Virtual Machine). Installing JVM in devices and software packages such as Windows has become an industry standard practice.	1

Java Classes	In Java all programs are classes, to me a class is equivalent to the perimeter of my house, it has walls, a floor, and a ceiling. Whether it is one bedroom apartment or a 20 room mansion it has a perimeter. Java programs are of all sizes, and their perimeter is the outside class. A program can be of the size of the Windows operating system (over a million lines of code) or as small as the program that controls the time and temperature of your microwave.	2
Java JDK	The Java Development Kit (JDK) is an Oracle Corporation product aimed at Java developers. The JDK has as its primary components a collection of programming tools for Java. Download (FREE) Java JDK from: http://www.oracle.com/technetwork/java/javase/downloads/index.html Make sure you download the proper version for your computer 32 or 64 bits.	1
Javadoc	Javadoc is a Java tool that creates html documentation from javadoc comments /** */ created inside the program source code. Javadoc allows you to attach program documentation descriptions to classes, methods, variables, and other tools such as constructors, and interfaces in the generated html documentation by placing Javadoc comments directly before their declaration statements.	17
Linked List	A linked list is refered to as a linear collection of nodes, they are also defined as a finite sequence of nodes. Except for the first node, each node contains one pointer field that points to the next node, and another pointer node that points to the previous node. The first node only points to the next node. The pointer in the last node points to null, which is always the end of the linked list. Linked lists have many similarities to single dimensional arrays the major difference is: Linked lists are data structures that do not have a set size as in arrays. What we know in arrays as indexes, in linked lists we call them nodes. In linked lists we can always extend or reduce the amount of nodes. In arrays we can not change their amount of indexes, once created.	15

Loops	In Java we have three types of loops: for, while, and do while loops.	6
Math Using Primitives	Java provide us with already made methods to do many math computations. The math class is called Math. Please see program mathExamples.java	3
Message Dialog Boxes	These boxes usually contain a system icon, one or more buttons, and a short specific message.	11
Methods That Accept Data	Methods that accept data are methods that are called by other methods that are passing/sending data of any type to the receiving methods, as shown in the following program. Please see program passingDataProgram.java	4
Methods That Do Not Accept Any dData	Methods that do not accept any data are methods that can be called without needing any data from the calling statement. Program noDataPassProgram.java contains two methods main and printMyInfo1()	4

Methods That Return Data	Java also has methods that return data to its calling statements/ methods.
	
	Note that in this example, in main we are making this type of call:
	
	int result1 = printMyInfo3(myFirstName, myID);
	
	Also note the first line of the called method:
	public static int printMyInfo3(String myFirstName, int myID)
	
	Notice that instead of "void" we have "int" which means that this method will return a variable of data type "int".
	
	The last line in this method is:
	return(myID * 2);
	returning the int value of (myID * 2)
		4

Methods. Calling Methods	In programming it is very important to be organized, good use of methods is the best way to achieve organization in Java.	4
	In Java we can have as many methods as we want. The main(String arg[]) method is the entry point of Java. I use it to create variables and as the central control point from where I call all methods. We can also call methods from inside another methods.	
	To show how to use methods I say that Java has three types of methods with variations: methods that do not accept any data, methods that accept data, and methods that return data.	
	Let's use four regular methods called printMyInfo1, printMyInfo2, printMyInfo3, and printMyInfo4 to implement the three different types of methods mentioned above.	
Methods. Java Methods	A method is a section of code inside a program (class) which contains instructions written by you. Methods always go inside a class.	2
	Methods are independent logical units of programming instructions, and can be re-used as often as necessary. If we have an error in a method, it is restricted to that method which makes finding and fixing errors easier.	
	Methods cannot see each other, however they can communicate among themselves by making calls capable of passing and/or receiving data to/from each other.	
Netbeans	A graphical user interface IDE to create Java programs. Download (FREE) from:	1
	http://www.oracle.com/technetwork/java/javase/downloads/index.html	

Numerical Operators	There are some special symbols called Operators that perform specific operations on one, two or three numbers, giving us a result.	3

There are some special symbols called Operators that perform specific operations on one, two or three numbers, giving us a result.

In math we say: x = 3 + 5
but we never say: x = x + 5

In computer science we can say both of the above, the second method needs the following explanation:

```
//creates variable basket and assign value 5 to it.
int basket = 5;
```

```
//add one to the current value of basket
```

```
//the new value of basket is 6
basket = basket + 1;
```

```
//takes 3 from to the current value of basket
```

```
//the new value of basket is 3
basket = basket - 3;
```

In the same manner we can implement multiplication and division.

```
basket = basket * 3; //note * means multiplication
basket = basket / 3; //note / means division
```

The following section shows other ways to use the math operators: =, --, ++, -=, +=, *=, /=

```
//create and initialize counter to 0
int counter = 0;
```

```
//adds 1 to counter, = 1
counter++;
```

```
//multiply counter by 6, = 6
counter *= 6;
```

```
//divide counter by 2, = 3
counter /= 2;
```

```
//take one from counter, = 2
counter--;
```

```
//take 2 from counter, = 0
counter -= 2;
```

```
//add 100 to counter, = 100
counter += 100;
```

Numerical Systems	Throughout the existence of humans, we have invented many numeric systems. In this chapter we discuss four types that we will use in this programming class.	3
Operating System	Windows, Linux, and Apple are the most popular current Operating Systems. An Operating System is the software that allows the user to control the hardware.	1
Operator &&	The operator && means logical "and" if(cold && raining) //if cold and raining	3
Operator %	The % operator also known as modulus and mod, means remainder when dividing two numbers, but the result is always an int, which is different than division. Division keeps the decimals in the result, again % gives you and int, dropping/truncating the decimals. % looks like division but it is NOT 5 % 2 = 1 //this is modulus means that 2 exists twice in 5 leaving 1 as the modulus 182 % 3 = 2 //3 exists 60 times in 182 leaving 2 as the modulus 55 % 7 = 6 //7 exists 7 times in 55 leaving 6 as the modulus 2000 % 4 = 0 //4 exist 500 times in 2000 leaving 0 as the modulus. The % operator is very useful in programming, allowing us to perform very complex operations easily.	3

Operator ||	The operator || means logical "or"
	
	//if cold or raining
	if(cold || raining)
		3

Operators =, = =, !=	This is where many people get confused and cause programming errors.
	
	The operator = means the right value is assigned to the left value e.g.,
	
	// 5 is assigned to the variable total
	total = 5;
	
	Operator = = means equivalence, we check to see if the left value is equivalent to the right value:
	
	//test if total is equivalent to 5
	if(total == 5)
	
	The operator != mean not equal, we check to see if the left value is not equal to the right value
	
	//if total is not equal to 5
	if(total != 5)
		3

Operators >= and <=	The operator >= means left value is greater or equal to right value, e.g.: 5 >= 5 same as in math, 5 is greater or equal to 5 5 >= 4 same as in math, 5 is greater or equal to 4 The operator <= means left value is smaller or equal to right value, e.g.: 5 <= 5 same as in math, 5 is less or equal to 5 4 <= 5 same as in math, 4 is less or equal to 5	3
Overloading	Overloading is a great tool in Java that allows us to use a single method name to accept different amounts of variables, of various data types, in different order. It behaves similarly to the System.out.print(? ?) Java command.	15
Pause Program	In programming we need to stop our programs at any place so that we can see what the program is doing, this is called debugging. Java has a class called wait() which allows us to stop a process for a specific amount of time, but it can be interrupted by other processes through a class called threads. However, when debugging we want the program to stop until we tell it to continue, we need total control. For this purpose I created a program called pauseClass.java which has a method called pause. I use this method all the time to do my debugging, and I think it will be useful to you.	4

Polymorphism	Polymorphism is an extension of inheritance. It allows us to use multiple- super-classes and multiple sub-classes from calling programs, which I refer to as main or calling programs. Remember that super-classes and sub-classes do not have the main method. Please review the following .java programs: ToolsSPClass is a super class VehicleSPClass extends ToolsSPClass and is a super class PolyMain extends ToolsSPClass TheVehicleMain extends ToolsSPClass FullSizeCarSBClass extends VehicleSPClass SportCarSBClass extends VehicleSPClass MiniCarSBClass extends VehicleSPClass	3
Primitive Data Types	Each primitive has its own name, occupying a specific amount of bytes, and containing a minimum and a maximum value. The amount of bytes and values depend on the computer the program is running on. Large computer systems have different values, the following are the typical values on today's standard personal computers. Today's Primitive Data Types use the Unicode Standard, all the values represented in the ASCII codes are in the same locations in the Unicode Standard.	3
Print Commands	Java uses three distinct commands to print. System.out.print, System.out.println, and System.out.printf	2
PseudoCode	PseudoCode is the method of writing down the steps to be taken to solve a problem. This is done using regular English words without the use of any programming code.	1
Queue	Queue is a data structure that allows us to place data items one after another. It uses the FIFO (first in, first out) processing method. The first item placed in the queue is the first item to be extracted/ processed.	15

		9
Records. **What is a Record?**	In Chapter 6: Data Structures – Arrays, we learned what arrays are.	

We can say that a text file with one record is a single dimensional array, and that a text file with more than one record is a two dimensional array. In other words, a record is a line of text in a data structure such as a file or an array.

Records such as: Joe Smith CS are composed of the following segments: Joe, Smith, and CS. Each of these segments are called fields and each field is given a unique name. The field name for Joe could be First Name, for Smith Last Name, and for CS could be School.

Records are separated (delimited) in many different forms, for instance spreadsheets use the tab symbol to delimit their fields, the above record example (Joe Smith CS) is delimited by the space symbol.

A file can contain thousands of records, and a record can contain thousands of fields. It is limited by the type of data structure, the operating system, and the Java file management class we use.

With today's technologies we have text files that can contain terabytes of records, therefore is very important to select the appropriate file class for the job. Java has multiple classes that we can use to work with files.

In this chapter we are presenting the following file classes: FileWriter, PrintWriter, FileReader, BufferedReader, File, Scanner, FileInputStream, DataInputStream, Formatter, FileOutputStream and DataOutputStream, and my favorite one which allows us to process files larger than 2 gigabytes:

```
BufferedWriter bw = new
    BufferedWriter( new

    FileWriter( filename ) );
```

Recursion	The term recursion has different meanings depending on the area being used ranging from logic to linguistics. The most common disciplines where it is used are mathematics and computer science. In computer science recursion is the process of creating functions where the function being created is applied/executed/called within its own definition. In other words a recursive method/function is a method/function that calls itself. Any recursive function needs to have a place where it terminates, otherwise it will be in a endless/infinity loop and will never end. This place is called the base case, when the function reaches its base case, it terminates. Recursion is used to solve many algorithms, QuickSort, the current fastest sorting algorithm uses recursion. Our recursion.java program is the implementation of calculating the factorial of any integer using recursion.	12
Reduce Typing. How to Reduce Typing.	Sometimes we wish we could type less to do the same work, in Java to implement a print routine, we need to write System.out.print();. When we do a lot of printing, this can be time consumming, the pl() method is an example of how we can reduce the amount of typing. I am placing the pl() method inside a class so that you can run it, or just copy the method and use it in any program.	17
Scanner Class Reading The Keyboard Using Scanner Class	We need to be able to communicate with the keyboard. The easiest way is to use the scanner class. In the program scannerClass.java we obtain input from the keyboard of three different data types: int, double and string.	4
Sorting. What is Sorting?	The fastest way of finding any information is when it is in order, usually when it is in ascending alphabetical order. When you look at the index in a book we know that the items beginning with m are after the a's and before the z's. Sorting is exactly that, a way of placing data in an orderly manner, either in ascending (a-z) or descending (z-a) order. There are many specialized algorithms for sorting, the simplest and slowest is called bubble sort, one of the fastest is called quick sort. In this chapter we will learn the bubble sort. All sorts require that the items being examined be swapped/moved when necessary. Our swap.java program will teach us how to swap records.	
Stack	A stack is a data structure that allows us to place data items on top of each other. It uses the LIFO (last in, first out) method of processing. The last item placed in the stack is the first item to be extracted.	15

String Tokenizer	When analyzing data, lets say the contents of a book, we need to be able to split the entire book into words.	7
	The string tokenizer is what we use to do so.	
	Please see program tokenizer.java	
Swap - Placing Data in Order	Swapping is the central process used in all sorting algorithms. Since all sorting algorithms require implement swap routines, I think we should learn how to implement them using small amounts of data. Here we will use three items.	12
	In the swap.java example we sort three items using our swap method, we need three variables and an additional variable usually called temp which is used to temporarily move the data items that need to be swapped.	
	Please examine our swap.java program carefully, we must understand this process before going into the sorting algorithms.	
switch Command	Limitations of the switch command:	6
	I look at the switch statement as a variation of the if statement.	
	The limitations of the switch class is that it only accepts integers or characters as input, while the "if" command accepts any type and amount of conditions. Also, the switch command does not allow for comparison statements as follows:	
	evaluations (=, >=, ,=, etc).	
	Please see program swithClass.java.	
System.out.print	Remember that all statements in Java MUST end with a ;	2
	When a print statement is too long to fit in one line we can split it at the + symbol, e.g.:	
	System.out.print("My name is : " + myFirstName + " My ID is : " + myID + "\n");	
	System.out.print displays whatever is between the () following these rules:	
	whatever is between "" will be printed the + adds the contents of the next variable the + adds what is between the "" the + adds the contents of the next variable the + adds the enter key which is \n in Java.	

		2
System.out.printf	This is the Java implementation of the ANSI C printf command, it is very powerful, and can do all, and more than the above print and println commands. When a printf statement is too long to fit in one line we can split it at the ", location. System.out.printf("My name is : %s My ID is : %d\n", myFirstName, myID); System.out.printf contains several distinct placeholders where the corresponding data variables will display. These placeholders must be inside "" and they look like these: %d = displays variables of int data type %s = displays variables of String data type %c = displays variables of char data type %f = displays variables of float or double data type to these data types (float and double) we can request the amount of decimals we want, e.g.: %.2f displays variables of float data type with 2 decimals. %3.2f diplays 3 whole numbers with 2 decimals. We can have as many whole and decimal places as needed. After the "" inside the printf statement we place a , (comma) and then the corresponding variables in the same sequence as the placeholders, e.g.: System.out.printf("My name is : %s My ID is : %d\n", myFirstName, myID); myFirstName uses the first placeholder %s myID uses the second placeholder %d	

System.out.println	System.out.println("My name is : " + myFirstName + " My ID is : " + myID);	2
	System.out.println is exactly the same as System.out.print, except that the command \n does not need to be added inside the (), unless you want an additional line print to be executed, because \n or line print is included in the System.out.println with the letters ln meaning add one line feed or carriage return.	
	The \n command can be inserted at any location in any of the three print commands, and as many times as needed, as long as it is inside "", creating an additional line feed or carriage return.	
Terminal Mode/ Command Line	To use editors such as Notepad, Gedit, VI, VIM, Pico, Nano, and TextEdit using terminal mode in Linux and in Windows.Command Line.	1
	Windows:	
	To go to to the Command Line select:	
	Windows: Start, run, cmd, enter	
	Linux Ubuntu:	
	Applications, Accessories, Terminal.	
	Now open the editor of your choice.	
	Create/Save your program e.g., myFirstProgram.java	
	Compile your program as follows:	
	javac myFirstProgram.java	
	The javac command creates the compiled program called: myFirstProgram.class	
	If your program has errors it will NOT compile until all errors are fixed.	
	To run your compiled program: Java myFirstProgram (note no .class).	

Text Editors	Text editors are programs that allow you to create your Java programs in terminal mode. After your first or second semester of programming languages, in my classes, I require that all work be done in terminal mode. The reason is that in most large companies, programmers and scientists prefer, and in some cases require to use computers in terminal mode. There are many free text editors available for all operating systems. In Windows we find Notepad and a third-party free editor called Notepad++. In Linux we find Gedit, Nano, Pico, VI and VIM, all free, and in Apple computers we find TextEdit.	1
This. What is this?	The Java 'this' keyword is very useful, it helps us identify if a variable is of global or local scope. We are going to use it in all the new programs when necessary. It has many uses allowing us to clarify which variables or objects we are referring to. It sounds complicated but as we start using it, we will see how easy it is to implement it. In the This.java program, in the main method, we create an instance of its own class/program named test1. In this section we use local and global variables, please refer to Chapter 4 for their definition.	10
toString	toString is a Java build-in method which is easy to implement, modify, and it is very useful. Here we create a calling program named the_toStringCaller.java, which uses the external class named theToStringExternalClass.java that has its own toString method which overrides the Java build-in toString method.	1-
toString. Overriding Equals and toString Methods.	Overriding equals and toString methods. The toString method returns a string representation of an object. It is a string that "textually represents" the object. It is recommended that all classes override the toString method. If you do not override the toString method and you call it, it will return a string consisting of the object's name, the @ sign, and the unsigned hexadecimal representation of the hash code of the object, similar to noToStringMethodDemo@384f14b0.	17

Unicode Standard	This is another coding system that can represent over 100,000 characters.	3
	The origins of Unicode date back to 1987. The latest version of Unicode consists of more than 109,000 characters covering 93 scripts, a set of code charts for visual reference, display of text containing both right-to-left scripts, such as Hebrew and Arabic, as well as left-to-right scripts.	
	All the values represented in the ASCII codes are in the same locations in the Unicode Standard.	
Using Iterator in an ArrayList	IteratorsAddNextRemove.java, shows us, in detail, how to use iterators in an ArrayList with multiple examples about how to create an ArrayList, add data/elements into it, print all elements using the iterator class, find out if the ArrayList has elements, go to the next element and display it, remove the elements and print an empty Array List.	8
Variables Scope	Variables in Java have an area inside the program where we can access them. This is called the scope of a variable. Java has global and local variables.	4
Variables. Global Variables	In the Methods section we learned that methods do not see each other, however they can communicate with each other by passing and returning data to each other.	4
	Java in general has two types of variables, global and local.	
	The global variables are declared/created outside of all methods and they can be declared only once. The advantage of global variables is that they can be seen by all methods, at the same time the disadvantage is that they can be modified by any method. To solve that problem we can make any variable global or local variable into a constant variable so that it can only be read but not changed (see Private – Final Variables section).	
	public static String firstName = "Joseph";	

Variables. Local Variables	Variables are created in, or passed to a method. Once accepted by a method the variable is called a local variable. What is usually hard to understand is that we can have local variables that have the same name in multiple methods, and they are different. The easiest example to explain this is: We get 200 persons called Maria and we send them to 200 different cities. Each Maria in each city is different. Think of Maria as the name of the variable, and each city as a method. Please see the following interesting example: Program : variables.java	4
Variables. Final Variables	Sometimes we need a variable to maintain its value throughout the project, making sure that even if its scope is global, its value is not be changed by any method. To do this process is very simple, all we need to do is to declare such variable as final: public final double interestRate = .25; Final variables are known as constant variables in other programming languages.	10
Variables. Private – Final Variables	These types of variables are also called constant variables because they do not change value once they are created. The following program shows how to create and use constants. Program: finalStatic.java	4
Variables. Protected Classes Methods and Variables	There are three types of access for classes, methods, and variables: public, protected, and private. Protected is the access mode that is between public and private, these are the scopes of the three access modes:	13

```
Modifier       Class Package Subclass Everybody
public          Y      Y        Y         Y
protected       Y      Y        Y         N
no modifier     Y      Y        N         N
private         Y      N        N         N
```

| What is a Variable-Length Argument List in Methods? | A variable-length argument list passes multiple amount of data items, usually used in for loops, when we need to process records from a file where each record has different amounts of fields or items, e.g.: | 10 |

2,74,6,8,5,60
2,74
2,74,6,8
2,74,6,8,5
2,74,6

Here we pass each record to a method that adds those items so that we can then obtain an average value.

With our current knowledge we would have to create a method for each record passed, based on its amount of fields, however, Java has implemented a way where we only need one method to process the entire file, regardless of the amount of items/fields per record in the file. They are called variable-length argument lists.

The data received by these methods must be of the same type, it could be ints, floats, string, etc., but again, each group must be of the same data type.

Program varLenArgumentsClass.java shows in detail how to implement this very useful tool.

Notice that the variable that is accepted by the method is automatically converted to a single dimension array. To access each value follow the single dimension array rules. Also notice that to access each value, we can use regular for loops, while loops, or enhanced for loop.

What is an Interface?	An interface is a class that contains methods that only have headings. It is also referred as "an interface is a group of related methods with empty bodies." These methods are considered to be "templates" without bodies. Interfaces can be implemented in any other class and all the methods in the interface must be used in the class that is implementing the interface. One of the main purposes of using interfaces is to establish uniformity in the software development, so that every class that uses a specific interface will implement all its methods. Another advantage is that each method in the interface can have its own implementation defined by the needs of the class that is using it. Everything in an interface is "abstract." There are two types of contents that we can have in an interface: methods can only be of type public and abstract, and variables are of type public, static and final. If we do not give a type to the methods or the variables, by default interfaces automatically treat the methods as "public abstract" and the variables as "public static final." Since variables are "public static final" we must assign a value to them when we declare them. Because we can not have definitions in an interface, we can not have constructors in an interface.	14
What is the Meaning of main (String arg[])?	Since the beginning of this class we have been using the main method: public static void main(String arg[]) but we have not mentioned what the purpose is of the (String arg[]) in the main method. Well it is similar to the (int ... variable) in the variable-length argument lists methods listed above. The String arg[] inside the main method is simply a single dimensional array arg of string data type which will accept any amount of items from another program or from the command line. For instance, you have a program written in C which produced multiple output values and it needs the Java program to accept and use these variables in a specific process. So, what we need to do is call the Java program passing these variables to it, and the Java program using the main method will accept them. The mainMethod.java is a program example of using the command line to pass data to a Java program.	10

while Loop, endless	We use the endless loop when we do not know when the ending condition will be reached. The whileLoopEndless.java program shows us a simple example.	6

while Loops	The while loop looks like this:
	
	 while(condition)
	 {
	 commands
	 }
	
	 When we compare the while loop with the for loop, what goes between the () in the while is the looping condition, same purpose but more flexible than in the for loop.
	
	 Assume we have variables that control the temperature, humidity, and altitude and we want to do a task while these three conditions meet some values:
	
	 int temperature = 50;
	 int humidity = 10;
	 int altitude = 0;
	
	 while(((temperature > 0) &&
	     (humidity<100) && (altitude>0)) ||
	     ((temperature < 100) &&
	     (humidity>0) && (altitude>0)
	     ))
	 {
	    //fly away
	 }
		6

While. do while Loops	The do while loops are different from the while loops in that they will be executed at least once. Please see program whileLoopDO.java	6

| Wrappers | As we learned in the primitive data types section, primitives do not have methods, however sometimes we need to perform functions on primitives. | 4 |

To do this Java has given us the wrapper classes. For the eight primitive data types we have eight wrapper classes.

Primitive Wrapper
  byte   Byte
  short   Short
  int   Integer
  long   Long
  float   Float
  double   Double
  char   Character
  boolean   Boolean

Notice that the first letter of the primitives is always lowercase, and the wrappers first letter is always upper case.

Index

8 bits byte samples, 34–35

A

Abstract class, 385, 418–420, 429
    defined, 432, 463
Abstraction, 385–389
Algorithm
    and recursion, 319
    and sorting, 301
    and swapping, 301–303
American Standard Code for Information Interchange (ASCII), 35
    alphabet, 36–37
ASCII code table, 35–36
    defined, 61, 467
    extended characters, 37, 38
    numbers, 36
ANSI C, 24, 28, 43
Apple, 1, 2, 13
    and GUI, 3
    TextEdit, 6
Applications, GUI simple, 283–295
Array
    adding space to declared, 139, 161, 464
    copying, 466

create, allocate, and load, 139–140, 162
declare and allocate, 139, 162, 465, 467
declaring one dimension, 138, 162
defined, 137, 161, 464
for.enhanced for loop, 164
enhanced for loops, 154–155, 164
load data to declared, 140–141, 163, 465
multi-dimensional, 141–152
one dimension, 137–141, 163
parallel, 152–154, 163
printing values inside, 140–141, 164, 466
string tokenizer, 156–159, 164
three dimensional, 147–152, 164
two dimensional, 141–147
two dimensional int, 143–145
two dimensional string, 146–147
ArrayList, 167–191
    copying, 182–188, 192
    defined, 192, 464
    iterator, 172–181, 193
    object data types, 188–190, 193
    ASCII codes program, 450–455, 458
    ASCII code table, 35–36
    defined, 467
Assembly, 2, 11

< 505 >

B

Base-2 numerical system, 33. *see also* Binary numerical system

Base-10 numerical system, 33

Base-class, 327

Basic tools, 33

Binary, 34

Binary code, 2, 11

Binary digits, 34

Binary file, 197, 227–231
    defined, 233, 467

Binary numerical system, 33–35
    defined, 61, 468
    purpose of, 34

Bit, 34

Boolean, 34, 40, 61, 66
    defined, 471

Boolean conditions in while loops, 117–118

Bubble sort, 303–319
    defined, 323, 468

BufferedReader, 198, 236
    defined, 478

BufferedWriter, 198

Byte, 34, 39, 62, 66
    defined, 34, 471
    samples, 34–35

Byte codes, 8, 11

C

C, 1, 2, 11

Caller method, defined, 432

Calling method, 72, 92
    defined, 468

Cast, 42, 43

Casting tool, 42

Char, 40, 62, 66
    defined, 472
    as input in switch command, 126–128

Class, 17, 27
    creating, 19–20
    defined, 19

Classes inside classes, 418
    defined, 432–433, 469

Class files, 9

Cobol, 2, 11

Code editor, 3

Command line, 8, 13

Comments, 18, 26
    defined, 469

Compiled language, 2, 11

Compiler, 3

Compiler (javac), 8, 11, 26

Compiling, 8–9

Complex programming, 417–431

Computer, 2

Computer program language, 11
    compiled, 2
    defined, 1–2, 11, 469
    interpreted, 2

Constructor, 250
    defined, 276, 470

D

Data abstraction, 385–389
    defined, 391, 471
    vs. interfaces, 389, 391, 471

DataInputStream, 198

DataOutputStream, 198

Data structures, 391
    array, 137–160
    ArrayList, 167–191
    files, 197–232

Data structures, implementations, 395–413
    linked list, 395–400
    overloading, 400–402
    queue, 408–412
    stacks, 402–408

Data types, 38–39
    defined, 62, 472
    problems with incorrect, 42–43
    and variable, 39

Debugger, 3

Debugging, 80, 81

Decimal, 34

Decimal format
    defined, 233, 473
    printing numbers using, 225–227

Decimal numerical system, 33, 63
    defined, 473

Dialog box, 283–291
  defined, 296, 480
Documentation, 17–18, 26
  defined, 474
Double data type, 40, 62, 66
  defined, 472
Do while loops, 120–122
  defined, 131, 503

E

Eclipse, 5, 11, 197
  defined, 474
  download, 5, 11
Editor, 2, 12
  defined, 474
Integrated Development Environment (IDE), 2
Text editor, 2
EditPro, 197
Endless while loop, 119–120
  defined, 131, 503
Enhanced for loops, 113, 122, 154–155
  defined, 479
Equals, overriding, 458
Error exceptions
  catching in data files, 198–199
  defined, 233, 468
Errors, in Java programs, 198–199
Exceptions handling, 210–214
  defined, 234, 474–475
Extends/inheriting, defined, 433, 475
External classes, 239–242
  defined, 277, 475–476

F

File class, defined, 236, 477
FileInputStream, 198
FileOutputStream, 198
FileReader, 198, 236
  defined, 478
Files
  binary, 197
  defined, 197, 235, 476
  large files, 477
  record, 198

  text, 197
FileWriter, 198, 236
  defined, 478
Final classes, 369–370
  defined, 374, 478
Final methods, 367–369
  defined, 374, 478
Final variables, 242–244
  defined, 500
Float, 40, 62, 66
  defined, 472
For.enhanced array, defined, 164
For loops, 113–116
  and counter variable, 113
  defined, 130, 479
Formatter, 198
Formatter class, defined, 236, 477
Frame, 291–295
  creating, 291–293, 293–295
  defined, 291, 296, 479
  full size, 293–295
  small, 292–293
  visibility, 293
Function, and primitives, 55. *see also* Wrapper

G

Gedit, 13, 197
  in Linux, 6, 7
Generic methods, 437–439, 458
  defined, 480
Global variables, 82
Graphical User Interface (GUI), 3, 12
  defined, 283, 296, 480
  dialog boxes, 283–291
  frame, 291–295
  input dialog box, 284–291
  message dialog box, 284
  simple applications, 283–295
GUI. *see* Graphical User Interface (GUI)

H

Hexadecimal numerical system, 35, 63
  defined, 481
HP-UX, 1

I

IDE. *see* Integrated Development Environment (IDE)

If command
  defined, 97, 109, 482
if, 97
if_else, 100–102, 109
if else if, 102–103, 109
  nested if, 104–106, 110
  plain if, 97–98
  plain if, examples, 98–100
  ternary if, 106–107, 110
If_else, 100–102, 109
  defined, 483
If else if, 102–103, 109
  defined, 482
If.nested if, 104–106, 110
  defined, 483
If.ternary if, 106–107, 110
  defined, 483
Imports, 18–19, 26
  defined, 483
Indentation, 22, 27
  defined, 484
Inheritance, 327–341
  defined, 374, 484
Input dialog box, 284–291
  defined, 297, 481
Int, 66
  defined, 472
  as input in switch command, 122–125
Int data type, 40, 62
Integrated Development Environment (IDE), 3, 12, 197
  defined, 482
  disadvantages of, 3
Interface, 379–385
  defined, 391, 485, 502
  methods content, 379
  variables content, 379
Interfaces, 418
  defined, 433
Interpreted language, 2, 11

Iterator, 172
  defined, 193, 485, 499
  using in ArrayList, 173–181

J

Java, 12
  compiling in, 8–9, 11, 469
  creating programs in, 8, 197, 471
  defined, 1, 485
  and devices, 1
Java classes, 27
  defined, 486
Java collection interface, 439–443, 459
Java Development Kit (JDK), 2, 12
  defined, 486
  download, 2, 12
Javadoc, 455–457, 459
  defined, 486
Javadoc comments, 18, 26
  defined, 469
Java indentation, 27
Java method, 27
  defined, 488
Java Virtual Machine (JVM), 1, 8, 11
JDK. *see* Java Development Kit (JDK)
JVM. *see* Java Virtual Machine (JVM)

K

Keyboard, and scanner class, 87–90, 93

L

Language, programming, 1
Letter value, ASCII, 38
LIFO method, 402, 408
Linked list, 395–400
  defined, 414, 486
Linux, 1, 2, 197
  Gedit in, 7
  and GUI, 3
  Nano in, 7
Local variable, 82, 84–86, 93
  defined, 500

Logical error, 198
Long data type, 40, 62, 66
    defined, 472
Loops
    Boolean conditions in while, 117–118
    defined, 130, 487
    do while, 120–122
    endless while, 119–120
    enhanced for, 122
    for, 113–116
    switch command, 122–128
    while, 116–117
Lowercase, and primitive, 55, 66

M

Mac-OS, 1
Main method, 21, 272–273
    defined, 279, 502
Main, point of entry, 20
Math, using primitives, 47–55, 63
    defined, 487
Message dialog box, 284
    defined, 297, 487
Method, 27, 72
    calling, 72, 92, 488
    creating, 20–22
    defined, 20
    that accepts data, 75–77, 92, 487
    that does not accept data, 73–74, 92, 487
    that returns data, 77–80, 92, 487
Multi-dimensional array, 141. *see also* Three
      dimensional array; Two dimensional array

N

Name, 41
Nano, 13, 197
    in Linux, 6, 7
Nested if, 104–106, 110
    defined, 483
NetBeans, 4, 12, 197
    defined, 488
    download, 4, 12
    using, 4

Netware, 1
Notepad, 6, 13, 197
Notepad++, 6, 13, 197
Notepad
    in Linux, 6
    in Windows, 6
Numerical operators, 43–46, 64. *see also* Operator
    defined, 489
Numerical systems, 33, 64
    defined, 490

O

Object data types, 270–272
    defined, 276, 473
One dimensional array, 137–138. *see also* Array
    defined, 465
Operating system, 12
    defined, 1, 490
Operating Systems for IT, 197
Operator, 43–46
Operator > and <, 45
Operator %, 46–47, 65, 490
Operator | |, 46, 65, 490
Operator, =, ==, !=, 46, 491
Operator, =, = =, !=, 65
Operator, other, 44–45
Operator &&, 46, 64, 490
Operator >= and <=, 45, 66, 491
Oracle Corporation, 2
Overloading, 400–402
    defined, 414, 491

P

Parallel array, 152–154
    defined, 163, 466
Pause program, 80–82, 93
    defined, 491
Perl, 1, 11
PHP, 1, 11
Pico, 13, 197
    in Linux, 6
Pingala, 34
Plain if, 97–100

Polymorphism, 342–367
  defined, 375, 492
  diagram, 361
Primitive, 39
  and lowercase, 55, 66, 69
  and math, 47–55, 63
Primitive data types, 39–42, 66
  defined, 492
Print commands, 23, 27
  defined, 492
Printing numbers, in decimal format, defined, 233
PrintWriter, 198, 236
  defined, 478
Private, final variables, 83–84, 94
  defined, 500
Program, documentation, 17–18
Programming language, 1
Protected classes methods, and variables, 370–372
  defined, 375, 500
PseudoCode, 9, 13
  defined, 492
  example of, 9

Q

Queue, 408–412
  defined, 414, 492
QuickSort, 319

R

Recompile, 9
Record, defined, 198, 275, 493
Recursion, 319–322
  defined, 323, 494
Remarks, 17, 26
Runtime error, 198

S

Scanner, 198
Scanner class, 87–90, 93
  defined, 236, 478, 494
Scope, of variable, 82, 93
Shannon, Claude, 34

Short data type, 40, 62, 66
  defined, 472
Simple constructor, 251–260
  defined, 276, 470
Solaris, 1, 2
Sorting, defined, 301, 323, 494
Source code, 8, 11
  transfer, 9
Stacks, 402–408
  defined, 414, 494
String class, 55–59, 62
  defined, 472
  first program, 57–59
String tokenizer, defined, 164, 495
Sub-class, 327
Super-class, 327
Swap/swapping, 301–303
  defined, 324, 495
Switch command
  defined, 131, 495
  and loops, 122–125
  using char as input, 126–128
Syntax error, 198
System.out.print, 23, 27
  defined, 495
System.out.printf, 24, 28
  defined, 496
System.out.printIn, defined, 497
System.out.println, 23, 29

T

Terminal mode, 6, 8, 13
  defined, 497
Ternary if, 106–107, 110
  defined, 483
TextEdit, 13
  in Apple, 6
Text editor, 3, 6, 12, 13, 197
  defined, 498
  Notepad, 6
Text file, 197
  BufferedReader, 203
  defined, 236, 477

exceptions handling, 210–214
FileReader, 202
FileWriter, 199–201
formatter class, 214–216
large files, 221–225, 235
PrintReader, 199–201
PrintWriter, 199–201
scanner class, 217–220
'this' keyword, in Java, 248
  defined, 277, 498
Three dimensional array, 147–152
  defined, 164, 466
Tools, 33
toString, 244–247, 443–449, 458, 459
  defined, 277, 498
Transfer, of source code, Windows to Linux, 9
Truncate, 42
Two dimensional array, 141–146
Typing, reducing, 449–450, 458, 459
  defined, 494

U

Ubuntu Linux operating system, 197
  Eclipse in, 5
  NetBeans in, 4
Unicode Standard, 38, 39, 66
  defined, 499
Uppercase, and wrapper, 55, 66
Utilities, importing, 18–19

V

Value, 41, 61
  assigning to variable, 43
Variable, 41, 43, 260
  defined, 278, 499
  global, 82
  local, 82, 84–86
  private, final, 83–84
Variable, assigning value, 61
  defined, 470
Variable-length argument list, 260–270
  defined, 278, 501
Variable scope, 82, 93
VI, in Linux, 6, 13
VIM, in Linux, 6, 13, 197
VM, in Linux, 197

W

Wait, or pause, 81
While loops, 116–117
  Boolean conditions in, 117–118
  defined, 131, 503
Windows, 1, 2, 13
  and ASCII characters, 38
  and GUI, 3
  Notepad, 197
Wrapper, 55, 66, 69–72, 94
  defined, 504
  and uppercase, 55, 66, 69

CPSIA information can be obtained
at www.ICGtesting.com
Printed in the USA
LVOW02s1145230416

483717LV00001BB/1/P